NORMAN LINDSAY

ON ART, LIFE AND LITERATURE

Norman Lindsay was a celebrated and controversial Australian artist, who also wrote novels and children's books. His influence on Australian life extended beyond this, and he frequently gave advice and encouragement to new writers. At times he provided illustrations free to a young author, knowing this would ensure the book would be published. His prodigious essay-writing continued until his death in 1969.

Keith Wingrove, a long-time friend of Norman Lindsay, visited the artist annually at Springwood in the Blue Mountains where they discussed his literary and artistic philosophy. He has collected and studied Lindsay's works in every medium, and items from his collection are often lent for exhibitions and for reproduction in books on the artist's life. Keith Wingrove is the author of *Norman Lindsay's Bears* and *The Comic Art of Norman Lindsay.*

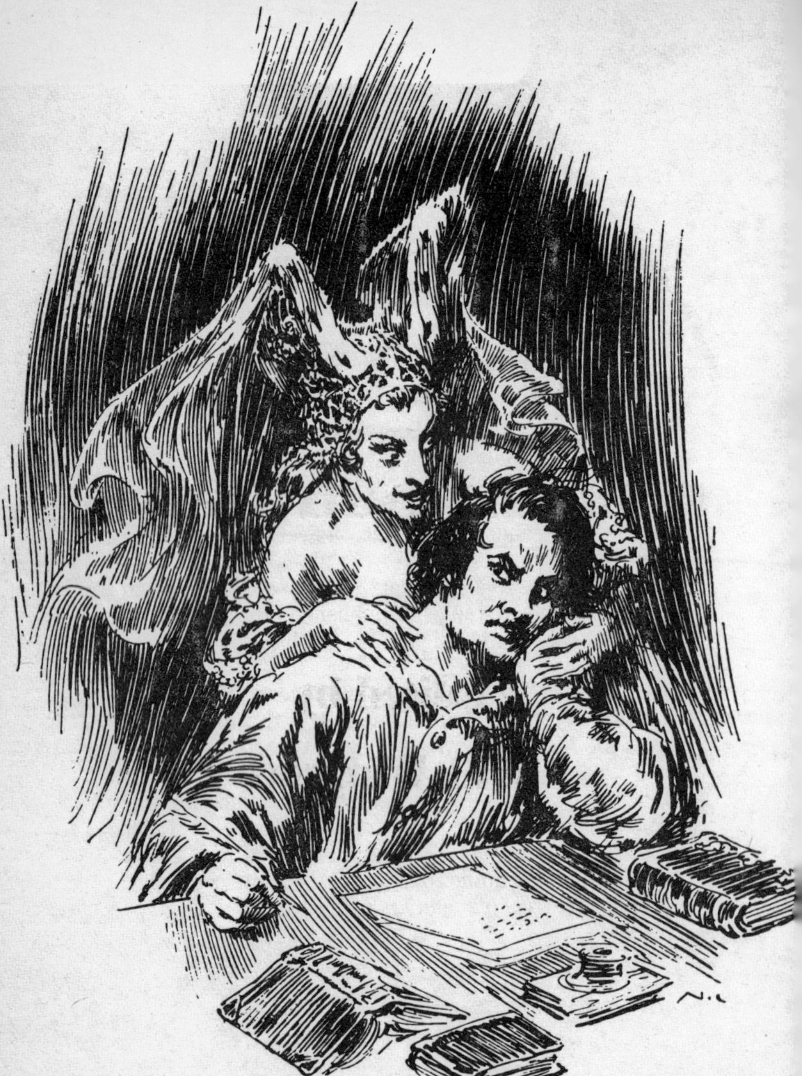

A homage to Balzac

NORMAN LINDSAY

ON ART, LIFE AND LITERATURE

Edited by

Keith Wingrove

University of Queensland Press

First published 1990 by University of Queensland Press
Box 42, St Lucia, Queensland 4067 Australia

Typeset by University of Queensland Press
Printed in Australia by The Book Printer, Melbourne

Distributed in the USA and Canada by
International Specialized Book Services, Inc.,
5602 N.E. Hassalo Street, Portland, Oregon 97213-3640

Cataloguing in Publication Data

National Library of Australia

Lindsay, Norman, 1879–1969.
Norman Lindsay on art, life and literature.

1. Lindsay, Norman, 1879–1969 — Written works. 2. Lindsay, Norman, 1879–1969 — Correspondence. 3. Artists — Australia — Correspondence. 4. Art criticism. 5. Literature — History and criticism. 6. History. I. Wingrove, Keith. II. Title.

759.994

ISBN 0 7022 2227 5

Contents

Acknowledgments

Extracts from letters are reprinted here with the permission of Jane Glad and Angus and Robertson, publishers (*Letters of Norman Lindsay,* edited by R.G. Howarth and A.W. Barker, Angus and Robertson, Sydney, 1979).

The sources and dates of first publication are shown beneath each essay. My indebtedness to all concerned is acknowledged. My thanks and appreciation are extended to them.

Introduction

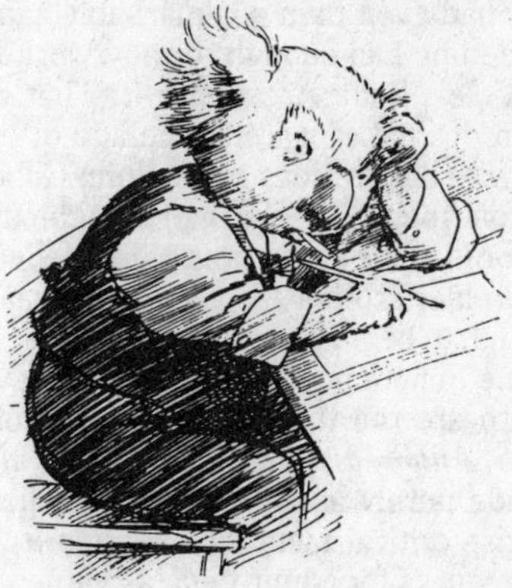

Norman Lindsay maintained throughout his life that he was a picture maker and never made any claims to being a writer. Writing to him was purely a release and escape from the stresses and labours of his avowed job of picture making.

From about the age of five he was for some years afflicted with a skin irritation, which prevented him from participating in any vigorous games or activities. He was compelled to spend much of his time as an observer of the world around him. As a result of this and by inclination much of his time was occupied in reading and drawing.

In a letter to me he tells of his reading and writing:

> To your query as to whether I wrote when young, the answer is yes. I wrote several small novels and illustrated them. They were all on one theme, escape from the home to an enthralling love affair with a delectable wench in a confined space. Parents were the villains of those works, from which I argue they were mainly inspired by conflict with my mother over going with girls. I usually made them into small neatly bound books and gave them to girls, no doubt in the hope that they be inspired to indulge a love affair with me in a confined space. I don't know why the confined space was considered essential, unless it survived from the early passion

every small boy has to build a small pleasure house, usually of chaff bags, and aspire to live in it in preference to his home.

Yes, I was an industrious reader of poetry from the earliest exercises in deciphering type matter, but I really owe Lionel a debt there for at least stimulating my interest in poetry. He had a very good library of the standard English poets even at the age of twelve, having had even then a remarkable capacity for acquiring money, and when he had enough for any work he wanted, used to send down to Cole's Book Arcade for it. That was how I acquired my first edition of Shakespeare at the age of eight. It was an old Dick's edition with illustrations by Sir John Gilbert, and Lionel sold it to me for four pence, as he had bought a Globe edition for himself. His words to me at the time were, delivered in the peremptory tone of the elder brother "You've got to read Shakespeare and you're old enough to begin now".

It interests me to note now that the three plays which fascinated me in my youth are the three which I still consider his greatest works, *Macbeth, Antony and Cleopatra* and *Hamlet*. Such a selection in youth is made purely as a personal predeliction. One does not bring any precise critical faculty to bear on it, as one also selects plenty of minor works for admiration, as witness my illustrations to Kipling, Conan Doyle, and Dumas done at the same period. And one reads plenty of minor poetry with gusto, such as Macauley's *Lays of Ancient Rome* and the verse of Adam Lindsay Gordon. Still, the poem that I read incessantly till I almost knew it by heart was Shakespeare's *Venus and Adonis*, which should be impressed on every adolescent reader to inspire a lyrical adoration of girls. Another work incessantly read in those days and which I still read at intervals, was Byron's *Don Juan*. For the rest, I industriously read all the standard poets, thanks to Lionel's bookcase, and some of the moderns of that era, Swinburn, Tennyson and Browning, and also James Thompson's *City of Dreadful Night*. The poet who took the strongest hold of my adolescent years was Browning and though I satisfied myself early with Tennyson and Swinburn, I read Browning today more than any other poet. I should have added Burns to the early list of poets who still remains for me one of the eternally young and fresh.

It must be noted that his writing was done for the sole purpose of providing material to illustrate. Drawing was his great and abiding interest. He never gave any serious thought to becoming a writer. His sole aim in life, even then, was to become an artist.

In a letter to his brothers Percy and Lionel in Melbourne

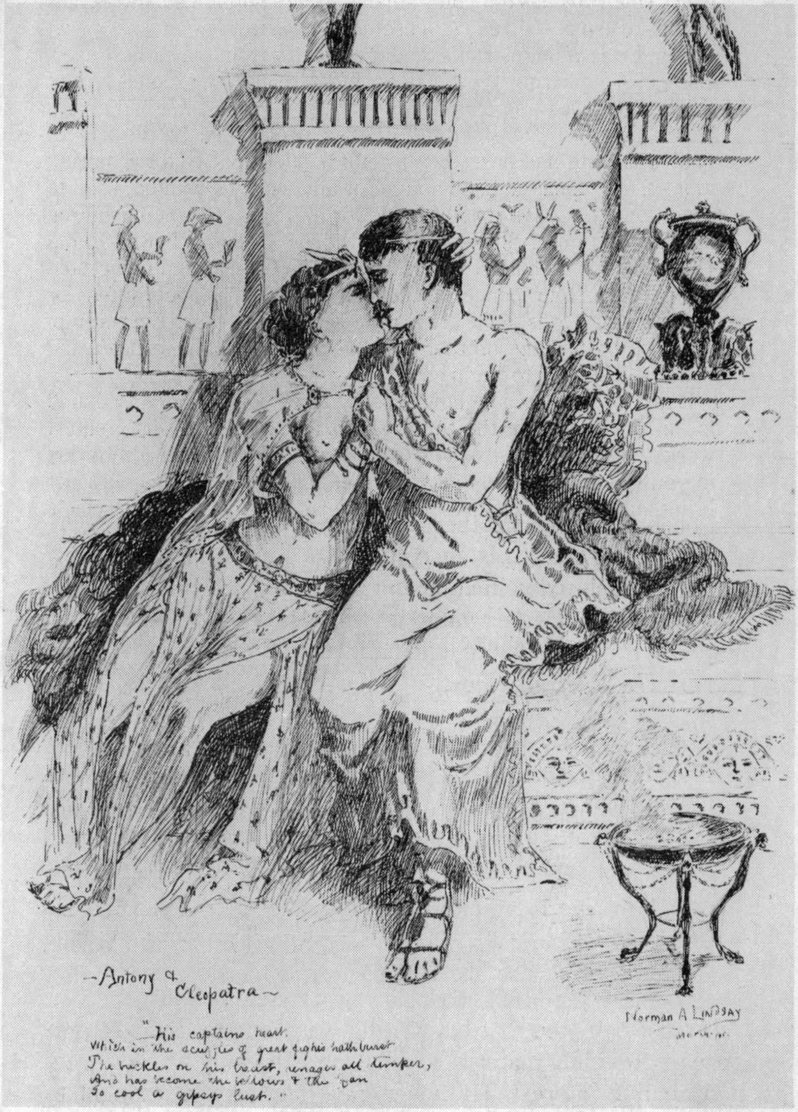

A remarkable drawing by fourteen-year-old Norman Lindsay. It is an early indication of the direction his art would take when he became a professional artist.

written about 1893 he gives an unusual and amusing view of women for a fourteen-year-old boy:

> I don't give the Mater any trouble about going out at nights. Look here, Woman havent any-sense in some things they never look below the surface.
>
> You know before, about a year or so back, how the Mater used to worry because kind friends used to come & tell her things about me. Then I used to do everything openly, being innocent myself, I believed I was doing no harm in tracking about in broad daylight with females of my own age and innocence. In fact, I used to think I was doing rather a fine thing — & fancied I was playing hell — but I was'ent, naturally. Now, having wisdom, I go about carefully, so that, if there are any sins on my soul, I put them Down to those Kind people who were the cause of the change, & thus I am absolved.

During 1895, his last year at Creswick Grammar School, he revived the school magazine the *Boomerang*, which previously had been run by his brothers Percy and Lionel. The grammar school, only a short distance from the Lindsay home, was a small school founded in 1869 and closed in 1903. Many prominent Australians were among its scholars. He wrote all of the material, transcribed it in long hand on to the old gelatine pads and printed it. He also illustrated it with many drawings.

Writing to Percy and Lionel he comments on a special issue of the *Boomerang*:

> Next week I am bringing out a double number of the *Boomerang*, which is to galvanize the Literary world. I tell you, I'm a reguliar power in the land. From my elevated standpoint as editor I observe humanity in a particular peculiar sphinx like fashion and express proper contempt for all petty affairs of gossip — regard religion from a purely logical point of view — disbelieve in Adam — believe in Darwin — critize the sermons, sneer at the minister and altogether make an objectionable prig of myself. Behold me.

In 1904 his pen drawing *Pollice Verso* was widely attacked in the press as indecent and religiously offensive. Norman did not attempt to reply to the attacks himself. Instead he asked Lionel to reply. He explained his position in the incident in a letter to me in 1947:

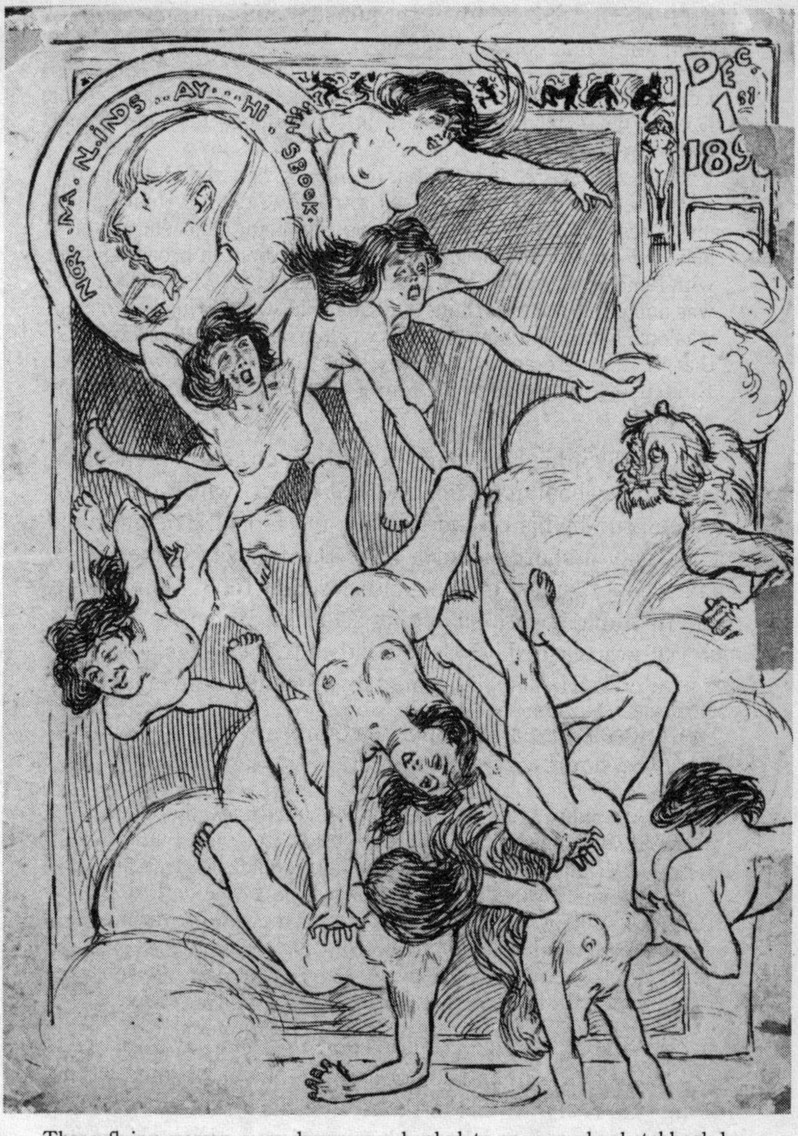

These flying women were drawn as a bookplate on an early sketchbook by Lindsay when he was seventeen. He included a self-portrait (top left).

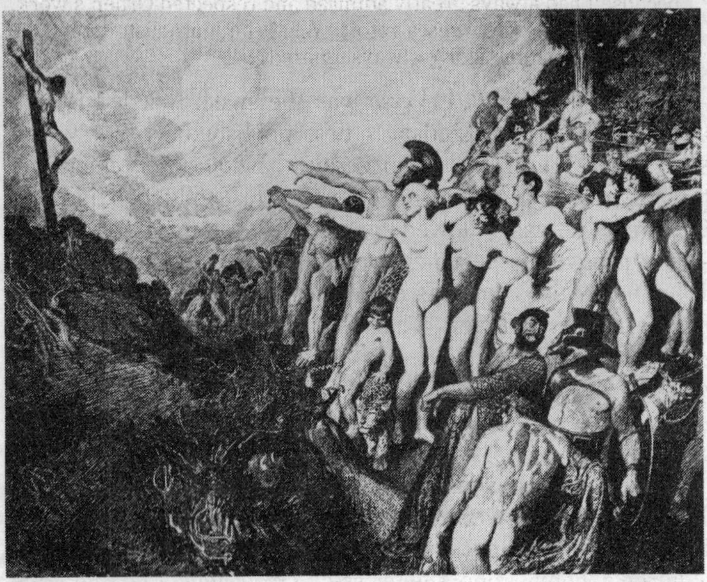

Pollice Verso (In possession of the National Gallery, reproduced with permission National Gallery, Victoria, Felton bequest).

One queer thing about the urge to write was that I never thought seriously about trying to handle prose till the first attack on my work, which was on that early pen drawing *Pollice Verso*.

I got Lionel to write an answer to the attacks, which I signed and which was published on the Red Page by A.G. Stephens. Old Hop of the *Bulletin* accused me of having got Stephens to write it, which I was able to deny, but I was ashamed of posturing under a false claim to Lionel's more or less fluid ease as a writer, and I set about trying to find a prose style for myself, foreseeing that I could expect plenty more attacks on my work. I worked extremely hard seeking to put my thoughts into a clarified form in words, trying out all sorts of exercises, but when at last I did find some ease in expressing myself I never attempted to use it to defend my work. The only attack I ever answered directly was that which Orpen* made on my exhibit in the 1923 show in London, and I did that

*Sir William Orpen RA (1878–1931), prominent English artist noted for his portraits, war paintings and landscapes.

> because I had always greatly admired and respected Orpen's work, and felt that he deserved a retort. What the journalists mob have scribbled about me I have always ignored.

The attack on *Pollice Verso* was the spark that led to him becoming a writer. Lindsay's first published writing was a short story "Saturdee" published in the *Lone Hand* magazine for July 1908, being recollections of his childhood days at Creswick. It was followed by a series of stories of similar youthful adventures which were collected and published in 1933 in a revised form as a book bearing the same title. His first essay or article "That Popular Myth — the Lady" appeared also in the *Lone Hand* in February 1910. His first venture into fiction was the novel *A Curate in Bohemia* published by N.S.W. Bookstall Co. Ltd in 1913 based on recollections of his student days in Melbourne.

Novels and essays followed down the years until his death in 1969. He also left several unpublished novels in manuscript. His literary output was considerable: eleven novels; two children's books, one the classic *The Magic Pudding;* five books of essays; a volume of bawdy short stories entitled *Micomicana;* and an autobiography *My Mask*. The autobiography and *Micomicana* were both published after his death. A selection of his letters was published in 1979. Several of the novels were published in England and America both in hard cover and later paperback editions. Sales ran into hundreds of thousands. *The Cautious Amorist* and *Age of Consent* were made into films for the international market and were successful.

The essays were contributed to the *Bulletin*, and other magazines and newspapers. They deal mostly with literature and art. His style is always personal, clear and forthright. You may or may not agree with what he says but you will have to respect his views, which are individual, and always of interest.

The works of no other Australian author, and few other authors, have been presented in so many different ways as those of Norman Lindsay.

On 1 September 1953, the Australian Broadcasting Commission broadcast a short version of *The Magic Pudding* to

Queensland schools. In 1960, Peter Scriven's puppet company created a puppet show of the book which toured Australia with great success. Then in 1970, the Marionette Theatre of Australia took a new version of the show to Expo 1970 at Osaka, Japan. The show then toured Korea, Hong Kong, Singapore and Djakarta. One cannot help wondering what the Asians made of Bunyip Bluegum and his adventures. The company presented a further version on another Australian tour in 1980. It is understood that an animated cartoon version is being made.

The novel *The Cousin from Fiji* was successfully staged as a musical play in Adelaide in 1962 by the Flinders Street Revue Company. In 1972 the television division of the Australian Broadcasting Commission presented a Norman Lindsay Festival featuring five of the novels, *Redheap, The Cousin from Fiji, A Curate in Bohemia, Dust or Polish,* and *Halfway to Anywhere.* The first two were each televised in three hour-long episodes, the others each in one hour-long session. Then in 1986 *Saturdee* was televised in a ten-part half-hour series, completing the televising of the *Redheap* trilogy on life in an Australian country town in the nineteenth century.

Five of Norman's literary works have been published in braille by the Royal Victorian Institute for the Blind. They are *Redheap* 1970, *The Magic Pudding* 1972, *Saturdee* 1975, *Halfway to Anywhere* 1975–1976, *The Cousin from Fiji* 1976. The Queensland Braille Writing Association also issued *The Magic Pudding* in braille in 1980.

The publishing houses Angus & Robertson and Ure Smith presented a Norman Lindsay Book Week in August 1970 at Proud's Gallery, Sydney, to help the New South Wales branch of the National Trust of Australia to raise funds for the purchase of Lindsay's home at Springwood in the Blue Mountains. The property was purchased and set up as the Norman Lindsay Gallery and Museum which was officially opened on 24 February 1973. The gallery attracts thousands of visitors from Australia and overseas annually.

In addition to novels and other writings there are the hundreds of letters he wrote throughout his long life. He was a has long ago been recognised by the world. It is too often forgotten that he is also a great Australian writer.

It is with Norman Lindsay's genius as an Australian writer, novelist, critic and philosopher that this number of *Southerly* is concerned. Australian writers — novelists and poets — have paid him homage for many years and the articles published here represent only a small section of their gratitude for the stimulus of ideas, encouragement and practical achievement which he has given to Australian literature during the last half-century.

It is true that, among the petits-maitres of contemporary painting, the Angry Young Pansies and the frustrated European migrants who drink sweet sherry with each other in the studios favoured by Sunday newspapers, it has become fashionable to decry him as a mere "illustrator", a "literary" artist, as though literature and the graphic arts should have nothing in common.

Some of the third-rate imported art-practitioners from Switzerland and Hungary and other countries, indeed, have felt their tiny egoettes so flustered by the impact of Lindsay's positive ideas that they have descended to terms of Port Said to express their hatred. He is, of course, a "literary" artist as much as he is an "artistic" writer, if only because his art is a full art of the concrete and not the abstract, and because (like that other "literary" artist William Blake) he has the perceptive powers of a poet as well as those of a delineator.

I know of no other Australian author, who has done so much to promote our literature as Norman Lindsay. This is all the more extraordinary in view of the huge volume of artwork he produced. In this he is unique. His place therein is assured.

KEITH WINGROVE

prolific and voluminous correspondent. His letters were addressed to a wide circle of friends, and writers and artists both established and budding. Many of them run from a couple of pages to eight or ten, and in some cases more. Many are in fact little essays as so many of them set out very clearly his ideas and philosophy. The few remaining letters from his teenage years are remarkable for one so young. The ideas expressed and the words used are those of a much older person. They are also early evidence of the clear flowing style he developed in his later letters.

Because the material in this book is drawn from a variety of sources, over more than sixty years, a consistency in spelling was sought, and, where possible, obvious typographical errors were corrected. In some cases the essays have been edited down for length reasons.

I omit all reference to the series of books on his drawings, etchings and paintings as they are not relevant here.

Although some fellow artists and many art students sought his advice, Norman was never closely associated with the local art world or artists, as he felt no affinity with them. Also he was too busy working at his home at Springwood to socialise. In a letter to me he writes:

> I have always lived as far outside the studio world and its denizens as possible, and dodged communion with artists, who of all practitioners in the arts, live in the most rigid limitations on any other concept of life save those externals which may be transcribed in paint.
>
> Also, its trade jealousies and utter intolerance of all values save those which engross a present movement in plastic art make sane communion with it impossible. Artists, as a class, read very little and are blankly indifferent to the psychological significance of culture generally as evidence of moral energy, or a lack of it, in the human ego. No doubt the competitive struggle for a place in the art world demoralises in them both a sense of the real function of art and a sense of humour in its practice.

Norman Lindsay's contribution to Australian literature is large and often overlooked. First there are his own literary works and secondly his efforts in the promotion of the works of other authors. His assistance to many authors included illustrating their books without charging a fee. It was a well-known fact that any book with a Norman Lindsay jacket or illustration would sell. His sole aim in providing the illustrations was to try to ensure the particular book would be published.

He was the prime instigator in 1932 of the Endeavour Press, persuading the Bulletin Newspaper Company to establish the press for the publication of Australian books. Appropriately their first publication was Norman's *Saturdee* published in 1933. He read and assessed very many of the manuscripts submitted to the press for publication, no easy or light task, and very time consuming, for which he was not paid.

The list of established novelists and poets who sought out Norman Lindsay is extraordinary. Poets Hugh McCrae, Leon Gellert, Robert Fitzgerald, Ronald McCuaig, Kenneth MacKenzie, Douglas Stewart, Francis Webb, Ken Slessor, novelists Louis Stone, Leslie Meller, Godfrey Blunden, Brian Penton, Lawson Glassop, Brian James all benefitted from his advice or support. In addition there were so many unknown aspiring authors, who also benefitted by his advice and encouragement.

Douglas Stewart pointed out so truly in his introduction to *Paintings in Oil,* a book on Norman's oil paintings:

> Writers came to him, not only because of the understanding he brought to their work, but because of the tremendous enthusiasm with which he received it — if it was good. When he talked to a young writer about the novel, he talked with the authority of a practitioner and critic, who has read and re-read the masters till he knows everything that can be known about them.

The Sydney branch of the English Association published a "Norman Lindsay Number" of their quarterly journal *Southerly* in 1959. In the introduction Ken Slessor, then editor, wrote:

> This issue of *Southerly*, celebrating the eightieth birthday of Norman Lindsay, is intended to do honour to his achievement as a writer. As a painter, etcher, black-and-white craftsman and illustrator, Norman Lindsay needs no further tribute; his genius

Part 1

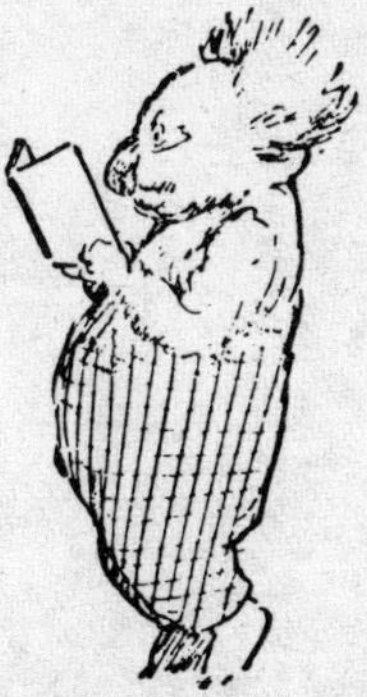

Boyhood Days

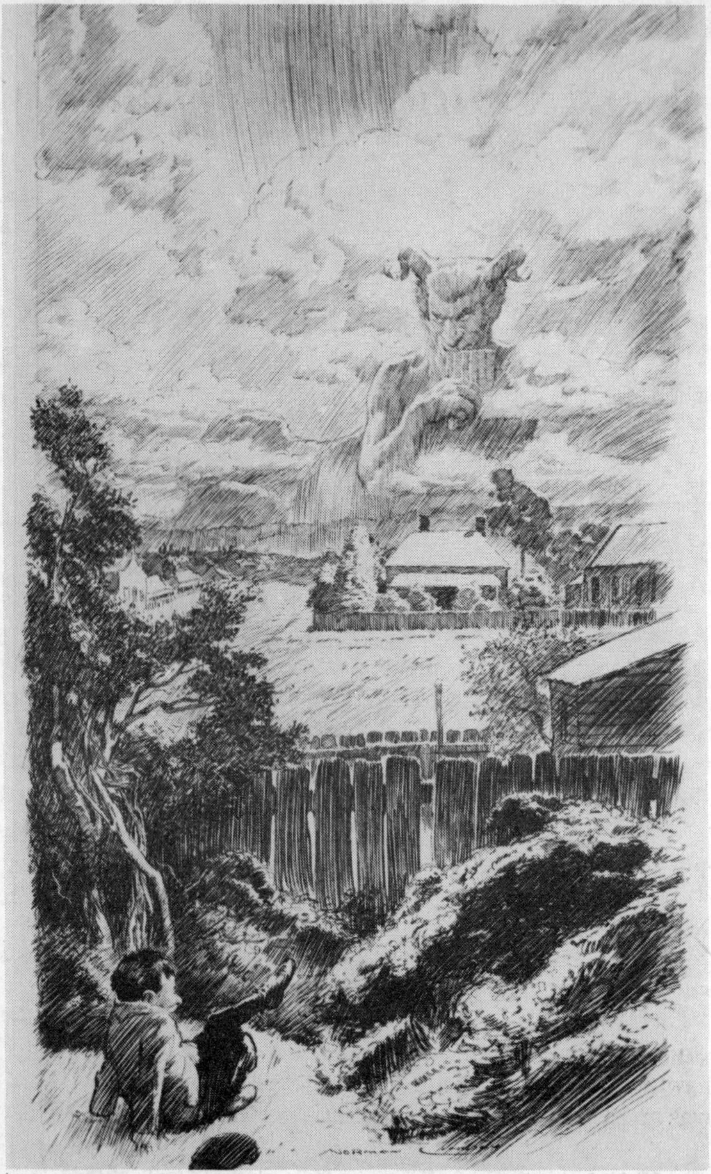

Peter sprawled in the grass so conscious of happiness that he hummed, too, like the bees

An Opulent Interlude

BEING ONE SPRING DAY IN THE LIFE OF AN AUSTRALIAN BOY

No doubt there are some rare moments when we are gifted with an extra sense, not of reason, but of refined perception – an epicureanism of sensation in which is revealed to us the divinity of external things. Our eyes discard the slothfulness of habit. We see the mystery of trees and the enchantment of back yards; discover the magic of blue skies, and find that cows are Nature's miracles. Such moments of true divination belong to childhood; for knowledge, the burden of age, destroys illusion. And illusion exists in externals. Nature made the tree a mystic thing, but man, in his madness, invented botany and destroyed its charm for ever.

Peter lay in the long grass behind old Mother Regan's back yard. It was a secluded place, overgrown with gorse and hawthorn, impenetrable to the eyes of people passing by. This was an essential condition of Peter's beatific mood, for he was

Published in the *Lone Hand* magazine, Sydney, 1 March 1916

wagging it from school, and so knew the true meaning of freedom — which is time filched from duty. It was a spring morning, and he had hours to squander in spendthrift leisure. The sun was of the right warmth, and the air was still and mild — a day that sweetens the skin with a sensation of perfect health. The heat drew out the full scent of the yellow gorse. Bees hummed their litany of perfect weather, and for happiness there is no sound like the humming of bees. On such a day Pan sits on the hillsides, piping his divine message of idleness and peace.

Peter sprawled in the grass, so conscious of happiness that he hummed, too, like the bees. A well-fed dog, lying in the sunlight, perhaps knows such beatitude. Warmth peace and security — these gifts the flesh acknowledges. Yet the eye must be enchanted too. Clouds loitered in the sky for Peter's benefit, too lazy to chart a course. Insects whirred in the grass, especially to be watched; ants, those imposters, burst themselves with industry for Peter's entertainment. Peter was stirred by an unusual emotion — a spark of that artistry which dreams of perpetuating beauty. The way the sunlight fell on the roof of the Wesleyan Parsonage seemed pregnant of this mysterious desire. The perfection of this scene must find some expression. Peter realised something of that true appreciation of beauty — a fleeting sense of sadness. If one could grasp this moment and make it eternal, wagging it from school for ever, watching the sunlight on the parson's roof, hearing the bees hum, and smelling springtime in the yellow gorse and dandelions.

The urgent need for articulate expression took Peter as it has taken many a wiser man. He produced a stub of pencil, sucked it for inspiration, and in a small, black pocket-book inscribed these words:—

Fairest girl on earth is she,
Ever in my heart shall be.
Ever how I long for thee,
I would like with thee to be
My Dolly, my own.

Peter read and re-read this lyric, amazed at the facility with which he had dashed it off. For here was a piece of paper, and behold, so marvellous is the intellectual process, here was an exquisite poem written on it! Peter had no weak misgivings as to the quality of his poem. He searched his pocket and produced the lid of a cigarette box, kept for its aesthetic appeal of color and a vision of female loveliness in Turkish costume printed on it. With extreme care he transcribed his poem on the back of that work of the printer's art, giving at intervals a chirrup of exultation. "I done a bit of poem for yer," he said aloud, rehearsing the moment of its presentation to his mistress.

After the stress of great emotional effort the mind seeks relaxation in lesser activities. Peter searched his pockets for fresh entertainment, for all small boys, like Mr. Wemmick, place their faith in portable property. He produced a piece of elderberry wood and began to scrape the pith out of it with his knife. This is a charming occupation, for the pith comes out easily, and then one has a fine wooden tube, designed by Nature to blow peas through. Peter had peas among his portable effects, and looking about experimentally, saw one of Mother Regan's fowls picking close to the fence.

"Supposin' that fowl's a lion," said Peter aloud, "an' I'm here with me gun, sightin' dead level for his brain."

His mind thrilled with exultation, on fire with the poetry of a hunter's life. For who would plunk peas at fowls when, by the wizard's art, he may crawl through African jungles hunting lions. Peter poised his gun, taking careful aim through the palings. The lion, pecking inadvisedly close to the fence, had a pea flipped off its comb and fled, clucking indignantly. Peter rolled in the grass enchanted at this success. He went on bagging lions till old Mother Regan came out to inquire into the fluster among her fowls, sending Peter post haste for cover. He lay close hid till this danger had subsided, and came out for fresh entertainment.

Old Poulter, the church organist, went past on the other side of the road, beyond the reach of peas. Peter hastily unrolled his shanghai, and fitted a stone in the pouch. He had nothing against Old Poulter, but for that matter, hunters have really nothing against lions. An uncontrollable desire urged Peter to lob a stone on Old Poulter's square, white hat. He stretched his weapon, quivering between fear and suppressed daring. He would; he would not! Such villainous decisions await one's moment of greatest moral laxity, a wilfulness more of the hand than of the mind. Peter's fingers snatched at the second of weakened moral tension — the elastic twanged, the pebble whizzed on its course, missing Old Poulter's head by a miracle. The target, his white hat, rolled in the gutter at his startled leap. He paused, recovered his headgear, and peered over the school fence, red with anger. "I see ye there, ye skulkin' hound," he roared, menacing a tree-guard. Peter dived like a rabbit for his burrow, where he squeaked and quivered with ecstacy. What sport, this big game shooting! He lay hid till Old Poulter, flouted by the tree-guard, was forced to take his anger and his hat about their business. When he was well along the road Peter pretended to some recklessness in singing out: "Hoot him, the bloke with the hat." A satisfactory defiance, especially when one is careful to sing out too softly to be heard.

Lacking a more exciting target he lobbed a few stones on Old Watson's house, thrilling to hear them bound and rattle on the tin roof. Old Watson, too, participated in this thrill, if darting repeatedly out at the side gate with a stick was any evidence in appreciation on his part.

After such stirring activities food is necessary. For lack of better nourishment one restores oneself with the pith of rushes, marsh mallow seeds, and hawthorn berries.

Refreshed, Peter found diversion in a small lizard, which he caught and skinned. A Bulljo ant came exploring in his kingdom, and Peter had a row with him on principle. "Fight me, will yer," he said, enraged, squashing the intruder with a stone. One takes no risks with Bulljo's, who have stings like redhot needles. From the school ground arose suddenly the clamor of scholars, let out for a brief respite of play. Through a spy-hole Peter could see them leaping and running, squeezing as much activitity as possible into their period of release. To him they seemed remote, ridiculous creatures, from whom he had long since severed all connection. The clanging of the bell that called these slaves to labor marked off for Peter yet another hour of freedom. In his secure retreat Peter exulted at the ignominy of their fate. "Hoot him, I'm waggin' it," he sang, as people sing whose hearts are light, who spend the patrimony of their leisure in kingly ease.

The afternoon saw Peter dragging unwillingly to school. His morning glory had departed, for what are sun and clouds and the pipes of Pan to a man whose vision is darkened, and whose heart is glum. It was a drab world this, that had him in its grip — a world of tattered books and greasy slates, where one was hounded to acquire knowledge, not as a gift, but as a penance.

Peter flopped into his seat knowing no philosophy to bear up against the weight of depression that crushed his soul as flat as a pancake. There was a hiatus between his ear and brain — a vacuum, through which sounds penetrated, without meaning. If a herring and a half cost twopence three farthings how many herrings might one buy for nineteen and sevenpence? His mind repudiated any effort to understand this gibberish, clothed with devilish cunning in a masquerade of sense. The second master had charge of Peter's class that afternoon. A tall, thin man, with a tall, pale face, to which was attached a long black beard like an ancient Assyrian's; such kingly beards as Nature, in prankish mood, sometimes affixes to the chins of mild and inoffensive men. Yet you would be wrong to rate this fellow by the meekness of his countenance; for, though sparing of the cane, he could, when so disposed, cover you with a certain ponderous ridicule — a dreadful weapon, the more effective since one comprehends such talk with difficulty. Corrected several times for inattention, Peter was finally convicted of a suspicious munching.

Boredom will drive men to desperate expedients, and Peter, as an investigation discovered, was doing his best to dissipate monotony by eating an unripe quince. It is difficult to see the breach of morals involved, the act being rather penitential than refractory; but school masters have their own notions of decorum.

"Come out in front, Peter Dickson," said the master, "and place that objectionable object on the table."

Peter crawled forth reluctantly, tugging at his quince, which, on the alarm, he had thrust into a pocket too small for it. To this fact was due the exposure that followed, for his pocket adhered to the gnawed and viscous surface of the quince, and its contents were strewn on the floor. The lizard and some minor articles Peter recovered; but a piece of cardboard, on which was inscribed certain metrical characters, fluttered to the master's feet. Peter's heart registered a thrill of horror. The master had picked up and was solemnly perusing the inspired utterance of his passion. Peter stood on one leg, frantic with suspense. Yet there was worse to follow.

"This, it seems, is a love poem," said the master, and with measured intonation, that clothed Peter's lyrical frenzy in a garment of tragic pomposity, he read the now shameful doggerel aloud. Such an agony of confusion fell upon Peter as nearly rent him in twain. He screwed himself into knots, twisting and writhing in the impotency of his shame, feeling himself exposed to merciless derision. The class, perceiving his anguish, exulted openly, pointing and jeering; the master, stroking his beard, regarded him with an air of scientific interest, such as one might use to inspect a peculiar beetle.

"So you are given to addressing verses to the ladies, Peter Dickson," he said at length. "You are a victim to the grand passion at the age of twelve." Much more in this strain he said, inspired by some ponderous sense of humour that belied the biblical gravity of his beard. Peter endured this badinage very much as a weak minded guest might endure a mouthful of redhot pudding, because he has no other option than to swallow the unpalatable morsel. When he was finally dismissed to his seat Peter was in such a hopping state of frenzy that an ungovernable impulse caused him to hurl a book from the desk in passing. The master recalled him to a more fitting state of mind by rapping sharply on the desk. "Pick up that book, sir," he said.

"Will I," shouted Peter, goaded beyond a redeeming sense of caution. Even the mildest beard could not permit so open a defiance of its authority, so Peter was had forth to the floor again. "You shall be punished presently," said the master. "Stand there, sir, and reflect on the unwisdom of giving way to the angry passions."

In the boiling state of his emotions Peter was glad of this projected punishment. To be publicly caned is to be at least restored to some degree of self-respect. He stood aloof, polishing his palms with gloomy zest. Let this bearded insulter of one's tender feelings do his worst. Peter would show him and his beard so lofty a contempt as would cause his cane to wither. Perhaps, who knows, Peter would bounce a slate off his skull. The worst of it was that Dolly, in order to repudiate any connection with Peter's poems, persisted in looking at Peter as if he wasn't there. So one is treated for burning incense to the beauty of these minxes.

The lesson went on, and Peter was left stranded on the floor, a tragic figure, polishing its hands. The master, glancing at his watch, saw that the hour of release had come and put up his book. He turned to find Peter, stern, implacable, presenting the defiance of an outstretched hand. The master contemplated him benignly a moment, stroking his beard. Finally he laid the cane on Peter's palm, with the air of measuring his stroke, lifted it, and gently replaced it.

"Well, you're not a bad lad, Peter," he said; "I think I'll let you off this time. Run along home now."

The effect of this anti-climax was diastrous. A wave of emotion shook Peter from head to foot. To his own unfathomable disgust he burst into tears; tears of an appalling sincerity; tears compounded equally of rage, shame and anguish. And this before a class that had already witnessed the shameful exposure of his poem. He saw grinning faces, peering and bending, hiccuped a repudiation of the master's leniency, and then, unable to face this intolerable situation, snatched the door open and fled like one hunted by remorse. He ran with demoniac energy to his lair behind Mother Regan's, and there cast himself down, wallowing in a fit of abandoned fury. Such anger and grief he experienced as can only come to one sunk in a very villainy of shame. He rolled and kicked and beat the ground with his fists. He tore up handfulls of grass and cast them from him with insensate fury.

For an hour Peter lay in the gorse, and every time the presentment of those shameful tears rose before him he went off into a fresh paroxysm of kicking and grovelling. He took his pea-shooter and hurled it from him. He had done with such vanities. His shanghai he stretched so violently that he snapped both rubbers. Damn the thing, let it follow the pea-shooter! What are such vanities to a man who has nothing before him but the seclusion of a hermit's cell. He crawled forth at length, for even the most blighted misanthropist requires his tea. Half way home he was arrested by the thought of his shanghai and his pea-shooter, and hastened back to retrieve them. He had reason to regret his intemperate renunciation of these valuables, for the pea-shooter was lost, and the shanghai broken beyond redemption. His gloom considerably enhanced by his misfortune, he resumed the burden of his blighted existence, all unaware that he who in one day experiences the extremes of joy and misery touches something of the best that life can offer.

Certain People of Importance

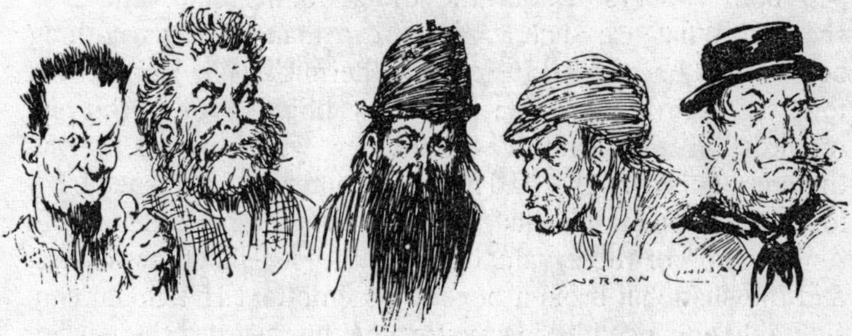

COMEDIANS OF REDHEAP

The notables of a country town on whom one placed the greatest entertainment-value were its less-reputable citizens – the less reputable the more their company was esteemed in our juvenile stratum. They revenged for us the soulless decorum forced on us by the home.

The most valued disreputable ancient in our estimation was old Bill Cannon, the custodian of the bowling-green.

He was a stumpy old man with a long, dank beard and bunion-distended feet encased in carpet-slippers, and he wore one of that era's immense broad-brimmed, high-crowned straw-hats lined with green cloth, under which his moistly tender red nose and libidinously winking old black eye existed in a perennial greenish penumbra, for I never remember seeing him without that hat, and I have suspicion he slept in it. I certainly recall seeing him seated up in bed wearing it, when confined there by a swingeing attack of rheumatics.

Published in the *Bulletin*, Sydney, 18 September 1957

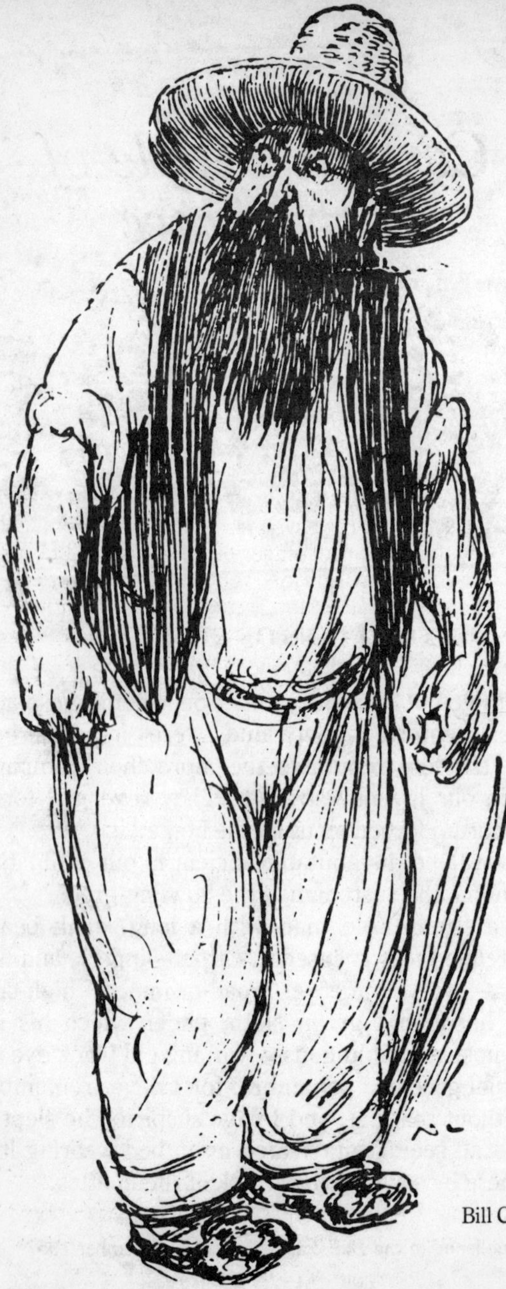

Bill Cannon

Bill was an old sailor, and how I regret now that I did not tap the wealth of reminiscence secreted in his memory, for his experience must have covered half-a-century of square-sail, and I daresay he had served in ships whose names are sacrosanct to those who love and mourn their lost splendor. Not that old Bill was one to see himself as the creature of a heroic tradition. His conversation was wholly devoted to another standard tradition of the sea; that of escape from it into every sailor's paradise — the port of arrival after a long voyage with a pocketful of cash, with the drabs of the waterfront lined-up to relieve him of it. If old Bill was to be believed, he had put up tremendous feats of venery in those days, to which he accounted the nemesis of celibacy now inflicted on him. Male self-esteem is usually reticent over a physiological debacle of that sort, but old Bill made it the subject of his constant lamentations.

The only event which distracted Bill's attention from this major grievance was a sacrilegious trespass of boots on the billiard-table perfection of his bowling-green, which never failed to bring him intemperately hobbling on his bunioned feet and vociferating malédictions which accused the trespasser of every unmentionable offence that Bill could lay his tongue to. As the tennis-court adjoined the bowling-green, with only a high cypress-hedge separating boozing bowlers from tea-drinking tennis-clubites, we used to caper with delight at hearing those refined ears of the social elect assaulted by old Bill's lurid vocabulary.

It was much complained-of by the ladies of the tennis-club, and Bill's dismissal demanded by them, but bowlers, whatever they may be off the green, are hearty, back-slapping, good fellows on it, so old Bill retained his office while his bunions and rheumatism permitted him to do so. His retort on those ladies was to indulge his talent for bawdy invention over their private lives — which was especially delectable to us, his junior court of sycophants, with those ladies tripping fastidiously back and forth with the impedimenta of the tea-tray.

But I find it impossible to Boswellise old Bill deprived of the unprintable nature of his vocabulary. Alas, that only simple men can use colloquial crudities without being offensive. It springs direct from the factual innocence of their outlook on life, which harbors no taint of prurience in recording it.

So pass, old Bill, hobbling on your bunioned feet off the earth's crust to a sailor's paradise . . .

A very different type of sailor was old Curly Coombs, who lived in a neat little white-painted, shipshape cottage on Hospital Hill, and who kept a fallen nautical way about him by wearing a forelock, two horns of hair brushed forward at the temples, and the Navy regulation of a shaven mouth but a fringe of chin-whisker from ear to ear.

He still wore, too, the regulation man-o'-war's white-duck trousers, reefer-jacket and tarred straw-hat.

Besides chasing slavers off the African coast and serving on the China station, Curly had been for a while on the Royal yacht Victoria and Albert, and always referred to the then Queen as "The old Gin-bottle" — but whether this inferred that the old lady was addicted to gin, or was referrable to her dumpy figure, the shape of a gin-bottle, is a question I leave to the researches of future historians.

Thought slightly irreverent when referring to his Sovereign, Curly was a tremendous stickler for the dignity of the English flag and, on some flag-wagging occasions when the Stars and Stripes had been hoisted above the Union Jack on the American Hotel flagpole, he threatened to cut down the pole unless the position of the flags was reversed; which was done, while Curly stood-by with an axe.

From Curly, at least, I might have garnered stories of the sea, for Curly was a garrulous raconteur; but boys are like ants, and keep to those itineraries which have to do with their affairs, and we rarely used Hospital Hill for a visit to Curly's cottage, unless making for Grub Gully, where we always went to roast potatoes in their jackets for an afternoon reflection.

We could have roasted potatoes in our back paddock, or down the flat, but tradition had it that potatoes must be roasted only in Grub Gully and, the slaves of tradition, we always tramped the three miles there to roast them.

There were other ancients who existed outside all status of repute or disrepute; derelicts hardly to be tabulated in the order of the human species.

Old Mick Reardon was such a one, a shambling homunculus with greasy long hair dripping from the brim of a high-crowned boxer-hat of some fungoid substance — it exuded a slime as of snails. He sprouted such a rank growth of dank whiskers that there was only space left on his face for his nose, which was a long, red tender snout of the shape and apparent consistency of a carrot, for he was constantly fondling and protecting it with one hand, as if he feared a sudden punch might snap it. He wore three or four coats in all kinds of weather, and possibly these had to do with a mystery frequently canvassed among us, which was that no one ever discovered where he slept, so that the supposition was that he carried his housing on his back, like a snail.

But the prime distinction of his being was that he had cultivated a tremendous stink, his *alter ego*, which pervaded space about him like a tangible substance. Noses coming in contact with it stopped with a jerk, and made a hurried itinerary round its perimeter to escape it. This stink was an undoubted asset to the single objective of old Mick's existence, which was to cadge beer. He would sidle up to the bar obsequiously smiling and furtively hiding his nose; and so stand, till in olfactory self-defence someone ordered him a beer, with which he would at once retire out of nosing distance. And as an attainable aspiration is the only solution to a satisfactory existence, no one can say that old Mick had not solved this oppressive problem.

Monkey Meggs was another old derelict, but one who had undoubtedly failed to find a satisfactory motive for existence.

The driving impetus of his being was a ferocious hatred for all mankind, and especially mankind in embryo, for if all the boys in our town had one collective neck he would have strangled it, so be he could get his clutches on it. He was a dirty, crook-backed, crazy old loon, with an underhung jaw sprouting a bristling grey stubble, and fierce little eyes darting glances right and left for causes of offence, while he shuffled along in a greasy old greatcoat that trailed on the ground, giving his progress the effect of going on castors. He was reputed to be an old lag, relic of the convict-system, and he lived in a squalid bush hovel on scraps of food collected at back-doors, which he carried about his person in greasy paper parcels.

For the diversion of the chase a cry of "Catch 'em alive-oh!" while hooking up one leg and imitating the simian action of scratching the ribs, invariably sent old Monkey into a hair-trigger release of frenzy, charging this way and that, snatching stones to hurl at us with intemperate aim, and even pelting his food-parcels when other missiles were not to hand. Fatuous to denounce boys for inhumanity and collective sadism. To know man one must also be man. How is one to divine the mass-mentality divided between stark primitivism and an acquired civilised consciousness unless one has been through both stages? A sound economic, to get the age of flint over early and settle down to enlarging the area of consciousness for the rest of one's life.

But entertainment-value is not solely the property of the town's disreputable denizens. A public performer on that score of the most distinguished order was W.B. Purdie, one of its most elect citizens. W.B. Purdie himself was not the protagonist of that performance, but its victim, in which he played the part of dummy and his leg that of low-comedian.

It was a sentient malignant, that leg, obeying no caprice but its own, and inflicting indignity on W.B. Purdie whenever he went abroad with it. From the waist upward he was the most dignified man in Redheap. His glossy top-hat was an importation from Paris. A selected flower always adorned his immaculate frock-coat. Gold-rimmed nose-glasses glinted on his high-bridged nose, and his beard was barbered to a precise point between his magnificent ram's-horned moustache. Only his prominent eye retained an expression of parboiled indignation at the low-comedy antics of his leg.

Its stage-entrance of a morning engaged the attention of everybody within view of W.B. Purdie's front gate, from

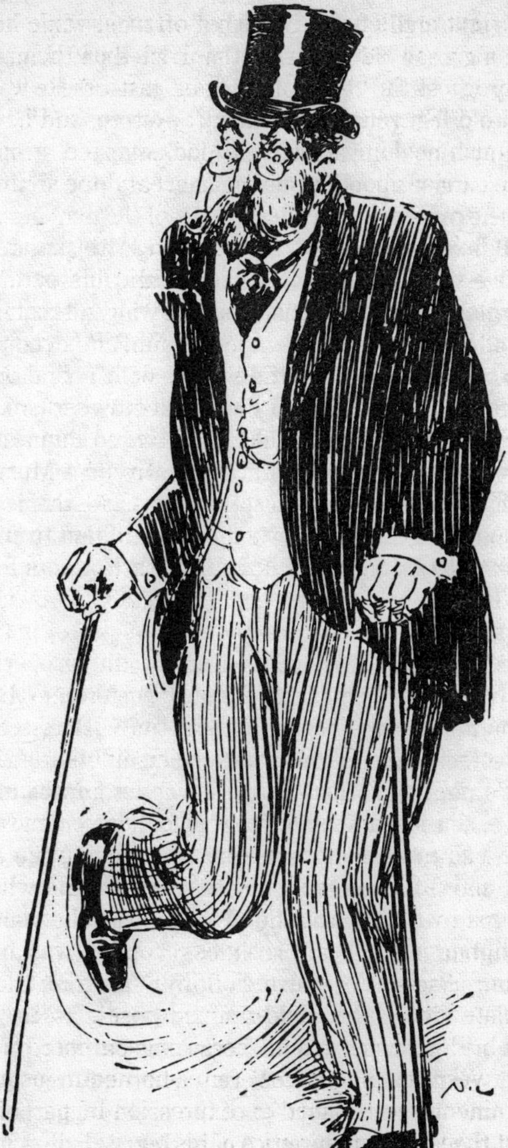

W.B. Purdie

which he emerged staggering about on two sticks, with his leg kicking out in all directions in the most spirited manner, and defeating all W.B.P.'s efforts to set a course with it, till it decided to go off with a bang, doing two steps to W.B.P.'s one, and forcing him along at a hoppity-kickety pace, with his sticks rat-tatting and his good leg doing a heel-and-toe shuffle to keep up with the procession.

W.B.P.'s objective was the American Hotel, dictated by the imperative of his scorching kidneys, and his parched gullet already making the motions of swallowing a sizzling brandy-and-soda. But his leg chose to reject W.B.P.'s chosen hostel, which lay well back from the street, with a fine open space before its frontage, and W.B.P.'s efforts to veer two points off his course kept him battling like a full-rigged ship clawing off a lee shore with a defective rudder. His curve hit Murphy's hay-and-corn store on the opposite corner, and the leg was off again, splurging full-tilt down the street again to perform its frustrating antics on the Bull and Mouth Hotel, or else dowse W.B.P.'s hot coppers in the horse-trough. Only by a practised tactic was W.B.P. able to grapple a veranda-post in time to get a half-turn on his leeway and rat-a-tat into the pub.

But even worse pranks the leg performed on W.B. Purdie's return-home at night after closing-time. Assisted by that notable effect of mental fuzziness which night-air inflicts on an evening's potations, the leg refused to let him chart a course for home, or sometimes precipitated him into homes where he least desired to be — in particular, the home of an acidulated spinster named "Granny" Buggins, whose house was next-door to his own. She was the town's most noted social purist and scandalmonger, so that it could only have been some perverse principle of attraction by repulsion that forced W.B.P., or his malignant leg, so frequently to barge full-tilt through her gate and come a crashing cropper on her front veranda. And, once down, there was no getting-up again for W.B.P. unless some wayfarer of the night lugged him upright and set him on his course. A just reprisal of scandal on a scandalmonger that old Miss Buggins, in curl-papers and a bedgown, should be exposed in the ambiguous posture of trying to lug W.B. Purdie off her premises while his leg was doing its best to take her virgin bedroom by assault.

In odd relationshp with W.B. Purdie was Uncle Dan Bodfish, the most prized of all our ancients. Both were uncles to an important member of our circle named Mucker Tweedie, and I never could work out how one nephew could have such a diverse combination of uncles, for Uncle Purdie dealt in mining-estate, with an important-looking office on the main street, and was of sartorial splendor and used a punctilious diction in a rich rolling voice, while Uncle Dan was a burly, bearded old man who had never worn a hat on his shock of upgrowing pepper-and-salt hair, and was never seen in a coat, and wore his shirt-sleeves perennially rolled up on his bronzed hairy arms, and did not inhabit the Purdie residence, but lived in a little hut down the yard with his mate, Sugarloaf George.

George was Uncle Dan's partner in the vocation of fossicker, and the pair of them were constantly going off in a leisurely way to sink a shaft or pan-out a prospect. Why be in a hurry to make a fortune when you must shovel away a few hundred tons of earth to get at it?

Uncle Dan's hut was any boy's concept of an ideal dwelling. It had bunks in it instead of beds, sawn-down barrels for chairs, a rough-board floor impervious to the clumping of dirty boots, and not an interdiction in it against a carefree deportment, smoking or swearing.

Moreover, Uncle Dan was a notable farceur, and liked an audience, and he found a perfect one in our circle, which was enchanted to find a burly and bearded comedian condescending to entertain it. His chosen device was one frequently employed by professional comedians, which was to hold conversations with himself in two character-presentations, one being Dan, and the other Bodfish to supply subject-matter on which comedian-Dan might exploit his wit. Sugarloaf George was frequently its subject, as well as supporting the character of dummy to Uncle Dan's performance. George did very well as a dummy, for he was a speechless, chunky little man with a chin-tuft, a wink, and a high-domed forehead, by which he had acquired his title of Sugarloaf. The wink was George's substitution for the lightning play of repartee. He used it, with suitable facial contortions, as comment on the brilliant dialogue between Dan and Bodfish, which was at its best at the Purdie dinner-table. Those excellent Purdie dinners, which were held in the kitchen, and so we were free of the starched decorums of a dining-room! Moreover, the Purdie young, nephews and nieces, were allowed to invite friends to them without bothering to consult aunts or uncles, which was a glorious prerogative, and proved their aunts and uncles to be the noblest of their kind. Dining at ease in the delectable company of girls, it was enchanting to have an Uncle Dan to keep the table in a roar at the brilliance of his patter.

"Eat hearty, Bodfish; I notice you ain't doin' yourself as well as might be expected. How so, Dan? It's owin' to exercisin' too much brain-power, Bodfish. A man as exercises his brain requires constant feedin', so I'll just arst you to have another go at that steak-and-kidney puddin'. To oblige you, Dan, I will. I wouldn't do it for anyone else, but as you're so pressin' I'll have another helpin' with an extra go at the cauliflower."

Captain Bunderby

When Captain Bunderby, escorting two ladies, walked past our house, on a wintry afternoon in the year 1882, he fixed for me an extreme point in time from that afternoon to the present moment. The past has nothing to do with its dated numerals on the recorded pages of history. It is a content of memory, and palaeolithic man is not a more distant figment of time and space than the adults who first emerged on the awakening vision of our infancy.

I am able to fix the date of Captain Bunderby's emergence, because I wore petticoats and the degradation of long curls, which means that I was about three years old. Of course, I must have been aware of other adults about the home before the caprice of memory decided to fix on Captain Bunderby as its most distant time factor, and I can account for this only by the fact that Captain Bunderby was himself a fixed time factor, concreting in his person the concept of his whole generation. It is due to my memory vision of Captain Bunderby that I enter-

Published under the heading "Uncles and Others" in *Southerly* No. 1, Sydney, 1955

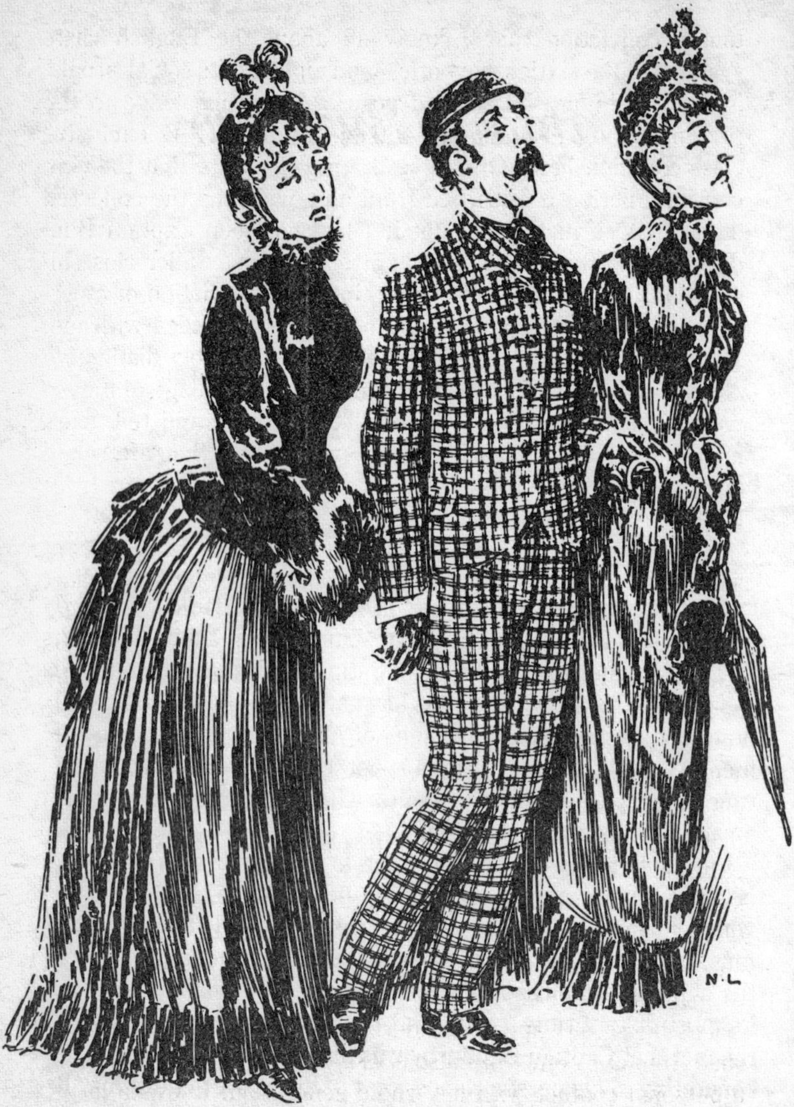

Captain Bunderby and his ladies

tain a conviction that I know all about the English caste systems of the sixties, seventies, and eighties, its social rituals, its spoken idiom, its studied pose of bored insolence to the pretensions of all humanity outside the pale of its exclusive class consciousness. Of course, I am well aware that the concept of a period is absorbed from its novels and the collected data of social historians; but if I had not seen Captain Bunderby in the flesh, and had his mystery house under close inspection, I would never have retained the conviction of a personal contact with his generation which still abides with me. And there must have been something remarkably distinctive about Captain Bunderby to have impressed an image of him so indelibly on my infant retina that three score and ten years later I see him as clearly this moment as on that afternoon when he strolled with an air of bored languor past our front gate.

He wore a little round basin-shaped hat with a narrow brim; which had the effect of greatly elongating his long pallid face, framed in two clipped sideboards and decorated by a drooping moustache. His eyelids also drooped to an alignment with his haughty, high-bridged pallid nose, which legend said he enclosed in a velvet nose peg at night to retain its aristocratic contour. His coat was buttoned up to its small lapels, revealing a black silk scarf tie, and his trousers were strapped down to his varnished boots. From one gloved hand he dangled a small flexible cane, and his cold, impassive gaze obliterated the existence of baser humanity within its line of vision. Of the ladies with him I retain only a vague period pattern of bustles, black velvet manteaus, and small bonnets on built-up chignons. Captain Bunderby engrossed all the attention I had to spare for lesser beings.

The house of Captain Bunderby, which was just across the road from our home, has also a lot to do with my conviction of a personal contact with his whole generation. It was a large, two-storied erection, originally designed to be a hotel, but converted by Captain Bunderby into a period-piece mansion, with a glassed-in balcony and long french windows through which, if the curtains were not drawn at dusk, one might observe Captain Bunderby dining in state with his ladies, all in evening dress, and attended by a butler in the correct garb of his calling. Yes, a butler; the only one who ever functioned in my native town. True, he was not precisely the clean-shaven, side-whiskered authentic butler of English tradition, as he had a great red beard. I wonder Captain Bunderby did not command him to shave it. Still, he made a majestic presence when taking the air of an afternoon at the front door of the Bunderby mansion. There was also a groom in green livery, white cords, top boots and a cockaded hat, when the ladies drove forth for an airing in the brougham.

The Bunderby grounds were extensive, with flower-beds, gravelled walks, a shrubbery and a croquet lawn. As they were on a slight elevation, the road had been cut down to the main street level, so that the fence on that side was some feet above the pavement, requiring our nursemaid to lift me that I might peer in at garden-party groups about the croquet lawn, the ladies in rustling bustles, high chignons and Dolly Varden hats, and very flirtatious with such males as might be entrapped into the insidious ritual of croquet, which in that era was what jazz afforded to the demoralised nineteen-twenties for an easy intimacy between the sexes. There was an aviary, too, but that was on our side of the grounds, and it was there, peering through a mystery hole in the fence, that I first saw peacocks. . . .

In short, Captain Bunderby had transferred intact the tradition of an English country house to an up-country Australian mining town, among its rough and tough denizens whose genesis was the goldfields of the fifties; and though the diggings were worked out, there were still big mines working which supported a large population of miners. Of course, the town in my infancy had simmered down into a normal division of classes: working people, shopkeepers, Government officials, and a small top layer of gentry, made up of doctors, lawyers, bankers, and those who had made minor fortunes in mining shares. Of these, Captain Bunderby took a place of first importance as Police Magistrate, for like a number of English

Army officers, mainly in the Indian service, he had thrown up his commission to take office as a police official in Australia.

But either as an official or a member of the upper class, he was not popular in the town. And that he was quite obtuse to the effect of his personality on others was made evident by a question he once asked my father: "Can you explain why I appear to be so unpopular in this demned town?" Recounting that passage to me long afterwards, my father said, "Deuced awkward question. *Noblesse oblige, savoir faire,* tact, and all the rest of it, put a man in a devil of a hole not to be offensive. Had to get out of it the best way I could, so I said, "Well, if you must know, Bunderby, it's because you're such an infernal snob."

If the gentry tempered their opinion of Captain Bunderby in that reticent style to his face, we have a fair estimation of what they said about him behind his back. And as the Bunderby ladies did not condescend to exchange visits with the ladies elect of the town, we don't need to inquire what *they* had to say about the Bunderby *mēnage*, either. So what a field day it must have been among the afternoon tea cups when the Great Bunderby Scandal burst on the town, blowing the roof off the Bunderby mansion, and exploding the legend of Captain Bunderby's haughty aloofness from vulgar contacts with the lower orders, to outcries of execration from the lower orders gathered in threatening array before the Bunderby mansion.

The event which detonated that uproar was an authentic episode from a Mrs Braddon novel; that of a squire of high degree who stoops to the undoing of the innocent daughter of the village blacksmith. In this case, it was the daughter of a tradesman, a pretty girl named Fanny Tregarth. Under what terms of a dark conspiracy of secrecy Captain Bunderby contrived to do his undoing of Fanny I have no data, but he certainly contrived to put her in the family way, and leave it at that. But Fanny had a brother . . .

He was still extant in the days of my nonage, a brooding, black-haired, beetle-browed man with one of those long pendent moustaches like the weepers on a mourner's hat, and his eye was charged with an expression of sempiternal gloom.

Possibly the Great Bunderby Scandal had affixed it there. For he was a brother of that era which chose for its impassioned slogan, "Sisters are sacred". When the fair fame of sisters was under discussion one heard that ferocious vindication of a brother's high sense of his obligation to preserve it in all its spotless purity: "I'd put a bullet in a bloke who laid a hand on my sister." Recalling the number of sisters who in that era were notable for allowing the town's amorous youth to tamper with their virtue, I wonder the streets at night were not littered with the tamperer's corpses. Yet to my knowledge no brother even blacked a tamperer's eye. The brother of Fanny Tregarth was the only one who had made a public announcement over his rage and grief at a sister's fall from virtue; and he did that, not by putting a bullet into Captain Bunderby, or punching him on his haughty, high-bridged nose, but by breaking every window in his mansion, while an outraged concourse of brothers burnt his execrated carcass in effigy. No doubt they were able to submerge an uneasy suspicion on their own account for laxity in vindicating the popular slogan that sisters are sacred by a collective denunciation of Captain Bunderby for having violated it.

And what of Captain Bunderby during all that uproar? Legend refuses to present him either as haughtily defying the base rabble, or as crouching in ignominy at stones crashing through his windows, exposed to his own butler as a philanderer with common wenches, and to the Bunderby ladies as one who had treacherously exploded a vulgar scandal on their refined exclusiveness. Legend is also vague about what happened on that score, though, of course, Captain Bunderby must have brought domestic cataclysm down on himself in the usual terms of an infuriated wife who has detected a husband going off the rails with a casual girl. I fancy there was a separation, and in any case, Captain Bunderby left the town either as the effect of that scandal, or very shortly afterwards, and his mansion was boarded up, and remained so in all my time in the town.

But for years I treasured a fantasy illusion that I had seen Mrs Bunderby, on that night of doom, drive off at midnight in the brougham, abandoning Captain Bunderby for ever. I might have been infected by a Mrs Braddon novel to have conceived such a crisis of drama, but I see now that it was an infantile effort to rationalise fragments of scandal caught from the remote, mystery world of grown-ups. From those I gathered a muddled conception that Captain Bunderby had been caught out by Mrs Bunderby doing something of an awful and unmentionable nature with Mrs Bunderby's sister, who was the other Bunderby lady. Knowing nothing of Fanny Tregarth's part in the drama at that time, but being aware that the unmentionable part of it had to do with some unidentified female, I naturally handed Fanny's part to Mrs Bunderby's sister, as the only other female to be identified with Captain Bunderby. The word "unmentionable" was much in ladies' mouths at that era when referring to conduct for which they lacked a precise synonym, and it must have come down to me from hushed and flushed whisperings over the afternoon tea cups.

The Bunderby mansion was left to decay. At times stray members of the lower orders squatted in it; an ironic tailpiece to the drama of Captain Bunderby's treachery to the caste taboos of his order in stooping to dally amorously with the daughter of a common Australian small-town shopkeeper. If he wanted that sort of thing he should have stayed in England and undone the daughter of the village blacksmith, assured that no concourse of enraged yokels would dare to burst his windows, or have the unparalleled effrontery to burn in effigy a member of the landed gentry.

A Cousin

He was the most lugubrious lad I have ever known. Resignation to martyrdom was the whole motive of his being. With a dolorous eye and a globular face the colour of suet, and of a fattish, lymphatic substance, he stood lumpishly about the activities of my elder brothers, knowing that acrobatic feats dedicated to joy were not for him. His name was Osbert, and he was the offspring of that bearded uncle who had taken offence at my embryonic exercises over the nude in art, and was constantly being left by that uncle on the premises of other uncles for indeterminate periods, and possibly his doleful outlook on life had to do with an enforced association with too many uncles. Certainly he had sad tales to tell of injustices perpetrated by those uncles on a suffering nephew. Their theme was that nobody wanted him, which was possibly true, for, putting uncles out of it, active cousins have no use for a lubberly lad imposed on them as a guest; and even aunts are apt to be a trifle intolerant of a martyred nephew peering in at the kitchen window where food is being prepared, but not for

Published in *Southerly* No. 2, Sydney, 1955

him, or announcing resignation to a joyless existence by lurking in the dark end of the passage at night, and giving them a severe fright as a mournful moon-face materialised out of the hall-stand overcoats. By day, he favoured a small embrasure between two tanks for standing about in. As he was fourteen years of age to my ten what time he suffered as a martyr cousin in our home, his status should have been guest cousin to my elder brother, whom I will call Bill; but Bill refused to function as host to such a lumpish parasite at Osbert, who therefore selected me to hear the sad story of his various martyrdoms, which he told in a flat, resigned voice, not complaining of them, but accepting them as evidence of his ordained lot.

". . . And when I was staying with me Uncle Ferdinand I fell downstairs and broke me back, and me Uncle Ferdinand said, If your back's broken walk upstairs to prove it, and I proved it was broken by being only able to crawl upstairs, and when they had macaroons for tea they never gave me any, and when me cousin Walter was asked to a party he never asked me to come too, and I never had any dinner that night because I was standing out in the yard and they never called me in, and me Uncle Ferdinand said, Serve you right going without dinner when we thought you were at the party, which only proved they wanted to starve me, and when I was staying with me Uncle Frintle I fell out of a high tree and broke me leg, and me cousin Henry just left me lying there, and I might have had to lay there all night starvin', only a kind man brought me home in a dray, and me Uncle Frintle said, If you prefer to stay out till this hour of the night you must go without dinner, which proved they grudged me the food I ate, and when I was staying with me Uncle Egbert I fell . . ."

Even at that date I was forced to remark a certain monotony about Osbert's martyrdoms, which had much to do with falling from high places and injuring himself severely, and being deprived of food by obdurate uncles, though it must be conceded that he did endure a considerable martyrdom when staying at our place, not by the malevolence of an uncle but by the insensate activities of a cousin. Osbert had been foisted on to Bill as a cousin to be entertained, and when Bill chose to entertain himself about the home, Osbert had to put up with it. At the back of our home were a number of battered trees, exhausted with trying to compete with Bill's arboreal proclivities. One lopsided pine had a suicidal house lolling in its branches, and boards were nailed casually across high spaces for strolling on from tree to tree. A trapeze dangled from a bough, and Osbert's martyrdom will be instanced by Bill dangling from the trapeze by his calves, with a purple face, and counting in a strangulated voice, while Osbert looked mournfully on, aware of a conspiracy by Bill to have him fatally injured.

"Eighty-four," said Bill, and fell off the trapeze on his face. That was nothing, and he leapt up to shout, "Prove you can beat eighty-four hanging by the calves."

"It's hard luck I can't prove it, because I've hurt me leg," said Osbert.

"Prove where it's hurt," commanded Bill.

Osbert pulled down his stocking and showed a small scratch. "The pain's agony," he said, limping to prove it. But Bill failed to register concern for a suffering cousin. He gave a hoot of derision at Osbert's scratch and ran at the trapeze to whip up on it, slide down hooked by the biceps, to whizz round in circles and whizz off on his backside.

"Nine times the muscle grinders," he said vauntingly.

It will be seen that Bill's performance as host was to depreciate the acrobatic status of a guest. He now proposed as a test of inferiority in Osbert that he should ascend to the roof of our house via the two tanks without holding on, which feat Bill performed, with minor abrasions. He would also have had Osbert drop from high boughs to the ground, swing from tree to tree with simian ease, and walk the tight-rope on a length of iron piping sustained precariously aloft, which feats Osbert's invalid condition would not permit him to essay. But he was induced to leap a hen coop, which was a mistake, as he caught his toe and came down a squelching wallop on his belly, and injured himself severely. But he did not complain. It was Bill's intention that he should injure himself, and he had now done so, and he got up limping and holding himself in a contorted posture, and sat down on a tank-stand, saying with resignation, "Me arm's broken. I suppose I've broken something internally, too. I don't suppose I'm really wanted here. I only come because me father made me, and I suppose you'll be glad when I'm gone. . . ."

But apart from those inflicted on him by Bill, Osbert did succeed in having one of his established martyrdoms while staying in our town, though he was not at our house when it befell him. It chanced that an uncle had been transferred to our town at that time, in charge of the Post Office, and by arrangement between aunts, Osbert was bestowed on him for a space, and this brought his martyrdom under the personal inspection of Uncle Archibald, who was a short, trenchantly upright uncle with mutton-chop whiskers and a Johnsonian habit of coming down sharp on all loosely authenticated statements. A dangerous uncle on whom to perpetrate a martyrdom which could be subjected to a strict inquiry.

Its scene was a Saturday-afternoon jaunt across the old diggings by Bill and his intimates for a swim in Puddler's Dam, Osbert going with the party, but not of it. He preferred to trail well in the rear of any bumptious, contentious, mullock-heap-bounding social event conducted by Bill, knowing well that its surface pretences merely masked a conspiracy to do some fell thing to him. So that when the clay-daubing interlude of refreshment was over at Puddler's Dam, and Osbert still not of or with the party, he was not missed, and remained missing till the dinner-bell went, and investigation failed to discover him, as usual, patiently starving in the yard.

And this much must be conceded to the reality of Osbert's martyrdoms. Greatly as he suffered at being deprived of food, he was prepared to forgo a meal when suffering a martyrdom. As usual, this one was inflicted on him by falling from on high; down a hole, to be precise. And as there were a few thousand old rotten holes for falling into, Osbert could hardly have selected a more propitious site for enduring a well-authenticated martyrdom, from which he did not arrive home till bedtime, with a sad story to tell of how he lay groaning from severe injuries down an old shaft of great depth, and

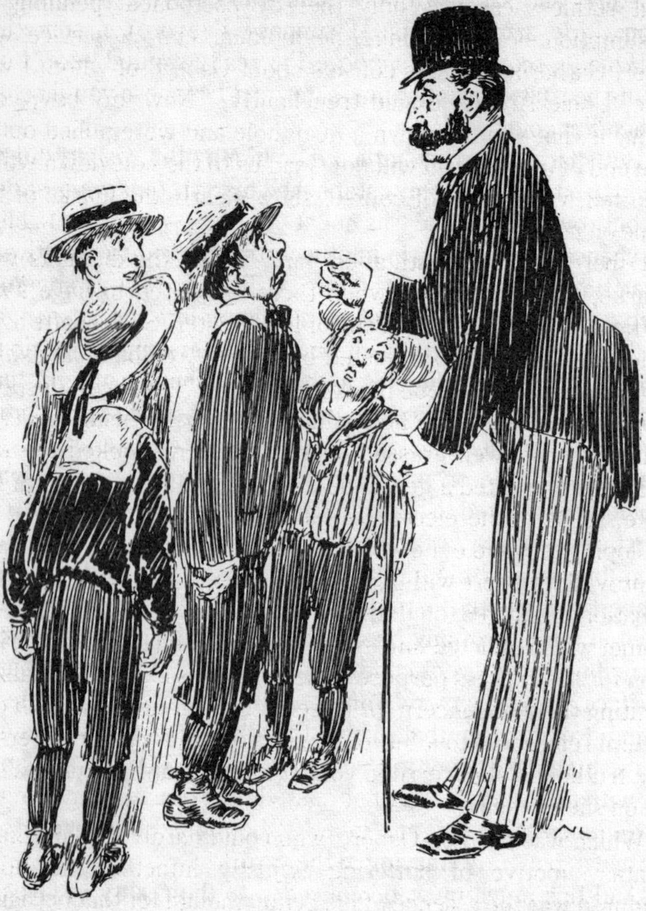

Uncle Archibald and Osbert

would undoubtedly have starved to death there but for his groans being heard by two kind men who happened to be passing, and who procured ropes and so pulled him out.

Uncle Archibald put Osbert through a precise cross-examination as to the particulars of this harrowing experience, and so far abated the ruthlessness of an uncle by sanctioning a late meal in the kitchen, and sending him thereafter to bed.

But ruthlessness was only thereby postponed, pending its resumption next morning, the moment church service was over. Gathering various cousins about Osbert, of whom I was one, Uncle Archibald said trenchantly, "Now, my boy, your story is that you fell down a deep hole and were pulled out at the end of a rope. You will now lead us to the hole down which you fell, which will, of course, show clearly the marks of the rope on its edges."

Osbert led the investigation party across the diggings with marked reluctance, and when there, appeared to have some difficulty in locating the scene of his disaster. Such shafts as he selected were at once rejected by Uncle Archibald, as exhibiting no evidence of rope marks on the rim. Finally, in desperation, Osbert selected a hole which had no rim, being merely a fallen-in shaft well grassed over. But he overlooked the fact that this presented a gentle declivity for walking up out of the hole, so be it one elected to fall into it, as we all proved by galloping into and out of it with hoots of derision. All the same, it provided Osbert with a valid infliction of martyrdom by the jobation bestowed on him by Uncle Archibald all the way home, which indicted him as one who concocted a base fabrication for the express purpose of deceiving his elders, and falsely inciting them to concern for a seemingly lost nephew, with collateral references to a future nemesis for all such perverters of the truth; and very terrible your trenchant, upright uncles can be on such a theme.

Which was hard on Osbert, who could hardly explain that a fantasy motive of suffering unjustly inflicted and nobly endured was the essence of his being, though for that occasion, I believe, he would willingly have reversed the roles of suffering nephew and malevolent uncle, for he said to me later, in private, with a certain dark significance, "You only wait till me Uncle Archibald falls down a hole and breaks his back and see how he likes it when I don't get a rope to pull him out again. . . ."

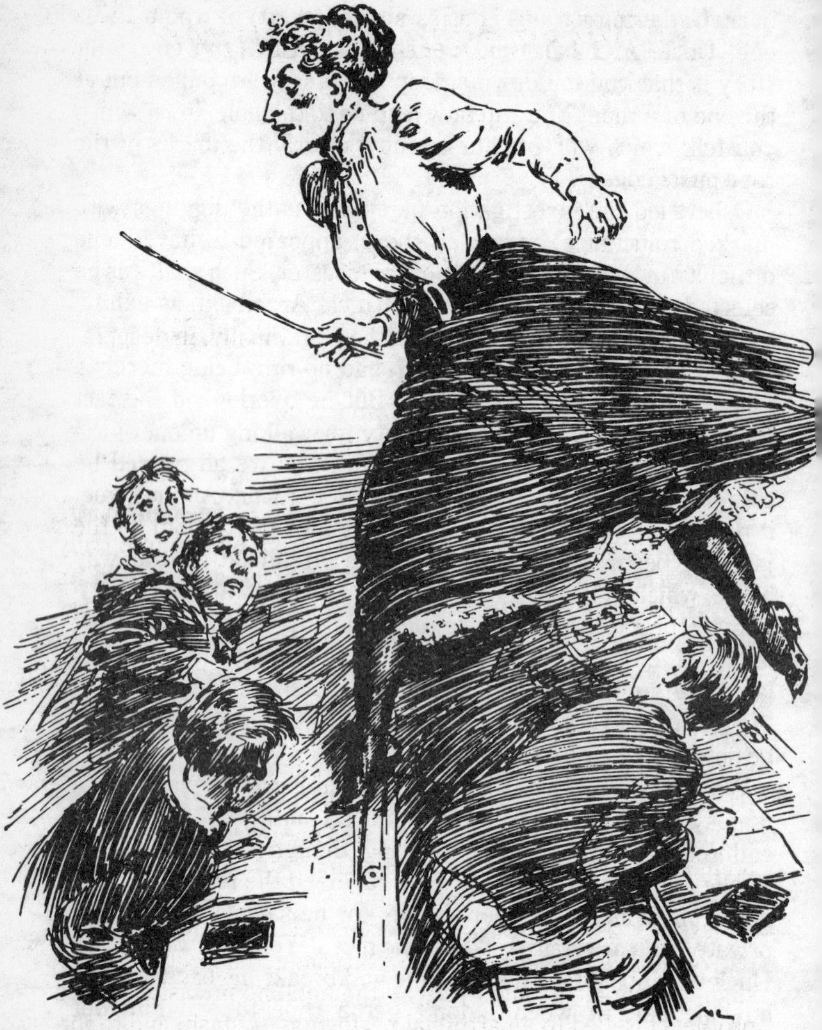

Miss Sadie Sabine

Miss Sadie Sabine

In my time at the state school, Miss Sadie Sabine had charge of the fifth class, which is to say that from nine to four daily she was brought into active conflict with the male ego in its mass content of some forty-odd lads about the age of fourteen. On the other hand, our collective adolescence was forced to support the impact of Miss Sadie's vitriolic femininity with a certain effect of confusion on its academic vocation. At this date I find it difficult to decide whether her femininity or her vocation was the disturbing factor in our relations with Miss Sadie. There were girls in the class too, but I rule them out as having any significance to Miss Sadie's vocation or her femininity. It seems to me that we alone supported her hectic assault on our embryonic masculinity.

Hectic is the key-word to a reconstruction of Miss Sadie's personality. It was conveyed by the dangerous glitter in her slightly prominent blue eyes, by the aquiline precision of her profile, chiselled to an artificial perfection of finish, and to the satanic activity of her stocky figure, which constantly

Published in *Southerly* No. 3, Sydney, 1955

threatened, and frequently performed, a lightning onslaught on the collective male backside. Later meditation inclines me to put the accent of Miss Sadie's femininity on that peculiar glitter of the eyes, which literally shot a diamond-bright spark from them at moments of emotional tension, even though sapient opinion credits that spark to certain intemperate ardours in the feminine being most remote from the austere vocation of schoolteacher . . .

Therefore that inference must be strictly ruled out as having any reference to Miss Sadie's conduct, in school or out of it. Lady schoolteachers are professionally doomed to celibacy; or were, in my time. They were under inspection by the community at large for any laxity in conduct or morals. The spiritual uplift of the young was in their keeping. A scandal would mean professional extinction.

Whether or not that scintillating glitter in Miss Sadie's eye had to do with ardours rigorously repressed, she certainly kept both herself and the class in a state of high tension, with a certain effect of exhilaration on its male components, even when attended by her method of enforcing discipline on them by lugging a delinquent up by the scruff of his neck and applying a stinger to his rump in a posture of indignity. Her speed of action caught one before duplicity could cover up from a misdemeanour. Such was the vigour generated in her handsome, muscular legs that she was able to take a standing jump from the floor to a desk in such an instantaneous manner that a misdemeanour was under inspection from that altitude no matter whereabouts it was being performed in the long classroom. It may be asked how we knew she had handsome legs in that era when no skirt was cut above ankle length. That was an optical thrill awarded us by Miss Sadie's lightning descent on a misdemeanour, which was not to go round the desks to get at it, but to speed across them in a series of tigerish bounds that left on the retina an impress of muscular legs in black stockings vanishing in a penumbra of white petticoat.

To such stirring adjuncts of the feminine on Miss Sadie's vocation of teacher, there was another confusion of both aspects of her being which had an exhilarating effect on her methods of imparting instruction, though at the time it had a slightly disturbing recoil on our adolescent reflexes. When touring the class behind desks to overlook an exercise in scholarship, or lack of it, she would pause to elucidate a difficulty by leaning over to reach one's exercise book in a posture which encompassed one between a pair of rounded arms and a resilient pressure of breasts on the back of one's neck. Embarrassing as it may be to be embraced by a lady in public, even on so remote a relation as a mathematical problem, it was impossible to dissociate Miss Sadie's austere vocation from her seductive contours, or prevent one's nose from frolicking with her alluring aromas. In any case, it confused one's reaction to the exotic feminine in Miss Sadie with the conception of her as a snotty bitch when she set about one with the cane. And that emanation of both the exotic and vitriolic in her was most in evidence when domination over a large and restless class sent her at one bound from the floor to a desk, there to stand lashing her skirt with the cane like a tigress lashing her tail, her eyes glittering, her nostrils distended, two flushed patches of temper on her cheeks, and her figure vibrant with vitality in leash for an assault on our reflexes.

Did I think Miss Sadie a handsome creature when I absorbed that presentation of her vitriolic femininity and her abounding sex vitality? No, I think not. Small boys have very little conscious reaction to the adult feminine canon in all its variations between beauty or a complete lack of it. Charm is displaced for what tolerance it may have to the needs and aspirations of the immature male ego. If Helen of Troy came down from Olympus to conduct a class on terms of harrying it with impositions, castigating its misdemeanours, keeping it in after school or getting it in for cuts in the office, she would be labelled a snotty bitch and dismissed as an obnoxious adult. Yet in spite of the snotty-bitch content of Miss Sadie's being, I think we liked her. Her explosive methods of maintaining discipline were discussed with a tolerant air. There was even a sporting element in what we called "Getting Sabine's goat", even if it brought down on one a slash on the rump. And she had one highly valued habit of suddenly letting her academic vocation go for a heart-to-heart indulgence in self-revelation, which used up time otherwise squandered on textbooks. It was usually on late afternoons, when tempers thin out, when attention refuses to concentrate, when boredom resorts to scuffling and shuffling, that exasperation with her vocation sought release from it in fantasy. And that fantasy had its being in the major compulsion barely submerged by her glittering eye and the driven vitality of her stocky body. Slashing the desk with her cane, she would shout, "Attention!" and when that was secured, she would eject intolerance at the class in terms of "Do you think I'm going to waste my time trying to knock some intelligence into a lot of numskulls like you if you haven't the sense to profit by it? If I was not devoted to my career I would not do it for two minutes longer. Let me tell you — Florrie Tucker and Edie Plummer, come out in front. If you must do each other's hair you can stay in and do it after school — that at my last school I received an offer of marriage which I dare say most women would consider extremely flattering. It was from a — Simmons, come out and put that filthy quince you are eating on the table — a squatter. With the largest run in the district. And an extremely handsome man, too. I may have been foolish to prefer my career to a life of luxury and ease, and it remains a question whether I may, or may not, yet decide to send in my resignation. I have every inducement to do so."

As I never saw Miss Sadie outside the school, other than striding away from it with that swing of the hips which gave her skirt the motion of a Highlander's kilt, I am unable to supply any evidence of what her relations with adult masculinity may have been. For that matter, no small boy believes that a schoolteacher can have any existence other than that of hammering into him the arid subject matter of textbooks. That such a one could have anything in common with the passions that agitate humanity at large is an assumption too preposterous to contemplate. Teachers may have some personal idiosyncracies in their methods of inflicting their vocation on me, but otherwise they are dehumanised by its stale repetition ticked off on the clock between the hours of nine to four. You have them classified mainly by the amount of discomfort they may inflict on you in forcing you to assimilate a mass of indigestible erudition, which you regurgitate mentally the moment you leave school, and remember nothing of in after life. Their personalities, therefore, can be summed up in compact terms which dispense with any subtlety in the way of sub-clauses. Black Sammy the headmaster, then, was just a plain bastard. Or, under the superlative sting of his mastery with the cane. a stinkin', lousy bastard. When he came panther-treading the classroom we knew it was not to inquire into our scholastic shortcomings, but to select a counter-irritant to his misfunctioning gastric process. We, not he, were the victims of an excess of bile in his pedagogic liver. Whiskers Thorpe, the second master, was not such a bad old bastard, as he wielded a temperate cane, though he was given to indulging ironic comment on one's intellectual deficiencies which made a blinkin' fool of a bloke when held up to the class's derision. Slimey Simmons, the junior master, was given Black Sammy's status as a bastard, mainly because of his habit of having you out before the class for an oral examination and lashing you across the stockinged legs when you got the answer wrong. Fortunately, he was only given the very junior classes to practise sadism on. Miss Quiddle had the virtue of being stout and lethargic, and not much given to enforcing erudition by castigation unless we made special nuisances of ourselves. What presentation of identity they may have made of themselves outside the school I have no notion. Miss Sadie Sabine was the only schoolteacher in my experience who laid claim to the bizarre possession of a private life, and that only in the fantasy terms of a lady pursued by a horde of suitors ardent to possess her stocky figure and the classic perfection of her profile. One might have assumed that reality would have found those feminine assets a marketable commodity, if their lady had been adroit enough to command a price for them. But if Miss Sadie's assault on our immature masculinity was any indication of her tactics with the adult male ego, I suspect she scared off anything in the way of amorous enterprise. She lacked the first principle of feminine strategy, which is to impose an illusion of sex dominance on an intending seducer. Moreover, she was in her thirties when in charge of our class. Celibacy, practised too long, can become a strait-jacket. If a mature spinster does manage to throw it off, she is apt to throw off all discretion with it. I have a suspicion that Miss Sadie had reached that crisis of desperation, even to seeking a solution to the frustrations of her femininity in such masculine attributes as a lad of fourteen may possess.

I may be all wrong in that assumption, since at the time I never had the wit to put its implications to the acid test of action. Those may have been merely functional of her vocation, which commanded her to investigate a lapse in conduct and morals, of which I and a pretty girl named Dolly Trimmer were the suspect subjects.

In most classes, boys and girls were seated in alternate rows, but in Miss Sadie's class, the sexes were segregated into two sections, with a space between them. It was my seat at the end of the desk which allowed me to hold communion with Dolly at the end of her desk opposite. She was a charming young creature, a little blonde Venus, with scented, silver gilt curls, and a gold-tinted skin faintly flushed with pink, which is the heritage of a distant Nordic ancestry, and already her body had mature curves under her knee-high print frocks. As she and I were both members of an out-of-school group which sported round about the W.B. Purdie home, where the young were strangely free from adult intrusion, ease of address was established between us; and it was in the casual terms of that intimacy that she one day passed me a scribbled piece of paper while Miss Sadie was engaged at the blackboard. It was a rhymed conundrum.

When gentle storms arise,
Shall gentle storms succeed.
I will not cause you sighs,
Sleep is the friend you need.
With these few words designed,
You will a question find.
My question please find out,
Love is a trouble when in doubt.

I studied this gibberish, but failed to elucidate the question it was making a fuss about, and Dolly, marking this evidence of intellectual obtuseness on my part, gave me a key to her riddle by whispering across to me, "Read the first words." Being unacquainted with that literary exercise, the acrostic, I kept on reading the first lines which got me nowhere, and I was still drivelling over them when Miss Sadie made one of her lightning swoops down on me and had twisted the paper out of my hand before I had time to smuggle it into the desk. Standing over me, she read it with a frown, while behind her, I marked Dolly clap a hand to her mouth in consternation. Apparently Miss Sadie failed to decipher the conundrum at a first reading, for she merely said abruptly, "Where did you get this rot?"

"I picked it up on the floor."

She strode back to her table and spread out the paper to study it intently, incited thereto by its express invitation, and by a trained suspicion that all furtive antics in the young are evidence of illicit behaviour. By the way she suddenly stiffened up with a dangerously glittering eye it was evident to Dolly and me that she had unravelled the cryptic message, and pointing an imperious cane at me she said, "You stay in after school."

I stayed in, very uncertain of what misdemeanour I had committed by reading a seemingly meaningless scribble during school hours. Alone in that large classroom with Miss Sadie, I divined something portentous in this affair by the way she strode across to bump down on my desk with her feet on the seat and demand truculently, "Who gave you that piece of disgusting drivel?"

Confused by that stigma of disgusting, I repeated my explanation of picking it up from the floor, at which she said scornfully, "One of the girls gave it to you. Tell me at once who it was."

"Cripes, no, straight dinkum. I just picked it up."

"That's enough of your lies. Own up that you got it from Dolly Trimmer."

"No, I didn't, absolutely. I just picked it up."

Regarding me with the danger signal of those two angry

flushes on her cheek bones, she said, "That girl's a young trollop. I believe you carry on with her."

Inquisition from that angle of the affair was alarming. What adults call "carrying on" with girls arouses them to special pharisaical frenzy, as I knew by personal experience in the home circle. And by what explicit terms can you deny its implication? All I could do was mumble the usual defence of "only knowing Dolly a bit to talk to". To that Miss Sadie said fiercely, "You must have gone a good deal further than talk if she hands you a piece of indecent drivel like that."

More confounded than ever at the assumption that my private relations with Dolly were implicated by that now portentous piece of drivel, I could only repeat once more that I had picked it up, and that Dolly had nothing to do with it, while Miss Sadie sat glaring at me with something much more intimidating in her sharp-edged profile than a threatened slash on the rump. And it could hardly have been by the effect of an inquisition into conduct and morals that she suddenly gripped me by the shoulders and shook me violently, exclaiming through her teeth, "The idea of a boy of your age carrying on like that with girls."

Possibly it was by the recoil from a slightly ambiguous intimacy with a boy of my age that she suddenly said, "Clear out. And if I catch you again —"

That threat remained suspended, and I cleared out in a hurry, still the creature of an emotional crisis difficult to acount for over a seemingly innocuous piece of doggerel verse. But enlightenment on that score was waiting for me round the corner of a fence opposite the school, where Dolly was hopping agitation to find out how far that inquisition into the affair by Miss Sadie had implicated her, which she burst on me with the question of, "Did you tell her I gave it to you?"

"No. I told her I just picked it up."

"What did she say about it?"

"Just picked on to me about it being hot stuff or something. Blowed if I could see where the hot stuff came in."

"But I told you to read down the first words."

"So I did. There wasn't anything in them. Just 'When gentle storms arise'."

"No, no. Not the first line. The first *words* of each line."

I called over those words, and their import burst on me with staggering effect. What would have been libidinous exhilaration under other conditions now carried a catastrophic threat with it.

"Cripes! I'll be in for it if she shows it to Black Sammy."

I had need for alarm at the effect of that piece of doggerel on Black Sammy's misfunctioning gastric process. Anything labelled "indecent" by him as issuing from our assumed vernal innocence of life's simple crudities sent him into a sadistic frenzy. He had once given Mick Hogan forty cuts for talking what passed for bawdy wit in our stratum to the girls, and that only on evidence from a sneaking informer. And Mick Hogan was a tough lad, able to stand up to a castigation of that magnitude. The thought of facing up to one on the concrete evidence of that acrostic iced my spine, and I went to school next day savouring the horrors of a physical coward threatened by the torture chamber.

But no belly-slumping mandate arrived commanding my presence in the office. I caught Miss Sadie's eye on me at times with an effect of adult intolerance for anything in the way of those ambiguous carryings-on in the young of the species, but otherwise she took the class at her usual intemperate tempo, and I escaped when it was dismissed gulping down a blessed surcease of the horrors, and with my morale still intact from the demoralising threat of a lashing. It was revealed to me that Miss Sadie was the noblest of her kind; one with evidence to convict me of a major criminality, who had refrained from putting it before the court. I had to find some means of expressing my sense of her magnanimity, and next day at the lunch recess I gathered a bunch of our best flowers, and secreted them in the school lavatory, being abashed at the ordeal of publicly presenting them. With school dismissed, I retrieved them from the lavatory and carried them to the classroom, where Miss Sadie was putting her table in order before departing. To my mumbled, "I just thought I'd bring you a few flowers," she took the bouquet, inhaled it, and put it down to seat herself and say, "Come here."

I came, and she drew me close to her, and remained with an arm round me while she studied my face with a frowning intentness that I found embarrassing. In a curiously constrained voice, very different from its normal strident dominance, she said, "Tell me the truth. How far do boys like you go with those girls you knock about with at night?"

It left me speechless. With the best of goodwill to answer it, by what possible idiom could I have conveyed to an adult lady teacher the inconsequential nature of amorous enterprise which lacked precedent, had no stabilised ritual, and never arrived anywhere save by the vagary of chance or the caprice of girls. An impasse in communion between a muddled adolescent and an equally muddled spinster lady. I can only suppose it was by desperation at bridging that gap rather than by a belated discretion that Miss Sadie thrust me off, saying in a tone of exasperation, "Oh, go home, you young fool." But as I reached the door she said abruptly, "Thanks for the flowers, anyway."

Poor Miss Sadie Sabine. Inadequate as I may have been to mollify the compulsions of a frustrated Sultana which you daily exploded on the class at large, how glady would I have put my humble endeavours at your service if you had only been a little more explicit about what you required of them. Your vocation of teacher should have assured you that lads of fourteen are crude factualists, and are not gifted with powers of divination over the submerged urges of adult ladies, teachers or otherwise. All the same, incompetent noodle that I was, I must have responded lyrically to the Sultana encased in the hard shell of the schoolteacher, for I recall now that you frequently figured in those bedtime reveries wherein we correct the frustrations of reality by the heroic achievements of fantasy. I am sure they would have vindicated your sex appeal at least to an adolescent of fourteen, in spite of his incompetence to make obeisance to it in your presence.

Sommerville Ponsonby

Memory has played its usual prank of mixing up time-factors in my recollections of Sommerville Ponsonby, for it insists that he first arrived on my vision as a guest to Sunday's dinner, what time I wore a sailor suit of plum-coloured velvet with an orange collar, an obnoxious garniture forced on me by maternal ruthlessness at the age of nine; whereas I could only have been about four what time I sat under a hall table and heard a momentous conversation between Sommerville and my mother which had to do with the major drama of Sommerville's being as a man, a bank manager, and his status as one of the town's social elect.

But let that go for the moment and allow memory to insist that I first saw him as a guest to Sunday's dinner, which was a midday dinner, as in the custom of that era. It must have been greatly impressed by him, for it registered the minutiae of his appearance as if for future reference as to the correct stylism of a gentleman of the eighties. He wore a full-breasted frock coat with sateen lapels, a white waistcoat with pearl buttons,

Published in *Southerly* No. 4, Sydney, 1955

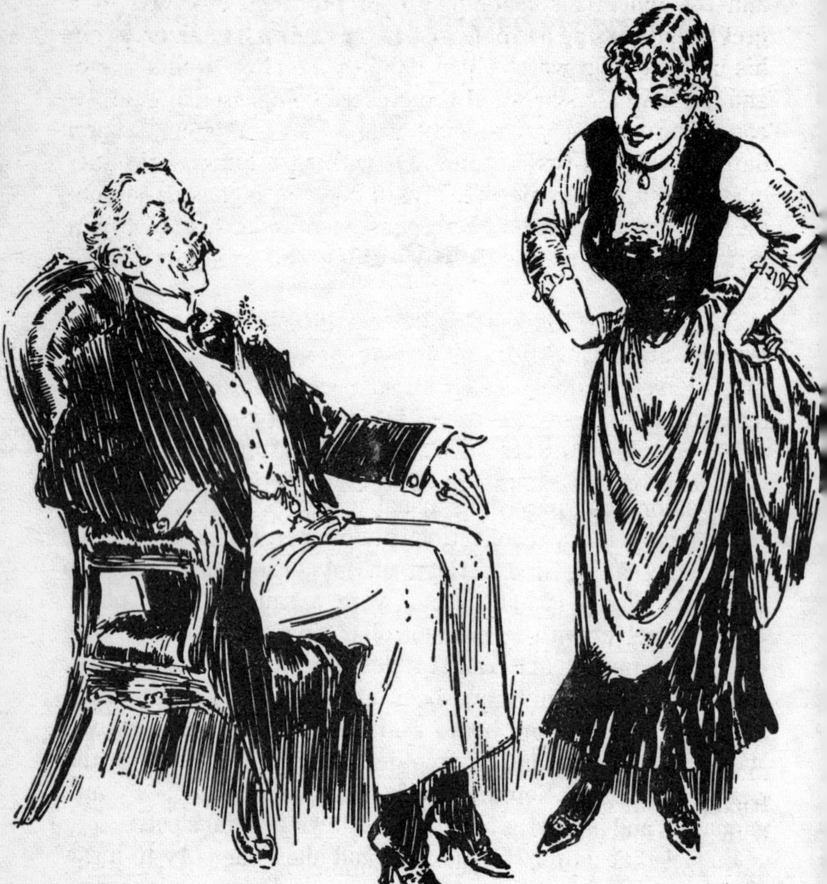

Sommerville Ponsonby

dove-grey trousers, and highly varnished boots. His cuff studs were of coloured bulldogs' heads under round glass covers, and the pin in his made-up tie of brocaded silk was of a greyhound chasing a rabbit, also under a glass container. From his massive gold watch-chain dangled a locket, a pink agate, and the masonic symbol of the crossed compasses in gold. Of course he wore a large signet ring — no gentleman's hand dared go abroad without one. Or without a button-hole bouquet, which in Sommerville's case had the ingenious attachment of a small bottle of water fastened under his lapel by a metal clip, so that his bouquet might not wilt for lack of refreshment.

This sartorial inventory has overlooked Sommerville himself, perhaps because he was of such a sandy consistency that his face was only a slight colour-variation on his gingery moustache, eyebrows, and hair brushed into two ram's horns at the temples. And also because he had a voice which abolished any precise statement of identity. It was such a thin, high-pitched treble that the ear was forced to entertain the concept of a ghost with a sore throat whispering through a keyhole. In that voice memory records him as saying, while we all stood round waiting for dinner to be served, "Ah! I see you have my Wilcannia chair here."

A drivelling thing for memory to make a point of recording. The chair was merely a Vienna rocking-chair of no distinction whatever, and I must surely have heard Sommerville make more revealing remarks than this. He was my father's dearest friend. I was often taken with them when they went fishing, both wearing the unseasonable garb of frock coats and top hats. In those days commercial cunning had not devised all those sport variations in man's dress which have so greatly added to his expense account when doing the correct thing as a golfer, cricketer, fisherman or tennis fanatic. Driving forth in the buggy, with me between them, those two exchanged talk with the gusto of male intimates, which must have had to do with matters strictly censored from a Sunday's dinner-table small talk, but I can't recall a word of it. They sometimes went on a holiday jaunt together, and if I know anything of my old man when holiday jaunting, a visit to the "little ladies" was included in it. They were both members of the Redheap Volunteers. Indeed, Sommerville was its commanding officer, though how he managed to do his commanding with that reedy whisper of a voice confounds imagination. But they put a deuce of a lot of style into their volunteering. It was a mounted unit, the uniform being copied from a smart Hussar regiment, frogged with much gold braid, with the correct bearskin shako adorned with a white plume, black leather belt with a silver buckle, and shining black top boots. For undress there was a scarlet mess jacket and a pillbox cap, worn jauntily over one ear. It was the Russians who were responsible for this warlike panoply and martial spirit. Good heavens! those Russians! The Sydney citizens in the fifties armed themselves with axes, the only lethal weapons they could come by, because the Russians were coming. In this same village of Springwood where I live, its denizens in the eighties used to secrete food in the gullies, to subsist on when the Russians came. My infancy was devastated by thrills of terror from talk caught from my elders about the inevitable coming of the Russians. And at this moment those ridiculous phantoms are disrupting the entire Western world with the imminent threat of their coming. Will it never wake up to the simple fact that those semi-Mongols have Yes-No minds; that their will to action is balanced on the inertia of nihilism; that they think in terms of the illogic of suicide, in which the act of dying is forced into instantaneous conflict with the act of living, so that its dupe is suspended in space, neither living nor dying? But enough of that damned metaphysic, into which I have been led by the Redheap Volunteers flourishing warlike sabres at a Muscovite phantasm.

In presenting Sommerville as a military dominant, gallantly galloping at the head of his small-town Hussars, I am reminded of a certain idiosyncrasy of his which appears to conflict with it, as savouring rather of a lady's boudoir than the stern realities of war.

When he first came to Redheap, he lodged with a family in which there was a young lady daughter, who is distinguished in memory as one who ate camphor to beautify the complexion, there being a local superstition attributing that virtue to camphor. It gave her a complexion, all right, but the wrong sort of complexion, for she turned as yellow as saffron by an attack of the jaundice. Her contribution to this brief memoir of Sommerville Ponsonby is that she wore high-heeled French shoes, and it was Sommerville's pleasure to take his ease of an evening with his feet in this young lady's shoes . . .

No doubt modern psycho-analytical scandalmongering would find this antic suspect, and attach all sorts of portentous terminologies to it. For my part, I find its motive to have been inspired by the simple fact that Sommerville was proud of his small feet.

At that time Sommerville was a sprightly gentleman, a carefree bachelor, a much sought intimate at the dinner tables and card parties of the social elect. The time was yet to come when his major objective in life was to put an obtuse plaster of booze between himself and the domestic cataclysm destiny had in store for him. As it happened, I was to hear its doom infallibly predicted by my mother to Sommerville himself.

Which brings me to that muddle in memory's time-factors which assures me that I heard the prediction while seated under a small passage table about the age of four, while my mother and Sommerville stood in the doorway facing each other, with the sunlit garden beyond them, silhouetting my mother's precise aquiline profile in silver and striking coppery gleams from Sommerville's ginger hair. That picture is irrefutably authentic, and no fantasy of memory. I can still hear my mother's voice keyed down to a tone awful with prescience as she says, "Ponsonby, as sure as you let that woman sit at table with you she'll end up by marrying you."

And that event simply could not have happened at that time and in that precise point of space, because that passage had ceased to exist when Sommerville broached the question to my mother of having his housekeeper sit at the meal table with him. A new wing had been built on to our house, and its interior construction altered, and the dining-room in which memory insists that I first saw Sommerville at the age of nine was built over the passage in which memory insists that I heard his doom as a carefree bachelor predicted by my mother at the age of four. Besides, at that time Sommerville was no longer boarding with the family of the camphor-eating daughter, and taking his ease of an evening in her high-heeled shoes. He had removed to the living quarters of the bank and had taken to himself of a housekeeper, and thereby established my mother as a prophetess of evil omen in those words which memory insists that I heard at least eight years before they were spoken, and under conditions which no longer existed when the housekeeper arrived to disrupt Sommerville's social relations with the town's elect.

Well, I can't help it, and I only instance it here as evidence that memory can transfer one association to another without reference to the time-factor of either. I can only assume that Sommerville paid a visit to our town what time I was aged four, and was observed by me from under the hall table in that authentic memory picture of him in conversation with my mother at that door opening into the garden, which later memory decided to dramatise by those words of doom from my mother which I could only have heard when I was about twelve years old.

Anyway, he married the housekeeper, and that was the end of Sommerville the sprightly bachelor, living an entirely satisfactory existence as a bank manager and a Benedict. To be sure, under cover of his frock coat, glossy belltopper and dove-grey trousers, he was a lank and reedy gentleman with that pointed, foxy type of face that goes with ginger hair, and doubtless under the strict deportment of a gentleman he was troubled by concupiscent urges, and those are not so easily disposed of by a bank manager in a country town, under constant inspection by the lynx-eyed ladies of the social elect. And those holiday jaunts with my father were too few and far between for those urges to be satisfied by taking a cabman into their confidence and bowling off in a hansom for a flutter with the little ladies. The theory is that with an unattached female on the bank premises they incited Sommerville to get into her bed one night, and so allowed her to blackmail him into marrying her. And she was one of those broad-bottomed, flat-jowled females who looked like a widow who had secreted a hatred for all mankind by keeping a second-rate boarding house, and she weighed about fifteen stone to Sommerville's nine and a bit, so that, though I have a good workable dirty-minded imagination, it falters at the spectacle of Sommerville Ponsonby guiltily treading the bank premises at midnight in a nightgown to perform a Tarquin act on that female bargee, who could have throttled him without an effort had she been so minded to defend herself from a ravishing.

I suspect that Sommerville had already committed himself to a fatal pact of marriage with her what time he came fishing for condonation of it to my mother under the more or less innocuous proposal of having her in from the kitchen to dine with him. Small chance he had of getting absolution for even an indiscretion of that sort from the ruthless caste interdictions of that era. When my mother voiced her prediction of its inevitable consequences, its implication was understood: "Ponsonby, if you marry that woman, don't attempt to bring her into *my* house."

And that would have been the sentence of social ostracism from every other lady of the social elect on the Man who Married his Housekeeper. Nor were Sommerville's male friends any less trenchant in denouncing a suicidal act of matrimony. Headed by my father, those soulmates of the American Hotel back parlour wrought tremendously on Sommerville, not to save him from committing a social indiscretion, but from the clutches of a female bargee. I remember my father darting out of his consulting-room to measure the hat-stand in a frenzy, exclaiming, "The man's mad — done for. Told him — marry that woman — cut your throat first. Only possible solution — end it."

He married her. Groans burst from my father whenever mention was made of that fatal subjection of Sommerville to his concupiscent urges. The ladies of the elect presented an embattled front of ostracism to the housekeeper. So it was a foredoomed inevitability that the housekeeper would take it out of Sommerville as a substitute for snooty ladies and groaning male soulmates. She was a virago, anyway, and already seething with spleen for having been forced to coerce him into marrying her, so she was primed to harry, disrupt, and make intolerable the home life of Sommerville Ponsonby.

Somerville went morally to pieces. He took to booze as the only solution left him of presenting a sodden, comatose defence against the rages of his termagant. Every night he was brought home by friends in a purblind condition, so that her only relief to present-moment fury was to scream its execrations at those friends for bringing him home in a state that defeated her need to explode it on him. I often saw that homecoming, for I was about twelve at the time, and well up in the town's adult scandals, and my spiritual home was the house of W.B. Purdie, uncle to my friend Mucker Tweedie, because it was one of those excellent homes where its young were allowed to invite friends freely about the premises, and to the family meal table, and as it was just opposite Sommerville Ponsonby's bank, we frequently saw Bob Lindsay and Johnny Brady the draper lugging the comatose form of soulmate Sommerville home to his nightly martyrdom. Arrived at the bank, we might hear Bob Lindsay say in trenchant tones, "Now then, Ponsonby — hold up. Stiff upper lip — stick to your gun, by George", as might be said in an awful formula to one about to meet his end on the guillotine. "My friend, have courage." He needed it, for at the first rat-tat-tat on the knocker the door would be snatched open by that large blousy virago, screeching, "So you have brought that drunken wretch home at last, have you!"

"Tut, tut! Poor old Ponsonby — non compos mentis — slight touch of the sun."

"Don't you tut, tut at me, Doctor Lindsay, after bringing him home in that filthy state."

"Filthy state be hanged. Poor old P. hasn't had more than a glass or two the whole evening."

"That's enough from you, Brady, stinking of liquor yourself this minute. *Are* you going to bring that wretch in?"

He was brought in, as far as permitted that termagant to fasten her talons on him, and whisk him inside like a straw-stuffed dummy, and bang the door on a husband's miscreant friends, who go off rumbling indignation at the immemorial martyrdoms of married men . . .

"Poor old Ponsonby — best fellow alive — man in a million — ruined — done for — life a perfect misery with that infernal trollop."

"By jingo, if I had her I'd put the boot into her."

"Boot, by George! Man would be justified in slipping poor old Ponsonby a dose of poison to drop in her morning tea . . ."

But chance, or rather, an astute inspiration by Bulljo Peddler relating to stamp collecting, permitted me to witness Somerville enduring domestic martyrdom within the bank itself. Of course, I collected stamps. Not with any special ardour; it was the correct thing to do, and I did it. In those days if one sent a thousand used stamps to an advertised address, one got in return an envelope containing about a dozen foreign stamps of no particular value, but still, collector's currency. Bulljo was the impassioned philatelist of our group, and it was on his suggestion that we petitioned the banks for permission to go through their waste-paper baskets of a Saturday morning in quest of stamps.

Thus, on a Saturday morning we were seated on the floor under Sommerville Ponsonby's office table, gathering stamps from his waste-paper basket, and cocking interested ears at an awful uproar going on off-stage in the living quarters of the bank, that virago screeching the roof off and apparently bursting crockery and bouncing tea trays on Somerville's person. If Sommerville was retorting manfully on this assault, we failed to hear him. Not the least of his martyrdom must have been the hopeless futility of trying to retort on that female bargee with his ghostly whisper. In the bank, the clerk and cashier went about their business without taking the slightest notice of the domestic cataclysm. Clearly it was to them a convention staled by repetition.

Sommerville arrived from it at a tottering run, and collapsed into his chair, huskily respiring execrations. To the furies of domestic cataclysm he was also enduring the hot coppers of a hangover, and there would be no surcease of either till he had poured half a dozen brandies and sodas onto his sizzling kidneys.

Off-stage his virago could be heard keeping it up, either in a squalling monologue or having a row with the cook. In either case it failed to relieve her of those stultifications of spleen which must be the major inferno of a virago's being, for she suddenly exploded into the office, upsetting every chair in transit and swiping everything off Sommerville's table in a perfectly demented concept of swiping Sommerville off the earth's crust, screeching like a damned soul, and exploding out again to a scattering explosion of papers, pens, inkwells and ledgers all over the carpet. It was like one of those circular storms which cause fearful havoc in the line of their trajectory, but leave the surrounding country untouched. The clerk went on calmly clerking, the cashier cashing, and we, perfect gentlemen, went on stamp collecting, assuming to be unaware of a slightly embarrassing exposure of the private life of Sommerville Ponsonby. He, too done up for any further response to cataclysm, merely went on feebly trying to gulp down his hot coppers.

In the end she resorted to a form of revenge on Sommerville which strikes one as extremely ill-advised from her point of view, as it threatened to deprive her of support by his professional income. She wrote to the head office telling its pundits that he had practically given up banking for booze, on which he was suspended, and recalled from Redheap, subjected to an inquisition by the pundits, and finally reinstated to a position in the head office, where he would be under inspection by its officials. But his termagant gained nothing by that, since she could hardly relieve her stultifications by exploding in there and swiping everything off his table on a top note of screeching . . .

But by that time Sommerville had matured at least one retort on his virago which must have added greatly to her stultifications, even if it imposed an extremely belittling one on Sommerville himself. Before he left Redheap, he called on my father for his professional opinion on its most perturbing manifestation, and by chance I overheard something of that consultation, because my bedroom was next to the consulting-room, and when both windows were open, I often heard snatches of secular communion between my old man and his patients. In this case, Sommerville's husky whispering failed to reach me, but I was able to divine something of the symptoms he was recording by my old man's hearty reassurances as to their innocuous nature.

"My dear fellow, that sort of thing is purely temporary. Temporary. Put the whole matter out of your mind. Don't dwell on it. Deuce of a mistake to get into a fluster over it. A mere temporary collapse of the muscular reflexes due to . . . well, damme, Ponsonby, don't tell me you want to have anything to do with that trollop. No need for me to give you a tonic, either. Later on, pick up a cabby who knows his oats and take a little run out to St Kilda. *That's* the sort of tonic you need."

It was sound advice and I hope Sommerville took it, not only as a panacea to his peculiar affliction, but as the only effective retort on a termagant wife.

Creswick Letters

TO J.E. TREMEARNE, 1947

Yes, you are right. The worst frustrations and defeats we inflicted on ourselves over the pursuit of girls are subject matter for memory to find purely humorous. And that really raises a very pregnant question: which is the reality, the factual event or the memory image of it? I say the image, because the event passed into the limbo of time within the very passage of its action, while the image remains a concrete and eternal thing, more vital today than today's actuality.

Cripes, actuality in those days of youth was half its time a boring, distracting, depressing business, abysmal with a conviction of futility and with the blankest sense of any movement into the future. I'm sure our happiest periods were when we loitered about together, content with the award of friendship, and discussing the complexities of life as those were inflicted on us. It's a queer thing, but though our conversations must have covered quite a lot of ground in relation to those complexities, I only recall distinctly those relating to girls and those which forecasted a future devoted to the arts. I particularly

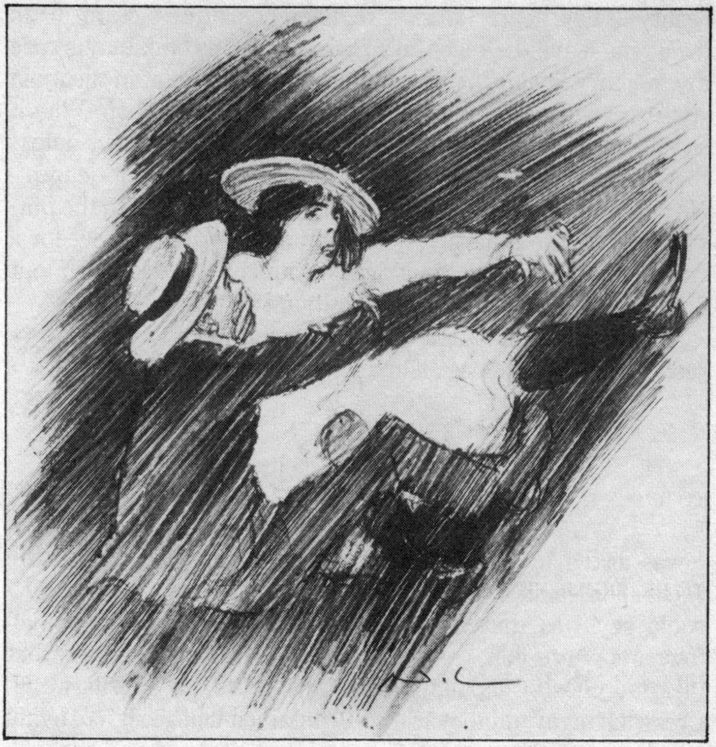

Attempt at an early seduction

recall a Saturday night's walk up the centre of the main street when, with arms about each other's shoulders, we swore that wherever the pursuit of art might take us our friendship was sealed on oath to endure. And it has endured, and grown stronger with the years; so that it is as much a part of us as any other integral content for our egos. I have the clearest memory of that walk and talk; the shops alight for the weekend carnival of shopping and parading, the carts and buggies drawn up at the kerb, the Salvation Army braying to its comic-paper God, and we two detached, absorbed in the projected vision of life together. I notice one queer quirk about memory images of reality. They nearly always register one brief picture of an event and leave the rest of it to be recorded as one. In this case my memory image suspends us eternally at a point in the main street between the town hall and Jebb's drapery shop. Why it should have selected that precise spot, I don't know, unless that was the spot where an emotional response went deepest. No doubt that Saturday night's event was dedicated to the pursuit of girls. No doubt we went up and down that street for a couple of hours, till hope was dead and we slouched our dolorous way home again in a moribund earth.

And what a fantastic space there is between Creswick as a reality and Creswick as an image!

TO BRIAN JAMES, 1964

I was asked by Geoff Dutton to write something about the Australian small town for an article on that subject, but all I could say was that the small town no longer exists. Small towns now are just sawn-off sections of cities. I've seen that metamorphosis happen under my eyes at Springwood. Creswick in my youth was a self-contained village. It had a mill which ground its own flour. A saddler who made all the saddles the district needed. The blacksmith employed half a dozen men who turned out all its iron work. The local tinsmith manufactured all its tinware. It had a brickworks for all bricks it needed. There was a coach-and-buggy builder. All it imported were such foodstuffs put up in preserved form — there was very little tinned food in those days. In any case, the people made their own jams and preserves. Also, the town produced all the labour it needed. Also, an important item, it devised its own entertainments, concerts and plays, very well put on and performed. I've recounted the presentation of *Faust* in *Redheap*, played in action and pantomime.

How much of personality is lost in the custom-built town of today it is hard to say. The constitution of the human ego never changes, of course, so I suppose the present-day writer, born into present conditions, will find all the material he needs, but I'm certain he'll never find such a rare collection of individual characters as we found in our time. Since I've taken to shopping once a week in Springwood, I haven't come across one that appears to be a unique human specimen. Its denizens look as custom-built as their shops and houses and motor-cars. It is nonsense to say that a nostalgia for our own youth allows us to assume that individual characters were more numerous and unique than they are under present conditions. A population under pioneer conditions has to fend for itself and manufacture the new procedure of existence. Such a procedure forces individuality on its members. Even on its youngsters. Rose's *Ma and Pa** gives documentary evidence of that individuality. So, I think, does my *Saturdee*. When I observe a bus full of present-day schoolkids, all neatly dressed in the same uniforms, I wonder how the teacher is able to distinguish one from another. Of course, personalities do emerge from the mass, but the social status and background of the unit will not be apparent at a glance, as it was in my schooldays. We had a class gamut from the professions down to the slum denizens of the creek hovels to consort with, and that is very important, when one comes to write about them in maturity.

**Ma and Pa — Childhood Memories* by Rose Lindsay, Ure/Smith, Sydney, 1963

Part 2

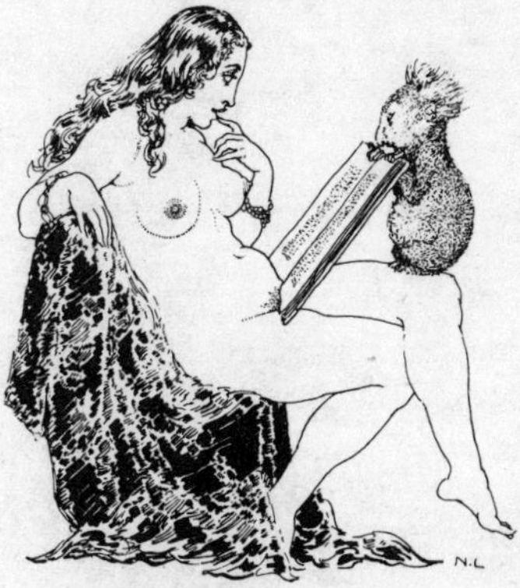

Essays

That Popular Myth — the Lady

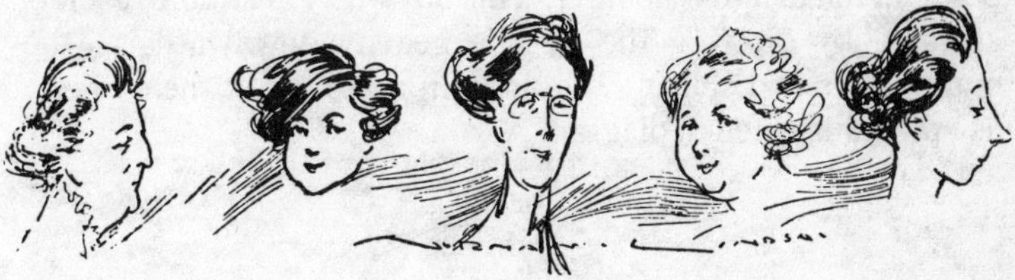

I have had my suspicions for some time that the title of "lady", as a class distinction, was not one to be any longer applied to the flesh, but existed only in the creations of the popular delineation of femininity. It was an intelligent shopkeeper who confirmed my suspicions. I was standing in his shop, when he produced for my inspection an inane-looking female head, with an immense coiffure of yellow hair, an out-size in eyes, and a complexion inclining to the mouse. This head was attached to a long, pale neck and a low-cut gown, and the title of it was "A Lady".

"I have sold," said the intelligent shopkeeper, with some pardonable evidences of exultation, "over five hundred copies of that head in a fortnight, at" — he added, fixing me triumphantly with his eye — "four shillings per."

That five hundred people had desired that depressing female head, not to speak of the myriads of others exactly like it that filled his shop, at the rate of four or more shillings per, was a consideration that filled me with a species of gloom. Ladies in

Published in the *Lone Hand*, Sydney, 1 February 1910

the flesh may be all shapes and sizes; but on paper, as portrayed by the popular artist aforesaid, they must be of only one sort, and the recipe for making them is quite as simple as the recipe for making Irish stew.

The most essential ingredient to ensure the immediate recognition of the Popular Myth is a demeanour of hauteur mixed with refined boredom. The expression required is that of one who had been given a bad oyster in the soup, but is too polite to make a fuss about it. This obviously desirable result is attained by drawing the eyelids heavily downwards at the outer edges and causing the underlip to droop at the corners, as aptly illustrated in diagram A.

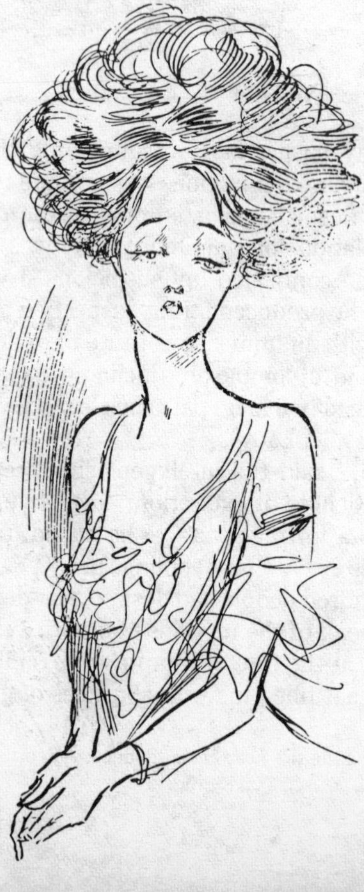

Diagram A

The next essential to the success of the composition is an immense amount of hair. Ladies on paper cannot have too much hair, provided they do it in the latest mode. It is an unfortunate thing for the popular artist that the mode so frequently changes, for an emblem of the Popular Myth in last year's hair, of course, ceases at once to be a lady. A glance at diagram A will show that the mode to-day betrays a gracious expanse of forehead. Observe the importance of hair to the creation of the Popular Myth. Remove it (diagram B). Bring it well down over the brows; remove the evidences of contempt for the rest of humanity, and the result is quite disastrous (diagram C).

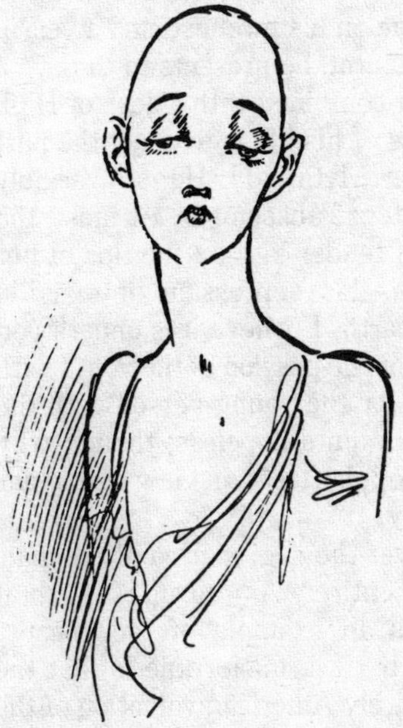

Diagram B

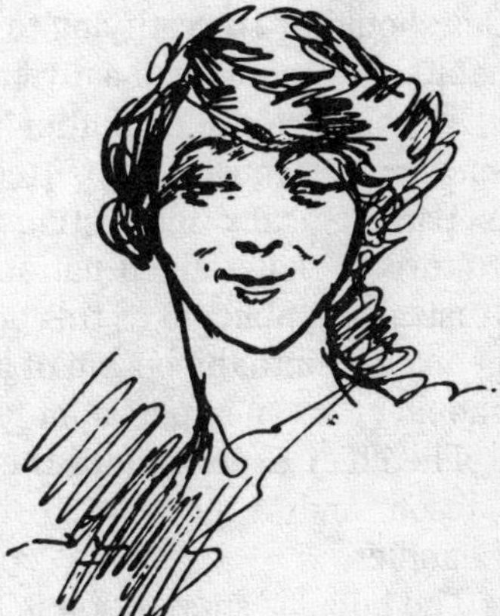

Diagram C

As for the popular fallacy's nose, it may be straight or it may be slightly tilted upwards, as favoring the expression of disdain; it must be small, but on no account must it be turned down. To draw a lady to-day with a nose inclined to the aquiline is to brand oneself socially an outcast. For other perquisites your lady must have an inordinate length of neck, and to mark her social status immaculate — a low-cut dress of costly fabric.

The Popular Myth may be said to live in evening dress, though there are occasions when she is allowed to escape into a short plaid skirt, a shirt waist, and a golf stick. A trifling innovation frequently attached to her presence is an immaculate youth with a high shine on his forehead and a yearning expression in his eye. In general, he presents to the eye a baffling mixture of beauty actor combined with a dash of High Church curate; and the business of his life is to enact the part of human poodle to the Popular Myth lady. He is invariably represented in an attitude of intense abasement. At most, the only intimacy he is allowed is a tender kiss on the tips of her fingers; and on such occasions his expression of maudlin ecstasy is like nothing else on earth. I believe it is understood by those who buy such prints that the passion of the youth with the high shine on his forehead for the young person with the oyster in the soup expression is quite hopeless; though why this should be so gratifying to popular taste, in view of popular habits, is something of a mystery.

All this pictorial exultation over the degradation of the male species is, it must be admitted, entirely American. As such, it is pathologically interesting as an example of the boasted culture of that refined nation; but the misfortune is that the Australian public takes this entirely American valuation of the genus lady into the bosom of its home as fast as, the intelligent shopkeeper can import it, at four shillings per.

The chief exponents of the Popular Myth to-day are C. D. Gibson and a person by the name of Howard Christie Chandler.

The popular supposition is that before the appearance of C. D. Gibson, ladies had not existed on paper. He is understood to have created the only genuine brand. I would like to correct his erroneous impression. A few years ago — but people have forgotten her — there was a creation called the Du Maurier Girl. For years she was understood to have exhausted every possible feminine grace; and there is an interesting anecdote told of Mr. Du Maurier, which shows how highly he appreciated the immense importance of having created her. He had been shown a drawing by C. D. Gibson, and at once, in a burst of prophetic solemnity, exclaimed, "This is the young man who will succeed *me.*" I confess to finding something extremely gratifying in this artless confession of Mr. Du Maurier's feelings on the subject of the Popular Myth.

The chief characteristics of the Du Maurier Girl were, in Mr. Du Maurier's own words, "Pootiness and virtue" (pardon me a moment while I wipe the perspiration from my brow, after using this expression), and an example of her in her marvellous tallness will be found in diagram D.

It was always said of Charles Keene, with much gloomy denial of any virtue in him that "he couldn't draw a lady". The fact was, he wouldn't draw the Popular Myth. He drew people so extremely true to life that, as the original of Mrs. Nickleby said to Dickens on the subject of Mrs. Nickleby, "it was impossible to believe that such ridiculous people ever existed". Keene's incapacity to draw what is called a lady was always used to his disadvantage in comparison with Du Maurier; but the verdict of time has had a trifling effect in restoring the balance of equality. Keene, who couldn't draw a lady, remains one of the greatest of black-and-white artists; while Du Maurier, who could, remains one of the worst. But Du Maurier was not the first exponent of the popular lust for the popular fallacy. While the Du Maurier myth was yet unborn, away back in the early days of London *Punch*, people talked about the Leech Girl as they talked later about the Du Maurier Girl, and as they talk about the Gibson Girl to-day.

After considerable research among the journalistic archives of that historic period, I have unearthed the recipe by which the cultured inhabitants of the Early Victorian Era recognised a lady. The various items that made for feminine perfection in

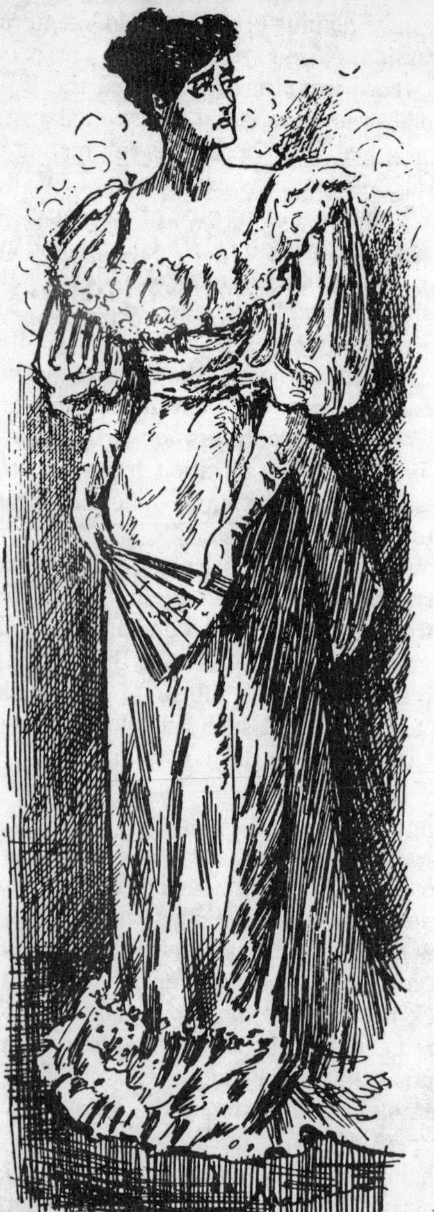

Diagram D

those simple times will be found correctly delineated in diagram E. It will be noted that an egg-shaped head, with the hair parted in the centre, and brought down in two geometrically correct curves, terminating in a species of hirsute sausage, was evidently considered attractive.

Another important attraction will be observed in the eyes, which are designed less in imitation of the human optic as in that of the gazelle — a refined animal, highly esteemed for purposes of comparison by the poets of that period. The lips of this tender conception were invariably much too small for such

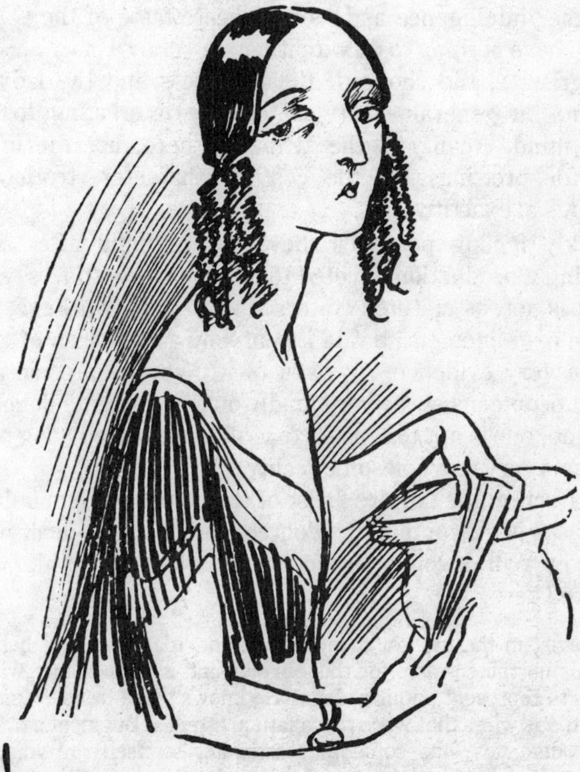

Diagram E

a vulgar occupation as the consumption of food; and the nose — let the admirer of the Popular Myth to-day avert his head — was invariably aquiline. I have a suspicion that the illustrious model for this species of nose was her late gracious Majesty, then — not as portrayed on later coins of the realm — of a slim and indefinite appearance in profile.

Our grandmothers may have felt a high moral responsibility in looking as like the Popular Myth of that period as possible; but nothing will convince me that they did, any more than a creation by Gibson or the person aptly called Chandler resembles a modern portrait by Sargent or Lavery.

This lust for the pretty face is essentially Anglo-Saxon in origin; but the American is the high priest of the cult to-day. The higher intelligence and more delicate taste of the Continent will have nothing to do with it.

The grisette, the shopgirl, the laundress and the lady — femininity in general — are all equally interesting to the French mind. Reality is the attraction here; not the inane desire for prettiness at the cost of character, truth and physiological exactitude.

A sickly feeling pervades the sensitive mind after contemplating a production devoted to the cult of prettiness. And this cult is not, as cultured editors would have us believe, the evidence of refinement; but in its parvenu assumption of gentility the very evidence of a lack of it. When a prosaic and plebeian people insists so very loudly on the exquisite delicacy of its mind, one is apt to suspect that all this sugared lying only covers up a very unwholesome reality.

The effect on the sincere artist of the incessant demand for pretty faces is distracting to a degree, and has been dealt with too well by Will Dyson in his lecture on "Black and White," to be omitted here.

> The artist in the earliest months of his novitiate, has left behind him his untrained taste for this obvious and insipid beauty which seems to represent popular ideals. He knows those faces — knows the fatuous wires that work those fatuous smiles. But an inexorable public demands, and sometimes arrogates to itself the voice of morality in doing so, that the artist must draw and paint these faces

> without cessation. His whole training makes him abhor them. It fills him with the blackest pessimism to think that his training should be wasted in problems as worthless as the presentment of this fatuous prettiness. . . . The feeling is from no innate viciousness or predilection for ugliness, but only a devotion to a beauty more enduring than is comprehensible to intelligences that look at these things carelessly.

It may be reasonably urged that the public has a perfect right to fill its homes with the vapid innocuousness of the eternal pretty face. I should be glad, for one, if the matter only ended in the comparatively decent privacy of the public's home; but this is the least of the evil. The demand goes considerably further afield than the four walls of the home. Not only does it swamp the print-shops and the periodicals of to-day, but it creeps into the artist's studio and puts a peremptory embargo on the treatment of any subject whatever concerning the portrayal of femininity; and I grieve to say that most modern exhibitions of pictures, from the Royal Academy upwards, only too clearly prove that the artist, base slave that the creature is, is only too anxious to deserve the ignominy of public appreciation. And nothing in the nature of the ludicrous can equal the frequent result of his misguided efforts.

What does it matter that the ladies of King Arthur's Court were robust dames who breathed an atmosphere of battle, murder and sudden death, or that a mangled corpse was the merest commonplace of their daily life? What that the bride of a viking could gaze with unblinking lids upon the smoking heart of a man? Paint them, as Mr. Blair Leighton does, with the pure and characterless faces of a lady's seminary and the British father will know that the purity of the home has been maintained, and that the truth has been secured against the sight of his daughter. Perverters of history such as Tennyson and the pre-Raphaelites, have all helped splendidly in upholding this sweet mendacity; and their creations would maintain irreproachably the chaste and rigid etiquette of the inhabitants of Clapham.

In no other countries but Britain, North America and Australia have we this etiolated prettiness for a feminine ideal;

so Taine was probably right when he said that the Englishman was afraid to face the commonest facts of sex, and that his innate barbarism, fearing the dire possibility of getting out of hand, takes refuge in the natural necessity for hypocrisy. We have here, I imagine, the key to our mystery. A spade must never be called a spade, and woman must be to us something more than an angel. The curious but unscientific notion that woman is a regenerator, purifier and uplifter of ignoble man must be maintained at any cost; and so, I suppose, afraid to face the facts of the eternally feminine as do other nations, the English-speaking world will go on maintaining, above such petty considerations as characteristic beauty and truth, inviolable and unassailable, the integrity of its Popular Myth.

A Modern Malady

I have noticed that three artists can hardly meet together now-a-days without presently seeking to impose on one another the personal definition of an artistic creed. The procedure is not so much conversational as ritualistic, the confessional passion of the devotee who must at all cost testify to the sanctity of his beliefs.

While such conversational testimonies go no further than an intellectual exercise, no harm is done, but too often behind them one discerns the clanking chains of conviction; the effort to move fettered limbs in the prison house of words. In plain truth, we have cast off a theological habit of belief without losing a theological habit of mind. We are as capable of calling a spade a sausage machine to-day as ever were the students of Duns Scotus, and though we no longer enforce belief with the thumb-screw and the rack, we can still drive a journalistic pen into the vitals of an enemy's beliefs.

To-day, the critic has replaced the priest, and as the priest, by his ritualistic antics, destroyed religion, so the critic, in the

Published in *Art in Australia* No.1, 1916

refinements of his virtuosity, has done a great deal to obscure the meaning of Art.

When one has ceased to discover, one sits down to tabulate the nature of one's discoveries. When one has ceased to create, one sits down to review the quality of one's creations. Criticism is the effect of sterility. To-day, the clamour of small artistic sects is a clamour for help. This uproar is the result of uncertainty, not of conviction. All issues are obscured by the wordy assertions of people without faith. We snatch right and left at definitions, as drowning people snatch at straws. God is no longer a problem to us, but there is still enough of priestcraft in our bones to make heresy a matter of the arts.

One effect of this theological passion has led to an extraordinary jumbling of the common stock of artistic technicalities. The musician has discarded utterly the assumption that his business has merely to do with the production of harmonious sound. Like a pirate, he has invaded the domain of literature, and, snatching the symbols of an alien craft, writes us a novel in a symphony, or a sonnet in crotchets and quavers. He has gone even further of late, and meddling with the artist's colour-box, affects to teach our ears to see colour. The artist has not so much retaliated as assumed, too, the aspect of a technical brigand. Colour, form, tone, all the accepted problems of his craft are discarded as things exploited and done with. He affects to translate the mechanism of movement, to express sensation, to tabulate in hasty paint the varying quality of emotion and even the passage of time.

The truth is this incompetent dauber has merely tried to substitute hieroglyphics of his own invention for the common alphabet by which we record the spoken word. He has done nothing more than resurrect the cuneiform tablet to express something that is more easily said in words, and if the truth must be told, the result is that of a savage experimenting with the art of writing. This relapse of the tired mind to primitive symbolism is a common phenomenon in all periods of low creative effort. Such back-stairs revolutions as Cubism, and Futurism, and all the rest of the modern art movements are neither important nor significant. The best that can be said of them is that they are sometimes amusing, as a comic paper is amusing, and the worst, that there is so little accomplishment in their production that they are as dull as a child's scribbling.

Their only claim to significance is that they express the theological malady that has attacked the mind of all modern art. The same irritated desire to express a theory, to paint a conviction, is apparent in better and more serious effort. The joy of work alone no longer suffices. We look with suspicion on any suggestion that we should associate gaiety with art, as though we were on oath to announce an ethical creed, instead of making it our business to express a joy in life.

It seems to me that though a sincere effort to fix a standard of appreciation must be of value to the community, any effort to live up to an accepted standard is a danger to the artist. It clogs the creative sense to live with a schoolmaster at one's elbow. So few of us, indeed, have the courage of our dreams and desires, or make of work a festival for our own entertainment. If others enjoy it, so much the better. If they detest it, so much the better still. It is personal vision that counts in Art, whether one is as intolerant as Nietzsche or as kindly as Dickens. For the truth is that all great art eludes a label. You can no more say that Dickens was a novelist than that Shakespere was a play-writer, that Rabelais was a satirist or that Cervantes a story-teller. To call Rubens a decorator is to miss seeing in his fecundity the brutal fecundity of life, to call Rembrandt a portrait painter is to see no mystery in the light that glows about his creations in paint.

The small uncreative mind is ill at ease outside the boundaries of a cult. It is lost without a label. The parrot cries of belief that we hear on all sides to-day are but the evidence of a feeble atheism.

In fact, this seriousness of aspect is not the seriousness of work. This pretentious activity is a mask for idleness, and what is worse, boredom. A passionate and unending labour to acquire perfection of craft can only come from a passionate joy in work. That all great artists were great producers is the proof that they found in work a saturnalia of delight. Our hasty scrawls in paint are the evidence of a tragic disinterest. I see always the effort of a bored and tired mind, seeking in work the stimulus of a drug. The modern novel is as shapeless as the modern picture. It sprawls from page to page with the gabble of a man too tired to articulate clearly, or to choose his words with care.

And the truth is that these wordy slabs of print are dull because the writers are drearily defending a belief in art, not a joy in life. And our acres of brightly daubed canvases are uninspired because the painters are vindicating a literary theory in paint, not a personal vision of form and colour.

The melancholoy conclusion is forced on one that most artists spend their lives in doing work that has no personal significance to them whatever. They labour under the curse of an intellectual conviction. I have known an artist in this desperate quandary, throw over all he had acquired of dexterity and a profound sense of beauty, and exultantly proclaim a metaphysical creed that not only killed all charm in his work, but killed all power to work at all.

The modern confusion of technicalities is the result of mixing metaphysics with the common necessities of a craft. Though art may be man's highest expression of passion and beauty, it is still tethered to the mechanism of his trade. Here at least is a fair subject for argument and dispute; but any subtler effort at the expression of an intellectual conviction is better left alone.

For the artist is notoriously a man who lives within the limited range of his own personal vision. It is this narrowness of outlook that is his peculiar virtue and peculiar vice. His savage and exclusive egotism is of immense value as a stimulus, though maybe what it gains in virility it loses in generosity. By intensifying his vision, it also narrows his vision; by looking only for needles in the hay, he often fails to see that hay, too, is beautiful.

What I would plead for to-day, and what I have been vaguely trying to arrive at in these remarks, is the wisdom of a little more light-heartedness. The wisdom, in fact, of occasionally having a lark with one's work. An effort is greatly simplified if one can remember in time to get rid of the burden of an intellectual conscience. Gravity is more often only another name for dullness, and the truly serious works of art are those produced in a spirit of delight.

Indeed, the emotion that produced Micawber inspired Giorgione's Sleeping Venus, and the tragedy of Antony and Cleopatra is moved by the same thrill of exultation that created Panurge.

Rocks and Mud and Novels

It is not enough to say that a people cannot have a national consciousness without an art; without an art it cannot have a consciousness at all.

A human being must recognise itself as a creature of fiction before it can be a recognisable content of life. It may generate within itself a certain dynamic of self, but that does not become a really sentient process till it has been made concrete in words or sounds or forms. That is only to say that some mental and emotional standard must be defined for the individual unit to make self-comparison with.

The mentality of the average bush type to-day is covered by the mentality of Henry Lawson. By jotting down notes of what he observed of their idiosyncratic variations as a species, they become those idiosyncratic variations, *plus* a sentient awareness of themselves as such. Before, they had been mere automatic reactions to the struggle for existence.

On those terms the mass of any people's consciousness must become an active process within itself, and a recognisable content from without itself. It is not distinguished from other

Published in the *Bulletin*, Sydney, May 1929

peoples by isolations of rock and mud, but by its peculiar outlook on life. And that, of course, can only be defined by art.

A people may gain a certain aesthetic value from the art of other nationalities, but their individual consciousness will not be deeply stirred by it. A Sydney girl may read of the emotional disturbances of a London girl in a novel about London and be entertained, but there the process ends. She must meet herself in type matter hurrying down George Street to bump into the boy at the post-office corner who takes her to Manly on Sunday before her own performance of that simple itinerary in the emotions becomes an amazing reality to her. The personality of a city which becomes so mysteriously an identification of the people who live in it, has nothing to do with architects and aldermen and kings and legislators, but with novels.

Who cares to know if Henry the Eighth built Lincoln's Inn? I don't know if he did, and I don't care either; but I do know I registered a thrill before it to recall that Mr. Tulkinghorn dwelt there, and the immortal Snagsby across the way in Cook's (they call it Took's) Court, Curseter-street. Types of human beings are created or wiped out under the terms by which they are defined in type matter, Dickens made the English people alter not only their institutions but their faces and manners too. He was so violently annoyed with the idle, bored man about town of his era, and castigated him so with ridicule, that the next generation of Englishmen were brisk, alert fellows, with a crisp, neat articulation, and never dreamed of throwing cushions on their heads like the debilitated cousin in *Bleak House*, who said ". . . Zample; better hang wrong f'l'a than no f'l'a."

In Australia we have arrived at that point in automatic national growth where its mechanism must be consciously defined, or there will be no further growth worth defining.

The novel *must* come, or we will remain unknown to ourselves and non-existent to other peoples, save as dumping-ground for their commodities, mental or otherwise.

It is very hard for an Australian in Australia to realise how vacuous is the glance cast at this country by other peoples. I found it quite impossible to give an intelligent Englishman or Frenchman who had not been here any conception in words of what sort of place it was. One might labor in vain to convince an Englishman just then that a Labor member did not wear bowyangs and smoke a short clay pipe. In the *Mercury* office in Paris a group of French journalists were looking over some illustrations I had done for Casanova's memoirs when one of them said, "Of course you came to Europe for your eighteenth-century material?" When it was explained that the drawings had been done in Australia that outraged Frenchman exclaimed, "Impossible . . . in that wild place!" Bill Dalley will recall that absurd incident, as he was my interpreter in a language that I speak, in its own idiom, "like a Spanish cow".

One can trace that inferiority complex of the Australian abroad, which he also defines by his boasting at home, to the depressing consciousness of his non-existence in type matter. Of all the novelists of the last generation who had its ear, only two, I think, mention Australia in their works: Conrad, for stray references to ports of call and one or two brief glimpses of Sydney; and Stevenson in *The Wrecker*, where the Domain, the Currency Lass (now vanished) and Paris House get a mention.

I never cease to regret that Louis Stone did not carry on the work he began so admirably with *Jonah* and *Betty Wayside*. There, for the first time, types idiosyncratically Australian moved through Sydney streets and those streets were brilliantly alive with crowds of people. If a dozen novels of their quality had been circulating in England since *Jonah* was begot, the coming Australian novelist would not have quite such a nuisance of a job before him. Some few hundred-thousand readers would have already travelled through the cities of his creations, and be aware of what skies and aspirations they lived under. Stone has the "locality" faculty highly developed; his streets and peoples are instantly vitalised and known at a glance. If he had only covered the social stratas as he began, with Jonah in the slums, and Betty in the suburbs.

Well, we have to admit that his reception as a novelist was not gracious. The inner history of his struggle to get a hearing for the novel here does not make pleasing matter for contemplation. But what genuine expression in the arts ever did? No matter, the novel must come, in spite of Australia's apathy or opposition to it. If it does not work, so much the worse for Australia.

For myself, I am strongly optimistic over the possibilities of the Australian novel producing a distinct aesthetic of its own; an obviously fatuous state of mind on my part, since the gods only exist to frustrate expectations of that sort. Still, I have read certain works in manuscript that impress me strongly with their vitality, frankness and courage; qualities, one has to admit, that may not endear them to the public. But that is a trifle; friction is the essential process that begets good fiction.

This much, at least, is obvious: Australia is manufacturing a background for the novel. I doubt if any city in the world could produce better human material, and a better setting than Sydney. A great pity, of course, that its night life is stifled by that imbecile early-closing law which forces more hard drinking into being than freedom to drink all night could do. In fact, we will never get rid of hard drinking till man is allowed to have his liquor when he will and how he should, which is in public and in a comfortable chair. One never sees a drunk in Paris because there is no pressure put on people there *not* to get drunk. This is not a subject extraneous to the novel. The mechanism of entertainment and release from nerve stress is as essential to the full experience of life as the emotional conflict of sex that begets it. True morality begins with that Roman principle which gives the largest area in the action of life for the release of the ego; which opposes the vulgar principle of bad and repressed peoples that life should be strangulated by by-laws and stultified by dulness.

Well, all that is in the hands of the novelist. He can make Australia not only a place worth living in, but a place where life exists. Life is the burgeoning of the human ego by a release of its emotional mechanism as a conscious impact, and not a blind automatonism that grubs for food and clothes. Pictures, poetry and music reach only the minority, and at that only of those already developed to react to an imagery of life, but prose goes everywhere. It is a rapier and a bludgeon, a brickbat and a hypodermic syringe; and, squirm, kick and struggle as it will the human ego must come into its operating theatre for clinical analysis.

All that is apart from the thousand bad novels that will be published for the one good one when novels are published in Australia. I hold no brief for aesthetic squeamishness on that score. Why shouldn't the people read rot? After all, even writing rot is better than sitting in a stockbroker's office or selling socks. Any sort of mechanism for the novel is better than none, and even in crude trade terms, it is a mystery to me why some reasonably intelligent business man here does not buy one of those printing machines which take in a roll of paper at one end and eject thousands of bound volumes at the other. Australia is now only a literary tip for English and American cheap novels, which could be equally well written and published here.

Australia and Australians

Published in *Fortune* magazine, New York, February 1932. The magazine told its readers that: "Following *Fortune*'s publication, in August, of an article entitled "Australia for the Australians," many comments were received from that continent. Recently one of Australia's most distinguished citizens, Mr. Norman Lindsay, liberal thinker, author of world note and famous for his work in water color, arrived in this country. Mr. Lindsay had read *Fortune*'s article and asked the favor of *Fortune*'s columns to comment upon it. Herewith Mr. Lindsay's manuscript:"

AUSTRALIA! Who knows anything about Australia outside Australia? Why even Australians know nothing about their own country. They refuse to know the only things worth knowing about it.

I don't mean things about wool and wheat and natural resources. The process by which a people exists has nothing to do with the state of mind under which it exists, and that state of mind will define whether it is mentally alive or mentally moribund.

Vitality is morality. Conventional labels have nothing to do with moral values. Bad forces are just as essential to a people as good forces, so that both are sufficiently forceful as to arrive at conflict. Conflict generates the defined statement of two opposites, and to define anything is to concrete it. Where one force overcomes the other we arrive at inertia and inertia is the death of morality.

Australia, isolated and overlooked as it is by other nations at present, has created a distinct dynamic and evolved also its hatred for that dynamic. I can only ask to be taken on trust when I speak of such poets as Hugh McCrae, Kenneth Slessor, Jack Lindsay, or such painters as Gruner, Heysen, George Lambert. They have yet to stand the test of world opinion, and my own estimate of them, as an Australian, can have no validity. Thomas Ewart, the English critic, has already placed McCrae on the line of English poets: I have brought a collection of Slessor's poems to New York, where it is to be published shortly and its quality may be estimated. If Australia is not to be dismissed by G.B. Shaw as a "place with sheep in it," something must be understood of its mass resentment against

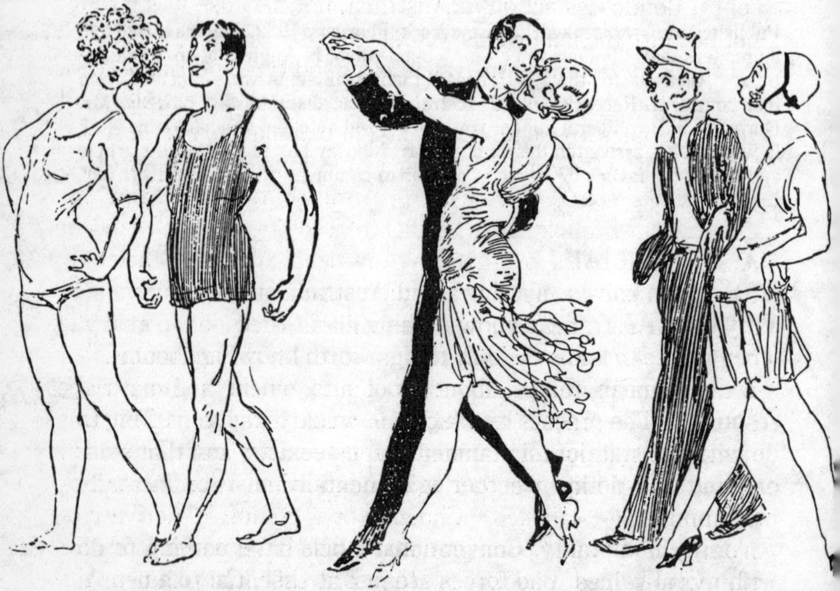

"The good Australian is a gay fellow and his girl is a gay girl. He is a good lover too."

the few individual creators it possesses. If I use the first person a little in discussing this matter, I assure you it is in no vulgar spirit of self-revelation, but because I have been forced into a peculiar relation with the Australian National Ego. For thirty years it has never ceased to attack me and my works, but it has also bought those works.

One must understand something more of the Australian ego to understand what is happening in Australia at present. I read the excellent article on Australia in the August issue of *Fortune*, and endorse it. As far as any generalised estimate of a people may go, it is a just one. But it leaves out something: something without which an estimate of a people must leave it floundering in any other anthropological limbo. I mean the effort of a small group to establish a culture in the face of a fanatic hatred of their effort.

I believe this hatred emanates from a minority, but at present it dominates action in Australia, not because it is strong, but because the majority is weak.

I think the average Australian is a good type, putting aside a lack of the graces in a social relation to other peoples. All young peoples are rude, boastful, and bad mannered; these are the reverse marks of ill ease and a consciousness of inferiority. Dickens did not very much over-caricature the American of his day, but how much has his attack had to do with the restraint and courtesy of the present-day American. If Dickens had only come to Australia, as he nearly did . . .

The pose of the average Australian is that of a sardonic cocksureness. He is foolproof: aware of the rottenness of human motives and not to be taken in by them. He derides everything – except himself. His weekly papers reflect this uneasy vacillation of national self-esteem by their incessant jokes at the expense of Englishmen, who are exhibited as semi-imbeciles labelled "Choom" or "Pommy"; derivatives from "chum" and "pomegranate" – the latter a similitude for the plump red cheeks of the Britisher. In return, the Englishman dislikes the Australian as a colonial and a convict-bred upstart without any social status.

All that is inevitable between an isolated group striving to detach its national ego from its parent nationality. All colonies replicate the resentment impulse between father and son.

Nevertheless, this annoying cocksureness of the Australian springs from two of his best virtues: his physical courage and his ability to think for himself in action. For a century he has been forcing a place for himself in a crude and difficult land afflicted by drought and an uncertain rainfall, and the War of 1914 demonstrated his tradition of toughness and endurance. His sporting impulse is one outcome of his passion for taking a risk, whether on a bad horse or by dying of thirst, or casually swimming in the company of sharks.

For the Australian is what all penetration into unknown lands has always been, the Roman legionary. Not the constructive Roman, the road-maker, engineer, builder, and lawgiver. Wherever I look at the faces of American men of affairs I see typical senators of the Roman Empire. Always in Australia I see the hard sardonic faces of Caesar's legionaries.

Years ago I produced an illustrated edition of Petronius and went to Pompeii for my material. When the book was produced, one Australian critic went for me because I had not drawn what he conceived to be Romans, but typical Australians. He was right; but faces I used were all from Roman portrait busts. During the War, English officers constantly complained of the Australian's disregard for the academic ritual of discipline. Very true; one of the marching songs of Caesar's soldiers began: "Look out, you women, we bring the bald-headed seducer . . ."

Also, the myth of the Australian as a lanky, loose-legged type has long outlived its day. Possibly the sons of the early settlers were like that, by the too sudden effort to adjust themselves to exotic conditions. The Australian of today is compactly built and of average height, as are all bodies built for endurance. The most perfect canon of male form on earth is to be seen on the Australian beaches. Australian women are apt to be stocky and too short-legged, but it is rare to find one broader across the shoulders than the hips, which is a bisexual stigma very common in European women.

I will add yet one more virtue to the average Australian; he is a good lover. Most Australian marriages are the result of a love episode and not an arrangement for one. At least this means that emotion comes before ritualism. It recalls another virtue, which requires of me to deny a statement in *Fortune's* article on Australia; that the Australian is a churchgoer. Australian churches are almost empty; the Australian spends his Sundays rationally in the open air, and Australian parsons have the hunted and harassed air of the uncertain wage-earner. They beg for a living, and I have known them to sell fowls and vegetables. One parsonage I recall as bearing the sign: "Motor cars attended to." In a recent trip down the coast where there were a lot of newly built bathing resorts, I never saw one church. Finally, the Australian term of supreme contempt is the word "wowser", which covers all aspects of the repressionistic reactionary sectarian mob.

Twenty or thirty years ago Australia was a miasma of sectarianism, and only its tradition remains. But a vicious tradition. It is linked with another; the convict system, though Australia is unaware of that. I was unaware of it myself until quite recently.

States of mind do not alter; they merely change their habitat. What *was* the parson and the convict official is now the bureaucrat. For its size, Australia has the largest bureaucracy with the lowest mentality in the world. The cost of maintaining the public service in Australia is such a joke that one can't laugh at it. The system arrived at is that it costs about nineteen shillings to earn a pound.

The financial madhouse is no affair of mine. I refer to it because this idiotic process which is strangling financial values in Australia has now stated its intention of destroying moral values too.

Up to this Australia has been a good place wherein to fight for an individual outlook on life and art. That is to say, conflict has been balanced between the endurance of the artist and the spleen of attack on him, which has taken the usual form of outcries by the press and in the press. I will pass over certain other activities by Australian Frustrates to frustrate movement in art there, for no one wants to be *too* ashamed of the country of one's birth. Left to the newspaper critic, he has done his job very well in his effort to destroy individual expression in any one of the arts. Very often he has succeeded. I recall a musician of great promise killed by him. The musician gave one concert, was viciously attacked, threw in the sponge and died. I recall a novelist who wrote two fine novels and an equally fine play. All were attacked by Australian critics. The attack on the play was arranged beforehand and squashed it after one night's performance. Disgusted, that writer has done nothing since.

No doubt this sort of thing is inevitable; mediocrity must fight to keep the standard of intelligence low in order to protect itself. At the same time, I am not going to throw all onus of responsibility on the disgruntled critic. For years past he has been driving every promising young writer out of Australia, but then the young writer has allowed himself to be driven. If he had stayed and fought it out, there would have been at least a space cleared for an Australian literature, but he has gone to Fleet Street and sunk his identity there.

For myself, I have no quarrel with Australia on the score of plastic art. I have seen a group of artists arrive from nothing to establish a sound tradition and a genuine culture. A very keen group of collectors has followed the movement and supported it. A sense for form is a very definite quality in the Australian ego, with a definitely sardonic outlook, as witness the subtle wit of Will Dyson's drypoints, Low's caricatures, Bateman's humour. These draughtsmen have left Australia because they needed a larger and more cultured audience than Australia possesses.

Only a prose literature can give Australia that. No country can have a national consciousness without the novel. And just there the Australian official moron has chosen to announce that Australia will not be allowed to have a literature other than one he approves of, which is to say that it will have no literature.

No one outside Australia can have any notion of the degradation Australian intelligence has been subjected to by the antics of its official morons. The censorship over books and motion pictures there would insult the mentality of a child of ten. Not one single book of high moral value from *All Quiet on the Western Front* to Hemingway's *A Farewell to Arms* has escaped being banned. In this frenzy of imbecility even Shakespeare's *Venus and Adonis* was accounted an indecent work and solemnly confiscated and burned.

For myself, I had always assumed as an understood thing that Australian officialdom was a poor thing still lumbering along somewhere in the 1850s, but I had no idea that it was still buried neck deep in the mud of the convict system. It went to a lot of trouble to demonstrate that to me personally over a novel of mine which was published in England and America, and was very courteously received in both places.

Nothing can explain the moral frustration of Australia better than the way it went on over that novel. Dementia, nothing else. For a start, it was banned by the customs as a matter of course. Then it was referred to the Minister for Customs, who wound himself into knots by alternately passing and banning it seven times. In a state of great moral debility at being unable to make up his mind, he referred it to the Solicitor-General and a Cabinet meeting, which finally allowed the whole solemn weight of the Commonwealth Government to ban the book.

But the rot wasn't over there. One of the newspapers made me an offer for the serial rights of the novel, to which I agreed, and its publication was announced. At once the Customs transferred the matter to the police, who arrived at the newspaper office and demanded their copy of the banned work. The paper then rang me to ask if I had a typed copy of the novel, which I happened to have and as that was my property which the police could not demand, it was decided to print from that. Thereupon the police passed the word to the

Post Office, who informed the paper that if the novel was published it would not be allowed through the post.

Pure convict system, one department passing the word on to another. Not even an appeal to the absurd by-laws which to the official lunatic are so many acts of God.

I take this affair to be a test case for Australia. It is a plain statement that its culture is not to be a fair exchange between creation and public opinion, but a matter to be settled by the arbitrary thump of a policeman's baton.

In short, on the only matter worth serious thought, the Australian is not going to be allowed to think for himself. I leave him to think about it.

The Australian Reader?

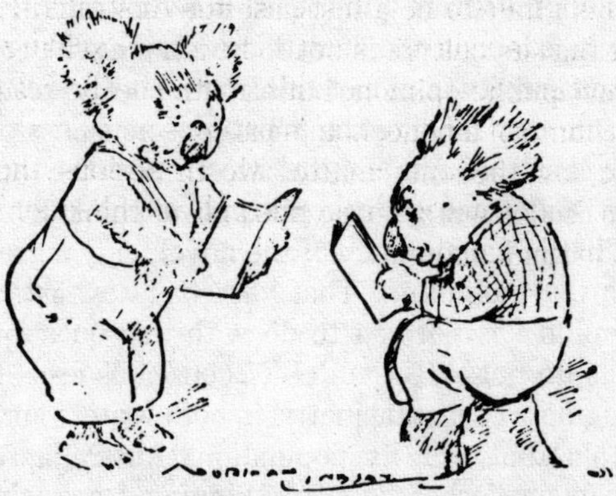

Having been asked to contribute so many words on the subject of the Australian reader, I find my mind a complete blank on it — or him, or her. Where does one arrive at an estimate on such a subject, anyway? Mostly by going about in people's houses, and listening to the things they talk about. If the people in those houses are intelligent they will, of course, talk about books. . . .

Books are the swiftest and easiest means of arriving at an estimate of intelligence, or a lack of it, in any average human being. A taste for good quality in pictures, poetry, or music, is always a specialisation of intelligence. Therefore, we are not offended if a man claims to have no particular interest in those three arts. But let him confess to no special taste in novels, or to prefer bad novels, then we ticket him as a nitwit straightaway.

For prose is the concretion of the people's average consciousness. The best prose is that which deals with the crudest

Published in *The Australian Author*, produced by the Fellowship of Australian Writers, Authors Week, Sydney, 1935 and commonest states of mind and life. The best novel of this era, *Babbitt,* is the record of a vulgar business man. And this novel has had such a staggering effect on American consciousness that it has almost become THE standard of self-criticism, by which the average American turns a scornful eye on every other average American. It is only by such novels as *Babbitt*, which label a people with crudity, that a people may be raised from crudity. I do not think that poetry, plastic art and music reach very far into the mass consciousness of a people. They are for the few — the elect. But the novel is for everyman, and it will not be a good novel unless everyman can read it. That is the anomaly of the novel; only a great novelist can reach the mob-mind. That very bad novelists also reach the mob-mind has nothing to do with this question, because bad novels do not affect states of consciousness at all. They are the stigmata of mental inertia in both writers and readers.

I am told that, for its population, Australia reads more novels than any other country. Judging from what English publishers have told me of the sales in this country of high-quality novels, I should say that the average Australian reader reads mostly trash. And, undoubtedly, the censorship on novels is a determined movement to see that he gets only trash to read. For myself, I really do not go about among people in this country enough to give an opinion on its taste in books, but on such chance occasions when I have heard books discussed, I can't say that I have remarked any special evidences of good taste or judgement. My personal opinion is that the average woman reads much better stuff than the average man. Englishmen travelling in this country have told me that they have no difficulty in talking to Australian women, but with the men here they are dumb, unless the subject is horse-racing. . . .

No, I think it must be pretty clear that books do not make the staple subject matter for intelligent conversation in Australia, as they do in other countries. I am reminded that this must be so when I recall the quality of many conversations in New York. There may be a hundred planes on which one may find the key of talk pitched, but the only talk worth having is that which discusses affairs for the motives that generated them, actions for the personality they reveal, or books for the special genera of which they are an example. All that, one got as a matter of course in New York. I never had better or more discriminating discussions on the novel than in New York. . . .

For my part, I do not intend to fall foul of the average Australian male because he reads only the sporting news in newspapers. He is an ass, no doubt, but that is because he is merely engaged in being what he is. If he is to be made into an intelligent reader of books, he must be given intelligent books to read. I mean, of course, intelligent books written in Australia about Australians. When an Australian author can puncture our average Australian Babbitt on the point of his pen, at least 40,000 Australian Babbitts will be roused to a frenzy repudiating the stigma, which will mean 40,000 readers suddenly stung into a state of outraged intelligence.

In short, readers don't make books; books make readers. When Brian Penton's novel, *Landtakers* was published recently, it aroused a great deal of interest and was widely read. That was because it was a powerful novel, and forced the reader's attention, whether he liked it or not. Whoever read that novel was, for the time being, at least, an intelligent reader of novels. I needn't stress this moral; there is plenty of rough material for readers in this country: it is the novelist's job to shape them by the standard of his own intelligence.

Commerce and Culture

AXIOM 1 — The commercial prosperity of a people depends on the vitality of that people's culture.

AXIOM 2 — A nation cannot have any future stability unless its national spirit is expressed in Art.

I am aware that commercial rationality will reject these simple truths, and always has rejected them, because commerce, and all that it implies of politics, industrialism and economics, is assumed to be the process which stabilises existence, while art is accepted as a paid dependant on the exertions of commerce, with a function to decorate and amuse its leisure, but with no place in the dynamic which keeps life in action.

And yet, since history has recorded the rise and fall of nationalities, no truth has been so irrefutably established as this — that only those nations which have produced great art have remained stable, while all those which failed to produce it have perished. At the core of every nation that has risen to

Published in *Australia National Journal* No.1, Sydney, July-August 1939 power there has been a great creative energy in art. The law of survival in a people appears to be defined by what power that people has to add its quota of culture to civilisation as a whole.

And this must be a living culture – one which may be translated into universal consciousness and so become an indestructible content of the human mind. It is not sufficient to raise a few impressive buildings and decorate them by the ingenuity of craftsmen and the spoil of trade with more enlightened peoples. For a brief period nations have risen to military and commercial power by such means: Carthage, Egypt, Babylon, Assyria, Phoenecia – but because there was no core of a universal culture in them they were doomed to extinction. India, China and Arabia retained just enough of an initial impulse towards culture to remain in existence as a people without dominance or power, but the Mayan peoples, cut off from contact with more vital nationalities, and with no core of culture to energise them, have retrograded to complete primitivism.

The principle which makes culture the central source of energy in a people is under our eyes in the records of a few hundred years. We may put aside the Greek explosion of creative energy, because the Greek was, and still is, the prime stimulus of all past and present efforts. In Greece was centralised the universal principle of culture which has become the property of all nations.

See what those nations have done with it. At the basis of Roman world domination were its poets and prose writers, who are still the perfect models of form and style. No nation rose to power in the long dark ages between Rome and the Renaissance, because no expression in art arrived to energise a people. But with the Renaissance the Culture-Power principle was vindicated with startling effect. Behind the potent Italian states were the first great painters. No need to call them over; we have only to glance at their works to see what a vital reaction to life they called into being. Venice dominated the commercial world *because* of Titian and the Venetian school of painters. At the centre of Spain's world dominion was the gigantic figure of Cervantes, with Velasquez and the Spanish school of painters and poets. Holland rose to commercial power because Rembrandt, Rubens, and all the fine Dutch painters functioned there. France became a great nation by its central stimulus of its two great rationalists, Rabelais and Montaigne, and has ever since produced great writers and painters. England exploded into energy and power with Shakespeare and the Elizabethan poets and dramatists, and has ever since drawn energy from the poets she had done her damndest to destroy. If there is a corruption of moral energy in England it is because her attack on poetry drove Keats to throw up the sponge and die, and Byron to half-finish his work and throw it aside in disgust and seek death too. Certainly ever since the destruction of those two great poets, who never fulfilled their destiny, poets and writers in England have made a cowardly obeisance to popular morality, and that is the death of integrity in art, and possibly the death of the nation that insisted on it. For if art can create the central energy in a nation, its refusal to create can also destroy that nation. There is a pretty damnable nemesis waiting for any nation which stultifies its artists, just as there is a nemesis on those artists who allow themselves to be stultified. We have seen quite recently how the German peoples were knitted into a national unity by the potency of its musicians and the vitality of its thinkers. And at this moment we have before us the confounding portent of the German people striving to destroy the very principle by which they became a people.

I must get rid of an accusation of confusing cause and effect in making a more or less stark statement of the principle by which culture must be the source of all other energies in a people.

We must dispose of the fatuous assumption that Art is an aesthetic; or that the people who create it are defined by their casual labels as Poets, Artists and Musicians. If we accept them as minds highly sensitised to the emotional complexity of life, and faculties highly developed to record its drama, its externality, and its moral profundity, and to define all these things in a symbolism of form, sound and word which may be assimilated by other minds, then we see that it is by this procedure alone that man has developed from a primitive savage to a civilised being.

It is art, not God, who has created man, just as it is man, not God, who took the few primitive seeds of the earth and turned them into the fruits which are the commonplaces of our meal tables. And man never would have developed wheat out of grass, and the apple from the crab apple, and the rose from the briar, unless his mentality had been quickened and developed by art.

We talk casually about forming the human mind, but how is it really done? Apparently by a slow accumulation of sensitive brain tissue which permits us a swift perception of all sensory impacts and the power to recognise them, analyse them, and understand their significance to the general content of our consciousness. A process physiological as well as intellectual. Thought must function on a mechanism, and that mechanism, the brain, is capable of expansion only on one system. The language of thought is not in words, but forms. For a form to be defined there must be a cell in the brain recording that form. Thus every form perceived is a cell formed in the brain. And when it is realised that of the two million nerve ducts functioning in the body one million is devoted to the eye, we do not need to say anything further about the profound significance of Art, by which alone an act of seeing may become an act of knowing.

All this is not merely a process for demonstration by a biological clinic, though I believe biologists are on their way to demonstrate it. The principle which makes Culture the central source of energy in a people is the living essence of the struggle for dominance going on between peoples and systems of government at this moment.

For the law of preservation for nations is also the law of preservation for ruling classes. Up to last century the aristocratic principle dominated because it was the aristocrat who protected and patronised culture. I believe myself that the aristocrat lost potency because he abandoned this special function of his class, and instead of patronising poets and artists and musicians, he took to jockeys and racehorses. Economists will explain that the rise of trade and industrialism gave power and wealth to the middle class, who thereby became the governing class. To be sure, it was the wealthy middle class which last century took to patronising the arts, and is still doing so, wherever that class had or has the intelligence to grasp the Culture-Power principle. We see it best exemplified in the American millionaire to-day, who is constantly giving vast sums to endow art galleries, libraries, conservatoriums of music, universities, and endowments to scientific research. I do not suppose that the average millionaire cares a dump for these things, but he has the protective cunning to be aware that unless he gives back to his country some of the money he has taken from it, the people will end by taking all his money from him, and perhaps slitting his throat into the bargain.

They certainly did this for him recently in Russia, and one cannot but confess that he deserved it, for the Russian aristocrat took everything from the people and gave nothing back. And today it is the Russian people who are now taking over the Culture-Power principle, or claiming to do so. I am told that there is now in Russia a genuine striving by its government to stabilise and encourage the arts, and there is a good deal of evidence to prove that this is so. To be sure, the uprush of communistic principles among all peoples has had one extremely disastrous result, for to their claim to a share of the world's culture the lower orders have taken to practising art themselves; hence the peculiar uproar of disintegrated values labelled Modernism. Later and more discerning generations will undoubtedly define this movement under the heading of The Wharf-lumper in Art. It is very annoying, no doubt, to have its exhibits constantly thrust under our noses, but it is a transient phenomenon which will pass once the Culture-Power principle is definitely established as a governing principle between the two great opposing factions to-day — Communism and Facism. The one that takes over that principle will undoubtedly win.

And what is Australia's reaction to this most pregnant of all present problems? A depressing question, unless we confirm the Johnsonian axiom of "Sir, if you see a fool rolling downhill, give him a kick to send him faster." Nothing can be more apparent than that the Australian monied class is blindly and suicidally bent on its own extinction. With the portent of socialistically-minded governments constantly taking large lumps of its income away by taxation, it fanatically clings to what remains of its hoarded wealth, when it could at least have the pleasure of aggrandising itself personally by endowing culture with the money otherwise taken from it by taxation, and thereby demonstrating its worth to the community and ensuring its own future safety. Conceive the blank and outraged stare of the average Australian capitalist at such a proposal. What! his security dependent on the exertions of a few artists and poets and writers and musicians. Could anything be more fatuous?

All right, have it your own way, you capitalists. Refuse to assist your country's culture. Refuse to endow its art galleries, museums, universities. Refuse to put Australian pictures on your walls and Australian novels and poems on your bookshelves. Go on refusing to bestow monuments on your cities and mural paintings on your buildings — the writing is on their very walls for you.

I must add a footnote to this, because Australia has an Art which has struggled for existence for the last forty years against disheartening conditions. That it exists at all is largely due to the patronage of a small group of picture buyers of moderate incomes, who have very often vindicated their taste at the expense of their pockets. I know of only a few rich men who have helped to stabilise our initial effort towards national culture.

In Homage to Julian Ashton

It astonishes me that I should have lived to have the privilege of writing a foreword to Julian Ashton's memoirs in his own lifetime, for Julian was in his middle age when I first met him in my twenties. In fact, I had just turned twenty, and meeting Julian Ashton was to be one of the most significant events of my life, as it must have been to many another young artist, for what he was to me as a friend and stimulus, he was to every other youth struggling to find a place in the difficult métier of art. Perhaps I can best define what he was to all those others by telling what he was to me:

It was he who first made an affirmative gesture towards my work by offering to raise enough money to send me off to Europe to study. He did this after seeing some pen and ink drawings of mine that a friend had taken to Sydney while I was still in Melbourne, and Julian wrote to me making that generous offer. I was extremely grateful for it, but my instinct warned me against the disruptive effect that Europe has had

From foreword to *Now Came Still Evening On*, by Julian Ashton, Angus and Robertson, Sydney, 1941 on so many Australian artists, and I decided to stay in Australia till I at least had some notion of where I wanted to go in art. As J.F. Archibald had made me an offer of work at the same time, I came to Sydney and joined the staff of the *Bulletin*, and it was to Julian Ashton that I then turned for an introduction to the period's movement in art. His generous and hearty welcome warms me to this day. He allowed me to work in his studio, he took me to stay with him at his home at Bondi, he put work in my way, and he made me a member of the Society of Artists, of which he was the president.

In those days the Society was just a small group of artists holding a yearly exhibition at their own expense, for there was never enough work sold to pay the expenses of exhibiting it. I doubt if it would ever have held together under the depressing conditions of those early days but for the energy and faith of Julian Ashton. He never announced a mission; but he had one all the same, and that was to establish a sound tradition of the dignity of art and its importance to a country's future stability. He stands at the very forefront of this country's effort towards a national culture, and for long years he fought to no other end than to see that culture firmly grounded. And to do that he must have sacrificed a great deal of his own personal effort as an artist. At that time he was the only distinctive portrait painter Sydney possessed, as his fine portrait of Parkes and many other such works attest. He did, of course, paint also a considerable number of landscapes, seascapes, and figure subjects, but he gave up a great proportion of his time to guiding the general movement here, and fighting for its interests.

The truth is, Julian Ashton is a born leader. He not only had the capacity for inspiring faith in his followers — he had that foresight in affairs and wisdom to act upon it that invariably added works to faith. We should never have got our initial struggle through all the difficulties it had to face without Julian's leadership.

My own personal debt to him goes very deep, when I recall how much I owe to his championship of my work under the antagonism it aroused from the public and the attacks made on it by the newspapers. Let me give one instance of the trenchant way Julian Ashton supported it in one of the earliest moral lion roarings over a pen and ink drawing of mine called the *Crucified Venus*. This work was exhibited in our annual show here, and later our whole exhibit went to Melbourne as a part of a general exhibition of pictures held there during some public celebration. I forget what about. Anyway, the Melbourne papers attacked the *Crucified Venus* as an immoral and blasphemous work and the committee responsible for the exhibition withdrew it from the show. Julian Ashton at once wrote to the committee saying that unless the picture was restored to the walls the whole exhibit would be withdrawn. The picture was restored, but the committee tried to take a middle course between Julian Ashton and the moral lions by hanging it with its face to the wall. This, of course, only exasperated public curiosity and brought down on the distracted committee Julian's final ultimatum. The picture must be turned face out or the exhibit would be withdrawn.

The picture was again reversed and the committee retired to give up the ghost, or to do whatever any other misguided beings did who fell foul of Julian Ashton over a question which concerned the dignity of art.

I know he had many such fights on his hands over my work, but exhibited it was yearly under his leadership, nor did he ever take the slightest notice of puritanic protests.

His affirmation of any other sincere effort in art was just as indefatigable as it was in my case. Streeton, Lambert, Hilder, Blamire Young, Gruner, all owe much to Julian's early recognition of their works, and the energy with which he fought to ensure their public recognition, too. To Gruner he was a wonderful friend, from the day that Gruner came to him as a student till Gruner was free to make the most subtle and profound analysis of light in nature that the art of landscape possesses. I cannot conceive what Gruner's diffident and reticent personality would have done without just such a strong and resolute spirit as Julian's to stir him into action. I saw the whole process from the first picture exhibited by Gruner, and can attest how much the initial impetus of Gruner's splendid contribution to this country's culture was inspired by Julian

Ashton. From the very first, Julian recognised Gruner's genius, long before its salient qualities were apparent in his work. I remember well the first picture exhibited by Gruner, which was just a passage of light through a mass of foliage, and I said something to Julian in appreciation of it as we were hanging the show. He said: "Yes, that's the work of a student of mine, and I can tell you he's going to do great work."

As for poor Hilder, sick and slowly dying, it is not too much to say that Julian Ashton literally nursed him through those last years which gave us his few charming works. And Lambert, when he returned to Australia, told us in public how much, as a student, he owed to Julian Ashton's stimulus.

But he did as much for any student who showed talent, or, for that matter, those who had little. When I think of the hundreds of young people who have passed through his school, all of whom have carried away at least a stimulated personality and a vitalised conception of the significance and importance of art to a country's moral energy, I find it impossible to compute the debt this country owes Julian Ashton. Without art as the central energisation, a people can have no stability, no integration as a people, and no assurance of movement into the future. No nation has ever established itself as such without an art. It cannot be said too often that art is not an aesthetic but a dynamic. It is the core of that constructive principle which forms the human mind. By defining form it gives to mental tissue a system of regulating the brain cells so that they respond swiftly to the needs of any special faculty. I am not forgetting that it can also seek to disintegrate and destroy this system, when it revolts against all those traditions and form images in art by which the human mind has been built, as it has done for the last twenty years under a general label of Modern Art. But that is only one facet of the destructiveness that is at present turning Europe back to the jungle. Europe invented modernism in art and now Europe must pay the penalty for its relapse into primativism and moral imbecility.

If that infection has up to this failed to demoralise Australian art, in spite of the activities of certain distracted iconoclasts, how much of its stability do we owe to Julian Ashton? He has given his life to impressing on the formative period of youth the soundest traditions of form and beauty. In the eternally interacting circles of human life, how many thousands had their values stabilised by principles emanating from Julian Ashton? Such a debt to the moral energy of a country cannot be paid. We can only record our respect, our affection, for the courage, the wisdom, the integrity and the faith which are the concentrated essence of Julian Ashton's spirit.

The Great Australian Myth

There are two obstructive factors at work on Australian writers today. One is the Commonwealth Literary Fund and the other is the Myth of the Great Australian Novel.

This myth is from two sources: Henry Handel Richardson and a forlorn conviction that the rest of the world knows nothing about Australia. Thus the novelist feels that he or she must explain everything about Australia while also writing an Australian novel. We have had a number of these complicated exercises published and we know their formula by heart. The arrival of a first family, its struggle to settle on the land, the begetting of a second generation against a background of the country's economic-sociological-political development, an arrival at the third generation and an effort to relate its states of mind, complicated relationships and various domestic dramas to the whole bedevilled content of the Australian background.

It can't be done. Not as a novel, anyway. As a chronicle, if you like, and a good deal of excellent, earnest-minded, Mit-

Published in the *Bulletin,* Sydney, 4 August 1943

chell Library research work has been done in these economic-sociological tomes masquerading as novels. As background material for the novel itself they may have done a genuine service. But as an art form they are impossible, in spite of *The Fortunes of Richard Mahony*.

No one can depreciate the profundity of that work, but it is not a great novel. Any one of its individual themes, worked out purely on its dramatic content, could have been a great novel, but, merged in the vast mass of its background material, each loses its special unity in the overlapping of other themes. Its central motive is too thin to carry the weight of 900 pages of packed prose, and Richard Mahony is too negative a character to vitalise that motive: a depressed Englishman whose nostalgia for England forces him back there only to find all his expectations of a homecoming disappointed, which drives him back to Australia and a miserable finality in senility and death.

If Henry Handel Richardson had split that mass of prose into its half a dozen separate novels, she would have given the Australian novel an admirable tradition on which to build its present effort. But *Richard Mahony* is doomed to become one of those works which everybody accepts as a classic and nobody reads. I have read it through myself, and it took me about a week to do so, and I am a quick reader. And this time-factor of its reading must defeat it as an art form, and will defeat all other art forms inspired by it. And that very inspiration, by the way, should warn Australian writers to leave the *Richard Mahony* form of novel severely alone. That a thing has been done well once is the best of reasons for not doing it again.

There is one simple and profound law to which every art form must submit itself. It is that no effort at creation can exceed the intellectual and sensory equipment that it is addressed to.

Sound cannot go beyond the gamut of response by the auditory nerves; the eye cannot record forms which go beyond its radius of vision, nor can the memory keep in sequence more than a limited mass of recorded material. If the Fifth Symphony lasted for three hours instead of half an hour, no normal ear could keep on responding either to its thematic unity or its massed sound waves. There are pictures in the Louvre so large that they reach from wall to wall of those large galleries. No one has ever seen them. They are not pictures, but panoramas.

Again, a drama by Shakespeare is designed to hold our attention for the time-space of about three hours. If it lasted for six, human endurance would throw up the job of trying to keep intact its sequence of drama and emotion.

If a novel cannot be read within the time-space of three or four hours, it cannot be absorbed and memorised in the foregoing terms. I put out of this consideration the old-time picaresque novel, which can be as long and rambling as you please, since it is really a collection of separate episodes strung loosely on a central thread. But the novel of today, defined by its greatest masters, Dickens and Balzac, has arrived at a form definitely fixed by our ability to retain its whole content intact in memory. And this demands that every separate facet of a work of art must have its reason for being and its special relation to the central theme. This does not exclude from the novel minor motives and separate character groups, but these also must exist strictly within the tonal setting demanded by the central theme, and must move with it, and not away from it. To do this effectively is difficult enough, but when the writer strives to impose on it a hodgepodge of economic-sociological-political-historical subject matter the job is bedevilled out of all possible order and unity.

No fatuity could be greater than the assumption that a great work of art demands a great mass of material, or that size itself has any relation to greatness. Just the opposite. All great works of art are based on the simplest of themes, and are worked out with a rigid rejection of all extraneous material.

The key word to creative unity in art is that of the law of Nemesis — inevitability. The theme must be struck at the outset and must dictate motivity to all that follows. Let anyone take the central drama of *Bleak House*, from the moment Lady Deadlock is arrested by the handwriting on a legal document to her self-willed death at the filthy graveyard where her lover lies buried, and, reading only the central theme, and excluding minor motives in the novel, see how sequence is driven on sequence to a finality as inevitable as that of the Fifth Symphony, struck from the fantastically slight germ of four unison notes, out of which Beethoven builds his whole concept of man at war with destiny.

The novel proper must concern itself with a single central motive worked out by the conflict of personality and dramatised by sequence of events forcing the motive to a final crisis. Take any great novel and you will see that this is the principle on which it is built. In *A Bachelor's Establishment* Balzac takes a handful of characters — a mother, two sons, an aunt, an old doctor with a weak-minded son, a gutter-brat girl and a tough small-town youth — and builds a splendid drama based on the scoundrelly son Phillip's rapacity, which is the thread leading all sequences of the novel to its finality. So with all great novels.

The great American novel is not one of those overloaded sociological tracts that have come out by the dozen these late years, in which the author's political bias sees his puppets the victims of a monstrous injustice by external affairs, and quite ignores the truism that all human beings are the creatures of their internal mechanism. *Babbitt* is a great American novel, and its theme is the simple one of a commonplace businessman's struggle to detach his ego from all the other thousands of Babbitts by trying to think for himself, and his failure to do so. That final crisis where Virgil Gunch breaks Babbitt's nerve by just looking at him is one of the subtlest dramatisations of a novel's theme that I know of. It was by Sinclair Lewis's earlier novel, *Main Street*, that the American novel became a world property, and turned our attention to the whole output of American prose. *Main Street* has for its theme nothing more than the disillusions of an average married couple against a background of small-town personalities, yet it brought America vividly before the world's eyes and sold over a million copies in Russia alone. Do you think any overloaded sociological propagandist tract could do that?

These are invariably "serious" works. The author's portentous seriousness of outlook on the subject matter of his novel is being accepted as a valuation of the novel itself.

And it is just in this matter of the author's viewpoint on his novel's material that all values in the novel exist. Unless an author can maintain a detached, ironic outlook on the creatures of his métier he is given over to the emotional sentimentality of third-rate art. Oh, I know Dickens floundered into that bog betimes, and so did Balzac, but the great content of their works is founded on ironic humour. I haven't space for instances to make that clear; it is sufficient to point out here that the great generic sources of the novel — Petronius, Rabelais, Cervantes, Fielding — based their work on laughter.

Humour is the sacrosanct property of prose; poetry cannot achieve it. Even Shakespeare had to fall back on prose for humour. I hope it is understood that humour, as the basis of all good prose, has more to do with the author's outlook on his subject matter than with the matter itself; though, of course, comedy and the mad antics of human personality must always be the best material of the novel. But any material, however tragic or violent, may be used effectively in the novel so long as the author maintains his ironic, sardonic balance.

I would place Conrad's *Secret Agent* as a perfect example of a tragic theme handled with inimitable good taste from the ironic angle.

What is its theme? The intense precautions of his mother and sister to protect the half-witted Stevie, which are the cause of getting him blown to pieces by a bomb. Think of what a loathsome mess a modern sentimentalist of the Steinbeck-Hemingway school would have made of such a scheme, and how at every page we would have to squirm at the spectacle of sternly repressed male tears.

I can conceive, and shudder at, the concept of Hemingway, with Chief Inspector Heat, bending over the slab on which repose the remains of Stevie, scraped up with a shovel. But Conrad carries us through that ordeal in a way that makes it a fascinating experience. So with the final murder of Mr. Verloc, which is visualised with such intense clarity that one has the sense of being actually in the room and watching the knife descend on Mr. Verloc's prostrate body.

But not for one moment does Conrad demand that we should suffer with Mr. Verloc or the unfortunate Winnie, or Stevie, or Stevie's mother. The whole sordid, drab episode of murder in the back parlor of the dismal little shop which sells indecent photographs is placed before us with ruthless precision but with perfect detachment from emotion for or against the creatures involved in it, and the effect on us is one of pure delight.

Can prose on a tragic theme ever give us that exaltation of mind that we get from poetry? I think not. Our response there is based on the conflict of two opposites: awareness of a tragic motive by the exaltation of its poetic image. But prose can come pretty close to that process where it fascinates an intellectual response by rejecting an emotional complicity with it. All bad prose tries to do just the opposite; it demands an emotional response at the *expense* of our intellectual detachment.

And that is what all "serious" novels of today are trying to do. By the weight, denseness, turgidity and solemnity in these works, it is quite clear that their authors set out with the label "great" already attached to them.

Let us get rid of the fatuity that such a thing as the Great Australian Novel can be written. It is an amateur's bedtime fantasy.

Great novels may be written in this country, but they will not be the Great Australian Novel, any more than a novel selected from the mass of English prose could be labelled the Great English Novel.

If such a unique standard could be fixed in any art it would be the death of that art. Yet there is no doubt that the myth of such an achievement is muddling the Australian writer today, and disheartening him and her from tackling the novel proper.

And here the Commonwealth Fund is adding its obstructive effect. For every writer suspects that if two novels were offered for its opinion, the one a novel proper, based on human personality and conflict, and the other one of the usual overweighted sociological tomes, it would inevitably fall for the latter, however good might be the novel proper. Don't ask why. Wherever a matter of aesthetics is referred to official or academic opinion, it will invariably discard a work of individuality and favour a work of standardised mediocrity.

I sympathised with Bob Menzies in his desire to help the arts by establishing the Literary Fund and the Royal Australian Academy, but I never have believed they would be any real use to either painting or literature. These State institutions always become the preserve of mediocre achievement.

The Making of a Novel

If the Australian novel has a definite nationalistic "direction", it would appear to be towards the picaresque, for the three most distinctively national works up to the present are in that category; *Such Is Life*, *The Peapickers* and Brian James's *The Cookabundy Chronicles*, which is making its first appearance in the *Bulletin*.

The Cookabundy Chronicles, though told in a series of short stories, is a coherent whole; and, insofar as it strolls about the countryside for its material, is in the area of the picaresque. *On Our Selection*, loose and casual as its writing is, might be included in the same category.

But these works are outside the classification of the novel proper, as is also that other type of prose work of which we have had a fair number of examples produced here; the semi-historical, sociological, three-generation chronicle, more or less in the vein of *Richard Mahony*.

But writers in Australia have dodged, and are dodging, the novel proper, because it forces on them a difficult problem in

Published in the *Bulletin*, Sydney, 22 May 1946

construction. And they must face it, if they are to be accepted as competent prose craftsmen. *Jonah* is the best example we have had yet of the true novel, though it is weak in construction; the two themes of Chook and Jonah being told in alternate chapters, neither of which has any integral relation to the other, so that the effect is of two separate novels.

The novel proper is based on a central theme, towards which all lesser motives move, and which is brought to a dramatic crescendo which finalises whatever may be its special motive. And all characters in it must have some relation to its central theme, and all extraneous combinations of personality and event must be rigidly excluded from the narrative. In short, the novelist must face precisely the same technique as the playwright. Whatever the suspense-motive of his work, it must build towards that crisis which reveals and finalises its theme before the curtain comes down on the last act.

To revert to the picaresque is to throw back to the genesis of the novel. Petronius, *The Golden Ass*, Rabelais, *Don Quixote, Tom Jones* – these great and enduring works will last as long as civilisation. But they ignore any constructive principle, and remain the explosive output of gay and reckless minds, fascinated by the mad spectacle of life, and grabbing up great handfuls of its material right and left. Scott's novels are also in the picaresque key, loosely held together by a casual hero and heroine thread. But once Jane Austen had written *Pride and Prejudice* the novel had to face a disciplined technique based on the dramatisation of a central motive, and all great or near-great novels since her day have worked strictly within that basic principle.

For the novel cannot escape the principle by which all other arts must function. It is only because prose gives the writer a larger mass of material, and a longer time in which it may be dealt with, that the novelist is able to evade constructive principles that would be glaring faults if applied to music, drama, or painting. Once a composer has given out his theme, all other phases of his work must be dominated by it. Once an artist has defined his salient curve or angle in a picture or a statue, all lesser rhythms must have their precise relation to it. For the playwright, of course, the mechanism of the stage insists on a more severe discipline than any other art. A nice mess he would make of a play if he threw in a few casual characters and events that had nothing to do with its theme.

If the Australian novelist of today confines his or her reading only to the novels of his own generation he may as well give up any idea of construction. Practically the whole modernist movement in all the arts has been an attack on established principles of construction, without being able to supply a constructive principle of its own begetting in return.

The bumptious young modernist has a contempt for all works outside his own meagre time-factor, and the meek ones have a vague sense of guilt in referring attention to past masterpieces. The modernist painter pins up a print of a Gauguin or a Dali beside his canvas and then tries to paint something like it, and the modernist prose writer reads Joyce or Hemingway or Steinbeck and proceeds to evolve a novel out of the state of mind engendered by these writers. And what a state of mind the novelists have exhibited to us! It has been one of dissatisfaction, fear and suspense, owing to the incessant threat of more war and to the moral disruption set up by the Russian revolution. Apart from its excessively depressing effect on the novel, it has seduced the novelist into assuming that the conditions under which man lives are of greater significance than man himself. He has surrendered to the supreme fallacy that affairs make man, and that by altering affairs man will become an altered being. Since Plato wrote that despicable work *The New Republic* this prime idiocy has been apparently ineradicable from the human mind. Its infliction on the novel these later days has been the miserable Leftist grouch against life and undergraduate jeers at it under the general heading of debunking all cheerful, courageous, and upright concepts of the procedure under which we *must* exist on earth.

Communism — or, in other terms, rebellion against freedom of action imposed by an elder world — is the normal state of adolescent youth. It is a stimulus to throw off parental authority and start out alone on the adventure of life. Once that adventure has begun, it should be discarded, having served its turn. If that state of mind persists after the twenties, the unfortunate being infected by it is doomed to futility.

As for sociology, who cares a damn today whether shipowners of the 'sixties were scoundrels or that lunatic asylums were mismanaged in that era; matters which sent Charles Reade into a frenzy of altruistic novel writing? The only work of his that survives is *The Cloister and the Hearth*, which has nothing to do with politics or sociology.

The novel must return to the constructive principle defined by its greatest writers, Dickens and Balzac, because there is nowhere else to go. And that principle is to take a central motive and build slowly towards its crisis, keeping all other threads in the novel interwoven with it and moving with it to a finality.

The central motive may be divided roughly into two basic principles. It may be a drama of passion and events which drives the characters into action, as in *Bleak House*, or it may be the effect of a dominating passion in one character dictating motivity to the lives of other characters, as in *Eugenie Grandet.*

Reduced to their starkest statement, the central motives of these novels may be stated in a few words. In *Bleak House* it is that of a woman who has had an illegitimate child in her youth, but has hidden that event, and, later, has married into a high social position. The early scandal of her life is wormed out by a morally blackmailing old lawyer and she is driven by the shame of exposure to a self-sought death. In *Eugenie Grandet* it is the ruthless acquisitive passion of a miser who frustrates the lives of all in connection with him. The themes in both cases are commonplaces of human relations; they are made profound by the revelation of human personality, by the absolute conviction of reality in the creation of character, and by the perfect artistry with which each novel, in the hands of these masters, is built to its crisis.

In *Bleak House* the constructive problem is much more difficult than in *Eugenie Grandet*, because of the mass of its characters, and the complicated threads which draw all those related to the central motive into contact with it. Consider what a hell of a job Dickens gave himself when he posited the beautiful and remote Lady Dedlock as a focus for such characters apparently impossible of any relation with her as Mr. Guppy, the crude little Cockney law clerk, his friend Tony Jobling of the whiskers, Mr. Snagsby, the meek little law stationer, Mrs. Snagsby, his nagging little wife, the oily Chadband and his wife, Mr. George, the ex-trooper, Mr. Bucket, the detective, and the astounding Smallweed family and their especially astounding old relative, Krook, the rag-and-bottle dealer. The only character who has right of contact with Lady Dedlock is Mr. Tulkinghorn, Sir Leicester Dedlock's solicitor. He is selected as the instrument of destiny who may expose Lady Dedlock or preserve her secret for her. It is by one of the most subtle uses of anticlimax that I know of in any novel that Dickens uses the murder of Tulkinghorn as the signal which releases the exposure of Lady Dedlock.

It is true that in this novel Dickens intrudes two minor extraneous themes: he attacks professional philanthropists on the one hand and Chancery practice on the other. But so many of the characters involved here are in contact with the central motive that they work into the general pattern of the novel. He gets some splendid fun out of Mrs. Jellyby and the philanthropists, but the Richard Carstone episode could be very well dispensed with. In it Dickens makes one of those annoying conflictions between presentation and motive that he so frequently does in his technically "good" characters. Richard Carstone is portrayed with psychological veracity as a shiftless youth, incapable of any sustained effort, who would make a mess of his life under any terms, but when he gets obsessed with the Chancery suit and dies (very unconvincingly) of disappointed expectations, Dickens tries to tell us that the evils of Chancery procrastination killed him. On the same sort of misplaced motivity, he pretends that he is presenting Esther Summerson as a sweetly unselfconscious young creature, while exposing her as a smug little prig, avidly recording every tribute paid to her and affecting amazement at her own goodness of heart as announced by all those around her. But that sort of thing in Dickens goes beyond innocence. He must have had spasms of disgust at times, for the concessions he made to popular sentiment never fail to arouse our dislike and derision for those characters who are ostentatiously introduced as sentimental dummies. But in reality they take up very little space in the mass of his work, and the drama of Lady Dedlock herself is carried to the end without a single resort to false sentiment.

In *Eugenie Grandet* the conflict motive is between father and daughter. Old Grandet is a miser, but a miser of Shakespearean magnitude. He is built up with such a minute attention to every facet of his personality that his reality as a human being carries complete conviction of the effect of that personality on the Grandet household. His wife and daughter Eugenie and old Nanon, the servant, accept his parsimonious dominance over their lives as the rulings of omnipotence. Eugenie, a simple, charming and affectionate girl, falls in love with her cousin, a youth whose father has committed suicide after sending an appeal to his brother Grandet to take charge of the youth's future. Grandet, to get rid of the lad, sends him out of the country, which also sends him out of the novel. But Eugenie has committed the unpardonable sin of giving the youth all her small savings, for which Grandet punishes her savagely, locking her in her room and allowing her only a prison diet, though old Nanon manages to smuggle food to the prisoner.

Later, Eugenie marries a dull fellow and is submerged in the drab life of a small provincial town. Her parents die, her husband dies, she inherits Grandet's fortune. But it is no use to her. Her will has been destroyed by the satanic dominance of her father. She gives her money away in charity and lives out her existence in the old house, religiously obeying all those parsimonious rulings laid down by her father for the administration of food and the necessities of life. Her one poor little act of rebellion, inspired by love, had been quelled at its source by her father, who continues to dominate her life from the grave.

A ruthless novel, but not a depressed one, because Balzac creates old Grandet with a satanic gusto, is fascinated by him and imparts that fascination to the reader. Moreover, the clarity with which the Grandet household and house are visualised is so vivid that we meet them as known personages, and could walk about the house blindfolded. Indeed, the unflagging care and zest with which Dickens and Balzac get everything possible out of their material give such a sense of vitality and fecundity to their works that after reading them most other novels seem only to be sketched in outline.

The construction problem in *Eugenie Grandet* is not one of gathering threads to a focal point, as in *Bleak House*, but of the gradually accumulated evidence of potency and ruthlessness in old Grandet and of docility in Eugenie, which makes his dominance over her so convincing. It cannot be too often emphasised that what an author says about a character has no validity. The character must reveal everything about himself by his speech and actions, and their effect on those about him. Reality in the novel has very little to do with factualism in itself, since factualism can turn out data which are extremely unconvincing, while the most bizarre event can bring a conviction of absolute reality, if handled with minute attention to its external dramatisation.

A perfect instance of this is the death of old Krook by spontaneous combustion. Whether such a death is possible is beside the point, though Charles Fort has dug up a great deal of evidence to the effect that such cases have happened. The reality of the event consists, firstly, in the visual projection of old Krook, with his liquor-fuming breath and his states of sodden coma, from which, when finally aroused by repeated shakings, he emerges in the full control of his faculties, as the evidence that he is no longer a normal drunk, but a man whose normality has been transferred to a liquor-sodden carcass; secondly, the prelude to his finality is so forced upon our senses that we feel the physical ill-ease of that close, hot night, and smell the stuffy atmosphere of that dingy little room in which Mr. Guppy and Jobling are waiting for the hour of twelve, when old Krook is to hand over the letters which will incriminate Lady Dedlock. The sense of suspense, of conspiracy, of waiting on an unmentionable event is forced on one almost intolerably by the awful significance of that smell of burnt chops, and of that filthy, oily substance that Mr. Guppy gets his fingers in, sending a shudder through our own as he frantically washes his hands, and smells them, and washes and smells till that obscene stench is removed from them. It confounds me that any novel-writer today should attempt to practise his mētier without having studied that masterly piece of realism.

I know that many aspiring writers suffer an illusion that the novel with a centralised motive requires an immense exercise of ingenuity in its invention and construction. Construction does require craftsmanship, but that is not an inspired process and is within the range of any competent literary carpenter.

And the centralised motives of all great works are not complex, but extremely simple. The Fifth Symphony is based on four unison notes. The destruction of Macbeth is made inevitable by the prophecy which assures him of an achieved ambition. Take the motive of any of Conrad's novels and it can be reduced to the simplest of formulas. A trusted employee of a silvermine is placed in a position where he can safely steal a load of silver and succumbs to that temptation. Out of that minute germ that long and powerful novel *Nostromo* is built.

In *The Secret Agent*, a mother and sister devote their lives to protecting the half-idiot Stevie, and are thereby the means of destroying him. *The Nigger of the Narcissus* – a malingerer is really dying of the disease he thinks he is simulating. *Heart of Darkness* – a highly civilised man goes into the African jungle to bring it the benefits of civilisation and the jungle reverts him to a primitive savage. *Babbitt*, a great novel built on the meticulous observation of trivialities, has for its motive the obscure and troubled urge of a commonplace businessman to escape the dull compulsions of his daily life and the opinions of his fellow dull dogs and live according to his own needs and aspirations. He makes one feeble effort at rebellion, which brings down a threat of ostracism on him, and in alarm he scuttles back, to submerge once more in the common mass of his kind. In short, the simpler and more commonplace the central motive, the better for the novel, since it will apply to the greater area of human experience.

It is not as an arbitrary ruling that we insist that the novel must be based on a central dramatic motive. Life itself dictates this principle. Every human unit has one special aspiration, passion or urge which dominates his or her lesser impulses, and every event involving conflict of personality must arrive at some sort of crisis before reaching finality. It is not proposed that Australian novelists should laboriously invent plots and then fit a set of characters to them. That is an industry for second-rate fiction.

There is the whole range of human personality and passion from which to choose a central motive, including the seven deadly virtues and the seven delectable sins. Love and hate may be the basic urges underlying all human action, but they are capable of infinite variations. No two human beings are created precisely alike, any more than out of a billion leaves we will find two with the same fibrous veinings. The material for art is inexhaustible. That understanding should be sufficient inspiration to the average young novelist to look about him for a few central motives on which to dramatise his novels.

The Craft of the Novel

For many years, in correspondence and in conversation, Norman Lindsay discussed with Australian writers the problems of their art. He was invited to write essays on the subject for the Red Page of the *Bulletin*. The first pointed out that there had been an indifference to constructive principles in the average Australian novel. The second essay, published on 12 June 1946 and reproduced here, was intended "to demonstrate practical methods whereby constructive unity and effective characterisation may be attained".

It is a dangerous thing to lay down arbitrary rulings for the practice of any art. At best, we can only suggest certain things that it is advisable not to do if unity in concept and construction is to be attained. Traced to their source, we find that most principles in art are already defined by the function of the human ego and the normal procedure of life itself.

Life creates the material for art and the human ego translates it into form, therefore form must be dictated by the senses which absorb the material of art. Thus in plastic art, it is the eye which defines the constructive principle: the eye focuses on a central point, and is aware of other objects only within its radius of vision. A picture, consequently, should have a focal point to which the attention is attracted, both by the emphasis of this central object and by the subordination and design of all secondary objects in the canvas. On the same principle, we focus our attention on the procedure and crisis of the dramas of life — on the fact of a murder, for example, and on the events which led up to it.

A picture is seen in its entirety at a single glance, whereas poems, novels or music have movement in time and are conveyed to the mind by a constant succession of fresh images, so that their constructive unity is a much more difficult thing to define. But the same principle must apply: each must have its dominant focussing point, towards which all secondary material must move in unity.

Inspiration may suggest the theme of a novel, but only sound technical craftsmanship can build it into a constructive unity. And I find, by the contemplation of many novels, published and unpublished, that the prime difficulty of the novel lies in its least significant aspect, and that is in the "bridge parts" which lead from chapter to chapter, and episode to episode, and which bind the narrative into a continuity of movement. Those "bridge parts" in a novel are what edges are in painting. In both cases, unless the salient subject-matter is bound into a unity by the subtle merging of edges, there will be abruptness and dislocation in surface and sequence. It is bad construction in the novel to jump from one episode to another where there is no relation between the two, or to leave one set of characters and shift to another without logical sequence.

A great deal of that sort of thing can be avoided if the writer starts his novel by first drawing a ground plan of its locality, and marking the dwellings of each character, and the streets or paths or roads by which one may be brought naturally into contact with another. And at the same time the writer may consider any communal interests, mutual acquaintances or events which will bring the characters into relation with one another. Writers enjoy the episodic meat of a novel but shy off the job of articulating the bones first. "Bridge parts" are not inspiring to write, and they frequently force one to a good deal of irritated meditation.

But, again, a great deal of that may be avoided if the end of one chapter contains a lead into the next. However slight the reference, it will be sufficient if it creates the illusion in the reader's mind that he is reading a continuous narrative. For a chapter gets him into a certain frame of mind. To switch him off in the next chapter on to a new series of events or personalities forces him to build up a new frame of mind, and the annoyance of having to do so very often causes him to drop the novel. The mechanism should sustain interest, and "bridge parts" are that mechanism.

Moreover, "bridge parts" may be used effectively to emphasise drama. As an instance of that, take the ingenuity by which Dickens overcomes the difficulty of getting Mr. Guppy, the crude little Cockney law clerk of *Bleak House*, into the remote Lady Dedlock's private apartment for an interview.

Mr. Guppy suspects that there is some family relation between Esther Summerson and Lady Dedlock, because of Esther's likeness to a portrait of Lady Dedlock which he has seen. As he is dismally in love with Esther, and hopes to gain her goodwill by tracing her relationship with the rich Dedlock family, he starts ferreting into her past.

Esther's father, Captain Hawdon, had died in miserable circumstances as an anonymous law-writer, and Mr. Snagsby, the law stationer, has been called in to give what information he may about him, and Joe, the crossing-sweeper, is also dragged in at the inquest to tell what he knows of the dead man. Mr. Snagsby, a kind man, is sorry for Joe and gives him half-crowns. These two are sufficiently remote contacts with Lady Dedlock, yet they lead to her.

Mrs. Snagsby belongs to a religious sect presided over by the oily Chadband. Chadband has married Mrs. Rachel, who was once maid to the austere aunt who brought Esther up. The Chadbands are dining with the Snagsbys when a policeman brings Joe, arrested as a vagabond, to Mr. Snagsby, as Joe has insisted that Mr. Snagsby will vouch for him. Mr. Guppy, professionally in contact with Mr. Snagsby, calls at the shop while Joe is being questioned, and hears his garbled story of a mysterious veiled lady who made him point out the filthy grave where the law-writer was buried. Making himself socially agreeable, Mr. Guppy is invited by Mrs. Snagsby into tea, and there meets Mrs. Chadband, and learns from her that Esther's aunt once confided to her that Esther's name was not Summerson but Hawdon.

With other matters emerging to his ferreting, Mr. Guppy has now enough evidence to warrant his writing to Lady Dedlock requesting an interview, and thereby becomes the mechanism which allows Lady Dedlock to discover that her illegitimate daughter did not die in infancy but is alive in the person of Esther Summerson.

Dickens could have avoided this extraordinary series of "bridges" if he had resorted to abrupt transition from scene to scene, but the slow building up of contacts from unexpected but logical sources and Mr. Guppy's pertinacity in following up their leads convey the sense of a ruthless closing-in on Lady Dedlock and the exposure of her secret, which is vitally important to the novel's dramatic intensity; inevitability must be the principle by which any drama carries conviction, but unless the writer shows the mechanism by which destiny brings it to crisis there will be no conviction of inevitability.

But the writer is advised to take care that the mechanism is not made too obvious. Nothing is so fatal to a suspense motive as to make the suspense too apparent. Or to forecast it. In that excellent novel *A House Is Built** a little boy and girl are playing in a garden, and the writers let slip the information that the little girl is destined one day to destroy the boy. That, for me, robbed the final drama of intensity. Whenever those two characters were mentioned the foreknowledge of their end nagged at the mind, making intermediate events tedious. The urge was to skip and find out how it happened.

Again, if a writer lets his preconception of inevitability color his presentation of a character or an event, he will defeat interest in its gradual development. Richard Aldington is a novelist who slips badly in this respect. Having tried as a stunt in *The Death of a Hero* announcing the conclusion of his novel before it had well begun, he repeated the device in all his other

**A House Is Built* by Marjorie Barnard and Flora Eldershaw, co-winner of the *Bulletin* novel competition in 1928

novels. One could detect their inevitable finality after reading half a dozen pages. In one of them — I forget which — the preconception of a character was so apparent that after a couple of pages of him I said to myself "I bet this chap commits suicide in the end." I looked up the end, found that to be so, and dropped the novel unread. And this was not because I had learned the plot, but because after those first few pages there was nothing to reveal in a character already revealed.

The interest in the revelation of character is, of course, in his or her unknown quantity. And that is based on the understanding that most human masks reverse the personality they cover. One constantly hears the phrase "Well, he is the last sort of person I suspected of doing a thing like that". The mask has slipped — the basic motivity of the personality has exposed itself. It is a commonplace that meek and sheeplike men secrete great malice, and that noisy fellows seek to cover up a meek and sheeplike ego.

In the terms of psychoanalysis, "the philanthropist is the sadist who overcompensates his craving". But there is no proposal here that the novelist should indulge in text-book psychology of that sort. He is advised to have nothing to do with Freud and the psychoanalysts, who have done a lot of damage to the novel by giving writers the illusion that they can learn about human motives from a book instead of observing their action in life. All psychoanalytical terminologies should be taboo — to use them in a novel is to impart an intolerably priggish air to the writer.

Psychology in the novel is based on a visual projection of a character in appearance, speech and action, with the ability to draw out at a given moment the hidden motive of his being. Dickens makes a cockshy of Sir Leicester Dedlock all through *Bleak House* as the fatuously complacent, arrogant and class-conscious aristocrat and then, in finality, turns him into a truly noble and dignified figure when, stricken down by paralysis, his one thought is for Lady Dedlock.

Since visualisation — in Conrad's words "to make see" — is the prime function of the novelist, I am convinced that, where a novel goes flat and a character has failed to come alive, it is because the writer himself has failed to get a clear pictorial image in his mind of the event, scene, or personality he is writing about. I have had so much to do in my time with illustrating stories and novels that this problem of visualisation has been expressly forced on me.

A properly visualised story springs to the mind automatically in pictorial form. Slovenly tricks which pass undetected as reading-matter are glaringly exposed to the artist who has to illustrate the book. A writer may introduce a group of people, label them, give a rough classification of each, and get away with it, but an artist can't escape by drawing a bald head or a double chin and leaving the rest of the face blank. I suggest that a writer should constantly ask himself how he would draw a scene or a face if he were an artist, and he will be astonished to find out how much material he needs to meditate over and select from, in order to make a reality of it. I suggest that he should go carefully through the manuscript of his novel and mark on the margin the word "Picture" wherever he detects flat passages of narratives which tell the reader about matters but do not present them to him pictorially, so that he may rewrite them in visualised form.

A danger to be guarded against in drawing character from life is the illusion that, because the writer sees the real character clearly in his own mind, the reader will see it also, and therefore he need not present it pictorially. I once illustrated a novel by a lady novelist which had for its central character a boozy loafer in an up-country town. Having a conscience on such matters, I searched the manuscript carefully for a description of this character, but could not find a hint of his external appearance, so I drew him as a fat fellow with a beer-eater's moustache. The lady novelist charged into my studio in a fury to demand why I dared have the insolence to tamper with her sacrosanct manuscript by putting a moustache on a character who was cleanshaved. The man she had drawn the character from, it appeared, was cleanshaved. Apparently she suffered from the delusion that by an inspired exercise of clairvoyance I could transport my vision to an obscure up-country town and study her character in the flesh.

A writer can save himself a lot of trouble if he first makes a synopsis of a character, writing down every detail of his appearance, his manner, his vocabulary, his way of speaking, his background, any personal idiosyncracy and particularly his salient mental characteristic, such as "suspicious", "tolerant", "sardonic", "stupid", and so forth. I am always falling back on Dickens for examples of mastery in the technique of the novel, but instances from his works simply jump into the mind unasked for. Take these lightning-flash portraits for perfect examples of personality and appearance conveyed in one impact:-

> Podsnap; prosperously feeding, two little light-coloured wiry wings, one on either side of his bald head, looking as much like his hairbrushes as his hair; dissolving view of red beads on his forehead, large allowance of shirt collar up behind.
>
> Twemlow; grey, dry, polite, susceptible to east wind; cheeks drawn in as if he had made a great effort to retire into himself years ago and got no further.
>
> Charming old lady Tippins, with an immense, obtuse, drab, oblong face, like a face in a teaspoon.

And so on, round a large dinner-table, every face drawn with that precision which selects the exact word which will convey it to the reader as a pictorial image.

If a character has marked characteristics, those should be referred to on his reappearance in the novel, so that the reader will recall who he is and his place in the narrative. Very few readers remember a character by name till he has been well impressed on the memory by repetition.

Reality in the novel is not based on factualism, but on the validity of character-drawing. A writer is constantly bothered by the mental question, "Can I make the character do this or that? What authority can reality give me for such a situation?" The authority of reality can be dispensed with if the reality of the character is established in the reader's mind. A writer should remind himself that in relation to his novel he is a god, and can make his creations do anything he pleases, so be that he has the art to convince the reader that they really did it. I have already used, in a previous article, the death of old Krook by spontaneous combustion as an instance of this truth.

A technical problem which every novelist must face is the "time-shift". It is bad construction to leave a present-moment narrative and go back into the past to account for distant events that are essential to the story. The past should be brought forward into the present.

In this problem, the technique of the detective novel can be used with effect. A crime has been done and the investigation into it starts at the present moment, drawing the characters into its procedure and, through them, delving into past actions and emotions and the conflict of personality till the motive of the crime and its criminal are revealed. In this way, the past is constantly woven into present-moment action, and the same device may be used in the novel proper. Conrad, indeed, used it as the method all through *Lord Jim*. Talk between characters is the most effective way of bringing in the past, but any object surviving from the past may be used, or a present event that had its genesis in some past action.

A rule that should never be violated is that the writer must not take sides for or against a character or an action. That is for the reader to do. I have used Dickens so often for instances of mastery over the novel that it is only just that I should give instances of where he violates his own high canon and falls into the excessively bad taste of attacking an alleged "villain" or overenthusing about a "heroine". In neither case is he ever convincing. He tells us that Esther Summerson is a dear, sweet, unselfish young thing, and convinces us only that she is a smug little prig. He shouts abuse at Carker in *Dombey and Son* as a base scoundrel and presents him as an admirable fellow in every respect. You have to ignore what Dickens says about him and pay attention simply to what Carker does and says.

Finally, a word on that most bedevilled of all problems, an overprizing of charm in the heroine. There seems to be a fixed illusion in the world of the novel that, unless a writer can convince his reader that his heroine is physically lovely and mentally charming, the reader will not think she is desirable. And that sort of thing has precisely the same effect as the efforts of the newly-captured lover to convince the world at large that his beloved is a houri from paradise while everybody is wondering what he can see in the wench. For in fiction to present a woman always as lovely and charming is to present a lifeless dummy.

Personality is much more important both in life and the novel than conventional good looks. A Rosa Dartle is genuinely alluring while a Dora is the sort of silly creature a man would dodge spending half an hour with. If the Australian novel can beat the heroine convention and still create desirable women in literature, this country will have contributed something very important to the mētier of the novel.

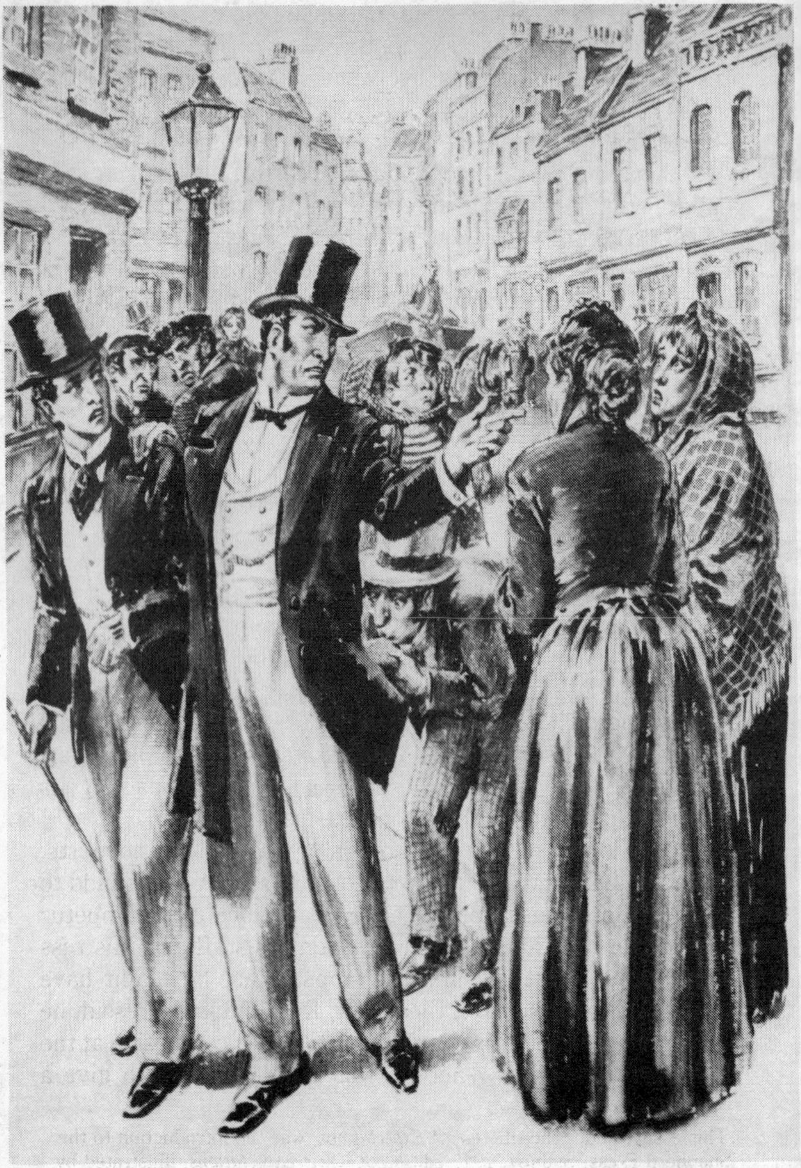

"If you come here bothering about your Bill, I'll make an example of both your Bill and you."

Charles Dickens and His Novels

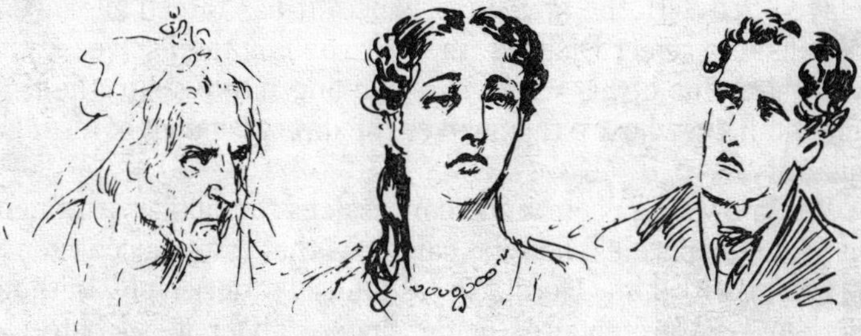

I have been reading Dickens all my life. I still read him. I will go on reading him while I can hold a book. When the urge takes me to pick up one of his novels, I know that once again I will be absorbed into its potent reality, which is much greater than the factuality that surrounds me as I read. Only great art can make us its creatures in such terms. Only great art transcends the procedure we call reality by compacting its disarticulated material into a concrete unity.

Dickens is last in succession of the great generic novelists; Petronius, Cervantes, Fielding, Scott, Balzac. We must add to those the prose passages of Shakespeare. The direct impetus of character-creation in Dickens is from Falstaff and Mistress Quickly. But there the impetus stops. What he might have transferred to prose from Cleopatra, Rosalind and Cressid, he evades utterly. And this evasion constitutes a corruption at the very core of his art. Where it was most essential to give a

This essay, under the title *Great Expectations*, was the introduction to the Shepherd Press, Sydney, 1947 edition of *Great Expectations*, illustrated by Norman Lindsay.

woman the full content of her femininity, he devitalised her into a dummy of popular sentiment.

I will not take upon myself the arrogance of accusing Dickens of this concession to mob morality. Dickens accuses himself of it. Its confession is written at large in his works. And because Dickens is the greatest of the great novelists, that false quantity in him must be defined, because it has broken the creative continuity of the novel as a form of art. It has played hell with the novel ever since. It has forced all sincere novelists to reject Dickens, thereby robbing themselves of the vital stimulus of his work, and handing him over to the sentimentalists, who are themselves the direct product of his false quantity.

We know that Scott made concessions to popular sentiment in his love episodes, but one can't feel that it was a conscience problem with him. He did it sardonically, derisively, without making any pretence of being sincere about it. "I hate the whole Jenny and Jessamy tribe of them," he said, and tossed into his novels a couple of stilted conventions labelled hero and heroine, and got on with his real job, which was the creation of Dugald Dalgetty, Nanty Ewart, Rob Roy, Bailie Nicol Jarvie, Dandie Dinmont, Dirk Hatteraick, The Antiquary, and all the other superb life-size male character creations. Some of his girls have charm and vitality. Julia Mannering is a gay minx, and Diana Vernon almost reaches full femininity. But motives in a Scott novel are never centred in women, save in the case of Jeanie Deans. They are based in a dangerous male earth of violent action; the life of action that would have been Scott's own, if destiny had not very wisely chained him to his job with a club foot.

With Dickens it is quite another matter. Women centralise and dominate most of his novels. He was passionately obsessed with the whole world of femininity. He adored women. Where their sex content is not touched on, his women are as alive as Shakespeare's. Indeed, Mrs. Gamp is even a richer creation than Mistress Quickly. But, where the dramatic intensity demanded that a woman should vindicate the integrity of her sex, he falsified the situation out of all relation to reality, or to his own deliberate projection of its drama.

And just here we have the maddening confusion between the concept of a Dickens novel and Dickens's deliberate falsification of it. The concept is always right — the falsification turns it into a piece of cheap popular fiction. Not only where the situation involves sex, but wherever it conflicts with popular sentiment it is mutilated and defaced. How far Dickens was the dupe of his own falsifications it is impossible to say. He had enormous powers of self-deception, and appeared to believe in any pose that appealed to his vanity. But he twists so flagrantly from creative integrity to popular fiction mongering that one is confounded for opinion between innocence and mendacity. At least it is clear that having made that first, drastic concession to the mob in relation to sex, he allowed it to pervert nearly every other situation involving human passion and personality. Invariably, those situations are superbly projected, so that their finality is inevitable. Almost invariably that finality is twisted into a falsification designed to gratify the cheapest taste in fiction.

Analysis of any of his novels must make that variation between concept and performance clear. *Dombey and Son* is a stark instance. This novel, as Dickens conceived it, might have been the greatest novel ever written. As he wrote it, it remains a mutilated masterpiece, emasculated of what should have been the apex of its drama.

That drama, in simple outline, is a wife's revenge on a husband she hates by taking as her lover the man whom her husband has used as the instrument to degrade her. Its essence is that the wife must give herself altogether to the lover, else her revenge is futile. Even a meek woman would have done so under the terms of Dombey's insolence to her. A proud and passionate woman like Edith Dombey would suffocate with anger till she had reinstated her self-respect in the arms of a lover. As if Dickens did not know that. Yet in his miserable effort to evade the finality he has built up with such superb skill, he tries to tell us that Edith only pretends to take Carker as her lover, and that Carker meets a villain's end by being absurdly run over by a train. And when he has brought Dombey to his finality by ruin — shut up in his deserted house, sick, frustrated, but at least rejecting all human sympathy in his tortured arrogance, Dickens makes a sickly pretence of bringing him forth as a good old man, chastened by misfortune, and maudlin with tenderness for little children.

It is enough to make one groan in misery to have before him the edifice of a great work of art, magnificently proportioned, superbly designed, revealing an unequalled power of creation, and to find that its interior is a hollow sham and that its foundations are built on sand. Such a work is not only an attack on the integrity of art, but on the stability of the human mind. A lie cannot be absorbed, because a lie has no existence.

I am convinced that in *Dombey and Son* Dickens did face a genuine attack of bad conscience. This is apparent in his treatment of Carker. In the true conception of the novel, Carker was cast for the part of a genuine lover, and in that character he got into the novel and remained as one, in spite of Dickens's frantic efforts to label him the villain. To make this clear you have only to separate the actual projection of Carker from all the rot that Dickens writes about him. He is constantly stopping the narrative to abuse Carker, which is not only bad taste, but worse art. He rants at him like a local preacher. Such intemperate conduct in a writer can have only one motive, and that is a fear that his real feelings about Carker will get out in spite of himself. They do get out. Dickens admires Carker extremely. He creates him as a proper lover for the lovely Edith. Carker has wit, assurance, and is perfectly at ease with life. He knows more about Dombey's business than Dombey, and manages it for him. He has a sardonic contempt for Dombey's megalomaniac self-importance, and mocks it ironically to Dombey's face. He has a fine taste in art and his house is handsomely furnished. He is a fine rider; always an image of masculine grace. He plays chess well; any game. He does everything well. He is the only character in the book who is never at a loss over the real motives of all the other characters. There Dickens uses him as a bad conscience device frequently used in his novels, which is to make his conventionally bad characters tell the truth about his conventionally labelled good characters. He had to relieve his spleen somehow over his obnoxious Cheerybles and Meagles, and he uses his Ralph Nicklebys and Miss Wards to tell the reader what he really thought about them.

What a writer says about one of his characters has no validity. What a character says and does in the presence of the reader alone counts as evidence of personality. There is no instance in the novel where Carker's speech and actions have any relation to the drivel Dickens writes about him. Nor is there any instance in Edith's relations with Carker where she expresses the hatred that Dickens says she feels for him. Carker is the only character in the book with whom Edith expresses herself without fear of being misunderstood. At their first meeting that relation is established. Carker sees at a glance that she has nothing but contempt for Dombey, and for herself, as a market commodity for Dombey's wealth, and he lets her see that he stands in exactly the same relation to Dombey by the neat irony of his talk. ". . . As Carker ceased speaking she looked at Mr. Dombey with a transient gleam of wonder in her face, not lost on one observer . . ." In short, a sympathetic understanding at the outset, which increases with every scene that brings Carker and Edith closer and closer to the last exchange of glances that confirms them as lovers. It is fantastic, the way Dickens gives those two inspired gestures of love, and then tries to scramble out of having done so. When Carker kisses Edith's hand, and Edith, left alone, strikes it on the mantelpiece till it bleeds, he tries to imply that it is because Carker has kissed it, and that while bringing before her eyes the hated image of her husband, to whom she has given that hand. Again, while trying to fob Carker off on us as the conventional villain of the period, who seduces women in order to ruin them, he gives him a true lyrical gesture, when, having kissed Edith's hand, he puts the hand that has held hers into his breast as he goes out; a charming symbol of the love embrace.

Conrad says somewhere, in so many words, that when two lovers fail to complete love in the fullest sense of that word, they have committed a crime against life. And a crime against art is the greater evil, for it perpetuates falsity in life.

If Dickens had not loved women, this sterilising of passionate intensity in them would not have mattered. He would have been on the other side, among the mockers and jeerers at life. No man looked on at its spectacle with such a fascinated interest. In spite of his falsifications, there are no lovelier women in prose than Edith Dombey and Lady Dedlock — not even in Balzac's wonderful gallery of femininity. You can search in vain for a literary device to account for their beauty. They are not even described, yet their beauty is as tangible as Titian's Laura Dianti or Goya's Dona Isabel de Porcel. He could give those women passion, violent and dangerous, but when that passion touched their sex, he fumbled the whole thing aside and tried to pretend that these living creations were just literary puppets stuck in a bookseller's window with all the other trash provided to gratify popular sentiment in the novel.

In *Bleak House* he evades facing the episode of passion by making it take place before the novel opens. We do not see anything of the tragic love affair which brought Captain Hawdon to a suicide's end in a filthy garret, and Lady Dedlock to a self-sought death at the churchyard where her lover lies buried. Still, the drama of exposure gradually closing in on Lady Dedlock is so superbly done that we miss nothing of its genesis in an illicit love affair. Objectionable qualities in that novel go elsewhere, to that smug little prig Esther Summerson and the overdone episode of Richard Carstone's death.

But, once again, a lie has no existence. Dickens was fascinated with sex and he had to squeeze its gesture in somewhere, and he did that by a fantastic and perverted device. Since he had sterilised his lovers, he handed over all the gestures that should have been theirs to sisters and brothers, daughters and fathers, women and women . . .

Oh, yes, it is all very pretty and innocent, and Dickens got away with it very well in the 'sixties and 'seventies, but it won't do to-day, even though those interested in the psychological revelation of human antics have given up reading Dickens. I am a hardened reader myself, and don't object to the incest motive in the novel, if the novelist uses it as such. The Greeks got tremendous drama out of it, but, normally, people afflicted by incest fixations are usually futile creatures, and not good material for art. I have read anything psychoanalysis has to say about this problem with interest, but I confess I can't read of Ruth Pinch coquetting with her brother Tom, or Florence Dombey's masochistic passion for her father, or Bella Wilfer's pranks with Pa Wilfer, or Louisa Gradgrind's overtures to her brother, without being incommoded by a consciousness of peeping through disgraceful keyholes. I never come on those passages without hurriedly averting my face and cutting in elsewhere on the novel. They excite a genuine sense of shame in us because they are so prettily petted with false sentiment and mendacious innocence.

As for women and women — putting aside those little instances where girls let down their hair and whisper confidences under its cover — I refer you to Miss Wade and her Diary of a Self Tormentor, in *Little Dorrit*. I do not know if Lesbians are self-tormentors, but Miss Wade is certainly a tormented Lesbian. How far Dickens was consciously innocent over Miss Wade I don't know, but he had mixed a lot with actresses, he had eyes in the back of his head for any human idiosyncrasy, and he must have seen something of Miss Wade's peculiar urges among all those flushed feminities. Anyway, he got her into the novel and allowed her to abduct the passionate young Tattycoram, and then did not know what to do about it. She has no part in the novel. She appears and disappears in the most irresponsible way, always under terms of obscurity in dark and dismal houses. There is a vague contact with the absurd Blandois, but there is no reason that she should know of his existence, much less that Blandois should leave with her a mysterious box of papers, which is the last thing a blackmailer would do with a comparative stranger. She appears briefly in the company of that magnificent old fraud, the Patriarch, but there is no explanation of what she is doing there. All we know is that she has got young Tattycoram hidden in one of her mysterious houses and is keeping the girl attached to her for reasons that keep Dickens floundering at an explanation till in desperation he pumps up some nonsense about an abstract revenge-motive against society to account for Miss Wade's obsession over the girl. And straightaway he explodes that imposition by making Miss Wade hand a written confession of her peculiar state of mind to Clennam, who is the last person on earth that Miss Wade would confide in. In these words she explains her initial reaction to her own sex:—

> She tormented my love beyond endurance. Her plan was to make them all fond of her and drive me wild with jealousy. When we were alone in our bedroom at night I would reproach her with my perfect knowledge of her baseness, and then she would cry, and cry, and say I was cruel, and then I would hold her in my arms till morning, loving her as much as ever, and often feeling, rather than suffer so, I would hold her in my arms and plunge to the bottom of a river, where I could hold her after we were both dead.

I think I have seen such abstract motives of a revenge against society in the case histories published in works on the psychology of sex . . .

One curious evidence of inverted conscience in Dickens is revealed by the parade of tenderness he made over the women he disliked sexually. As the women he loved were stately, lovely, passionate creatures, the women he disliked are all labelled Little, and are feeble, meek, spineless creatures, without the least feminine charm, with a perverted passion for suffering, and always attached to a degrading association — Little Nell to her imbecile grandfather, Little Dorrit to the loathesome Maggie, Little Emily to the bumbling oaf Ham Peggotty. But let it be noted that the recoil impulse of disgust from these depressing little creatures made him oppose to them a vital image of femininity — the delightful Marchioness to Little Nell, the vitriolic Fanny to Little Dorrit, the lust-tortured Rosa Dartle to Little Emily. Wherever there is no question of sex or popular sentiment involved, Dickens's women are the most alive in all literature. He created them by the hundred, too, and every one a full length portrait. Mrs. Jellyby, Mrs. Nickleby, Mrs. Clennam, Mrs. Varden, Mrs. Wilfer, Mrs. Merdle, Mrs. Pocket, Mrs. Gamp, Miss Tox, Louisa Chick, Susan Nipper, Lavinia

Wilfer, Flora — dozens more. It is not my purpose to call over the vast creation of his great characters, fatuously labelled "minor". He peopled an earth with them. In his first novel, *Pickwick Papers*, there are over three hundred individual characters . . .

The purpose of this essay is to define that basic corruption in his work which appears to be a concession to popular sentiment, but was really inspired by fear of the English puritanic hatred for all frank revelation of sex and passion. And the truth is that, having stultified his conscience on the score of sex, he let it play hell with the motives of his novels elsewhere. I will take only two instances where there is direct evidence that he intended to project the drama with psychological integrity, and then falsified it to gratify the vulgar reader's demand for a happy ending.

In *Our Mutual Friend* Dickens takes for his theme the corrupting effect of suddenly-acquired wealth. He sets out to show how a decent simple-minded old man like Mr. Boffin may be turned into a suspicious old miser by being left a fortune. And it is intended that all the other personalities relating to Boffin's money, from Bella Wilfer to Silas Wegg, shall also be corrupted by it. And he does build up this general corruption in a masterly manner till Boffin is presented as the universal symbol of the demoralised rich man. And then he turns it round with a shameless grin and tells us that it was all a bit of make-believe on Boffin's part to impress on silly little Bella Wilfer the evils of aspiring to be rich instead of being content with love in a cottage. Such mendacity leaves one breathless . . .

There is a final evidence in the case of Mr. Boffin that Dickens must have been eternally confused between his true and false projection of a novel. When Boffin is quite alone, after being blackmailed by Wegg, and there is no other person present but the reader, Boffin still carries on his true character of avaricious cunning, wondering whether Mr. Venus intends to go on bleeding him after Wegg has extorted his share of the money. This is a genuine slip of the pen, because, as the event shows, Boffin knows perfectly well that the will Wegg has got hold of is of no value as an instrument of extortion.

A secondary theme in this book is one of Murderer and Murderee. The point of conflict between Bradley Headstone and Eugene Wrayburn is jealousy over Lizzy Hexam. Eugene, the bored sardonic gentleman, drives Bradley, the passion-driven schoolmaster, to homicidal fury by jeering at him, forcing on him his own nagging conviction of inferiority, and, finally, tormenting Bradley into following him about the streets at night, on the presumption of going to meet Lizzy, who has hidden herself from both of them. If ever a man insisted on being murdered, it is Eugene Wrayburn. He is a man born disillusioned, utterly sceptical of all sincerities, finding life a tolerably bad joke, and unable to take anything — even his love affair — seriously. And Bradley is a predestined murderer. He seeks Lizzy Hexam with the full knowledge that she rejects him, because thereby he is given a valid excuse to kill. I do not know of any murderer in fiction so perfectly projected and understood as Bradley Headstone. And Dickens intended that he should murder Eugene. Writing the story in serial parts, he made the artist who designed the first cover, Storey, portray the murder. But when it came to that murder in the novel, he resorts to the cheap fiction device of a happy ending, in which Eugene is only battered by Bradley, is rescued by Lizzy, nursed back to marry her and renounce his idle ways and become a good industrious member of society . . .

But enough of this dismal theme of Dickens's treachery to Dickens. And this much must be said in extenuation of his submission to mob morality by fear of the mob attack. His destiny did to him the most damnably corrupting thing it can do to any artist; it gave him instantaneous success and popularity with his first novel. The roar of laughter that greeted *Pickwick Papers* shocked all the moral courage out of Dickens. He glimpsed what must happen if he carried the spirit of that novel on into his later work. Already we get the hint of a gay, non-moral earth in his spinster ladies running off with strolling players, his gentlemen mistaking ladies' bedrooms for their own, his girls kissed behind doors and his flirtatious married ladies causing uproars in the home circle . . .

We know that the puritanic hatred of life has only one taboo;

the glorification of the sex function. Degrade it, spit at it, make a joke of it, brutalise it, falsify it, evade it, and mob morality will approve. But lyricise it, love it, bring to its creation in art a passionate intensity, and the mob will crucify you. Or try to.

Dickens knew that. Every creator who loves life knows it. And Dickens could not face what must have followed if he had carried creative integrity, wherever it related to sex, into the power of his later works. He turned directly in his tracks and tried to efface creation of a gay earth by an image of murder. It was not at all in subconscious innocence that he called his next novel *Oliver Twist*. His spirit remained twisted for the rest of his life . . .

Well, he had brought down on himself idolatry by the mob and it became a drug to conscience that he could not do without. We can trace bad conscience in the feverish activity of his life, his passion for publicity, his posturings on the stage and the lecture platform. He had to drive down thought; he dared not be alone with himself. I cannot think of anything so degrading as the spectacle of Dickens reading his works in public, so crowded on by the mob that they lay on their bellies at his feet. Better have the vitriolic pens of a thousand frustrated journalists scribbling hate for one than to come to such an ignoble pass.

For, after all, the way had been prepared for Dickens by Fielding. We cannot accuse destiny only of malice in throwing mob idolatry at him. *Tom Jones* is not only a prose masterpiece; its psychology is profound, its outlook is ironic and sardonic, its women are satanically alive and sex is handled in it with astonishing frankness. A fatuous assumption has been urged that the times permitted what has been called Fielding's "licence" in that respect. There never was a more sneakingly prudish and "refined" period than the eighteenth century. Sermons were best sellers. Richardson wrote his mawkish drivel and that scoundrel Sam Johnson did his damnedest to destroy all frankness and clear thinking in literature. He was another who let funk of the mob bludgeon him into attacking the freed gesture in art . . .

But Dickens ignored Fielding and chose to pick up the tradi-

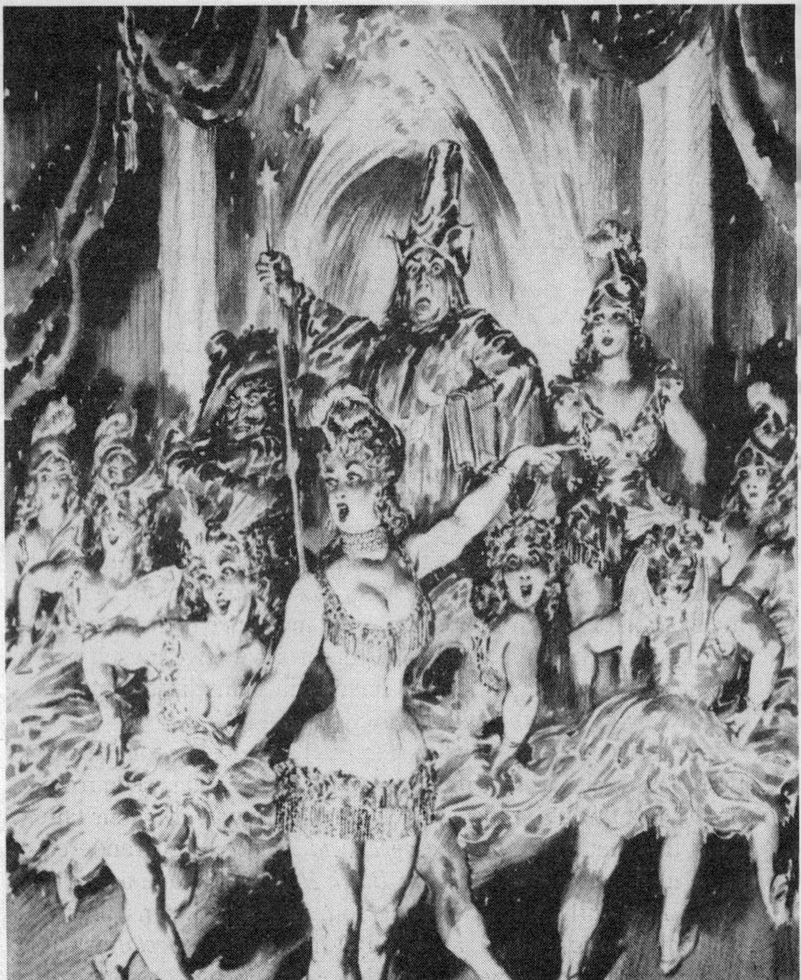

Mr. Wopsle in a high crowned hat, with a necromantic work in one volume under his arm.

tion of the novel from Smollett, who is a good enough rumbustious writer, but presents no conscience problem of integrity in the novelist. And in childhood Dickens had already turned to Smollett. Did he even then sense the conscience problem of his work, and make obeisance to fear? A depressing question; as depressing as the whole maddening complexity of his being, when we are forced to contemplate it apart from the immortal gusto of all that is great in his work.

* * *

With a sigh of relief we turn to the one novel in which Dickens affirmed the pact of creative integrity; *Great Expectations*.

In this novel there is no hint of evasion, no pandering to cheap sentiment, no false quantity anywhere in motive, personality, or emotion. One might almost think that Dickens said to himself here, "I will not squander in this novel a mass of life-size characters to distract attention from the hollow core of the theme. I will not involve the reader in secondary plots to hide my evasion of its central motive. I will introduce no humanistic tracts to reform some public institution. I will give myself one theme and every facet of the novel will bear directly on it. Finally, I will keep the author strictly out of it."

In all that he succeeded perfectly. The novel is told in the first person; the most difficult of all methods, and is seen from first to last through Pip's eyes, and not Dickens's. Dickens failed in this method in *David Copperfield*, where he surrendered to an idealised self-portrait. In *Bleak House*, he made a horrid mess of it with Esther Summerson, who is Dickens plus a falsely affected school marm. But in *Great Expectations* it becomes the perfect method for the revelation and exposure of Pip, who remains the creature of his own compulsions from his first appearance as a bothered, sensitive, submissive small boy to his maturity as an amiable, weak, fantasy-mongering self-defeatist. So with all the other characters. The key of their projection is maintained. No effect of events is allowed to turn them from human beings into popular sentimental dummies. Wemmick, in the debacle of Pip's great expectations, deplores the unwisdom of Pip's failure to get hold of them as portable property. Mr. Jaggers makes his last appearance in the novel indignantly ordering the snivelling Mike out of his office for daring to have "feelings" there. From first to last, Estella remains the cold little devil of a girl who smacked Pip's face to try to make him cry, and then allowed him to kiss her, that his desire for her should be assured of frustration.

Estella is to me the greatest of Dickens's feminine creations, because she is flawless. It was permissible for Dickens to believe that her character was the effect of environment and upbringing, for that fallacy was believed in his day, but the psychologist in him knew better. Estella is a cold, hard, sexually sterile woman because she is the product of criminal parents. Brought up in her normal environment, she would have gone on the streets. She rejects the refined and sensitive Pip and gives herself to the brutal Drummle because he is just the sort of crude male who might stir some response in her frigid sexuality. She will have him, in spite of Miss Havisham's protests and Pip's desperate supplications. Drummle is a typical bludger; the male complement of her genesis from a criminal and a murderess.

There is another instance in the novel where Dickens went infallibly to the core of sex-frustration in a woman. That is in the attempted murder of Mrs. Joe Gargery, which leaves her a speechless paralytic. No one but the woman herself knows that it is Orlick who has struck her down. And this woman, who has been a vicious shrew, to whom the simple Joe is only an incessant irritant, cannot rest till they have brought Orlick to her, so that she can fawn on him, and make those overtures to him which a woman of her type must use towards the man she needs; a crude brute to master her. It is by an inspired artistry that Dickens introduces this episode as a precise parallel with the frozen Estella and the brutal Drummle.

And Pip is as much the creature of his genesis as Estella; a boy of the labouring class who dreams of becoming a gentleman. He gives himself up to defeat at the outset, as all do who demand that fantasy will solve the difficulties of life and relieve them of its struggle. It is by that subtle urge towards unhappiness in the defeatist that he seeks Estella because he knows he will never forget her. He wanders vaguely into the procedure of becoming a gentleman because his defeatism knows there is no stability in fantasy's gold, and that it will one day vanish, as it does. Dickens descends to no hero- or heroine-mongering over Pip and Estella. He exposes Pip's weakness and snobbery with the detachment that never relaxes over Estella's cool feminine sadism. Yet he maintains the sympathetic bridge between Pip and the reader just as surely as he infuses into the reader's mind Pip's desire for Estella. She is one of Dicken's lovely creatures — that loveliness which is an emanation of Dickens's love for the feminine image, and which baffles any effort to analyse by the usual literary devices. It is made up of gestures, inflections of speech, the effect of Estella's presence on others conveyed through them to the reader's mind. Mr. Jaggers alone remains impervious to it.

Mr. Jaggers is the supreme masterpiece of this novel. Just as I do not hesitate at the conviction that *Great Expectations* is the best-constructed novel in the English language, so I accept Mr. Jaggers as the most perfect example of character draughtsmanship. Just as everything in the novel is told from without, and every facet of it built up under the reader's eye and laid before him without comment, so is Mr. Jaggers expanded into a reality that makes him much more alive than any shadowy wraith of a human personality in the flesh. That is the profundity of all great art, which is that the projection of any great creation in art exceeds the whole mass of whatever earth it defines. But I am not going to enlarge on that metaphysic . . .

The very first appearance of Mr. Jaggers in the novel is the purest art; groping his way down the dark staircase of Miss Havisham's mystery house to take Pip's face in his large-scented hand and turn it up in the candlelight for a ruthless inspection that detects everything Pip's face may tell him. That is the whole projection of Mr. Jaggers in a flash; groping in the dark spaces of the human mind till he has forced it to give up all its secrets. I have been reading Dickens constantly since the age of nine. I don't know how many times I have read each of his novels, excepting *Oliver Twist*, which I dislike for the black murk of bad conscience that pervades it, and *Hard Times,* which is only a bad Leftist tract, and *A Tale of Two Cities*, because its motive of self-sacrifice is too maudlin and false for my stomach. But I can never come on Mr. Jaggers groping his way down that dark staircase without a fresh thrill of delight. The conviction is of a mystery and a profundity to be revealed. But Mr. Jaggers keeps us as ruthlessly outside any intrusion on his privacy as the rest of the world. We get a glimpse into it only once, by a guarded remark of Wemmick's:

> ". . . Now I'll tell you something. When you dine with Mr. Jaggers, have a look at his housekeeper."
> "Will I see something very uncommon?"
> "Well," said Wemmick, "you'll see a wild beast tamed . . ."

On that, we get one brief picture of Jaggers and his housekeeper together, but it is more startling and arresting than the most intimate revealing of relations between a man and a woman. That sudden descent of Mr. Jagger's hand on Molly's, with the command, "Molly, let them see your wrist", and Molly's low-breathed protest of "Master!" before she slowly turns those hands up to the group of squabbling youths, her eyes going intently from face to face while Mr. Jaggers coolly points out the strong construction of those hands. Hands which have strangled another woman . . .

Only once is Mr. Jaggers thrown off his centre of gravity — when it is revealed to him that Wemmick is an impostor, with an aged parent and a mad little castle at Walworth and pleasant playful ways in private. And Wemmick's consciousness of a disgraceful exposure is another piece of inspired character revelation. Those two, Jaggers and Wemmick, are the perfect complement to each other, and are projected with a sardonic detachment from false sentiment which is the essence of good taste in art.

But there is no relapse on that score in any of the characters. If Miss Havisham, at the very last, falters into reality and self-knowledge, it is because Estella's cold malice forces on her a conviction of the futility of her whole life, given over to a neurotic self-revenge as a transferred fantasy of revenge on the world at large. How easily Dickens might have falsified Magwitch the convict, if he had let his popularity-mongering get a word in. But as he is projected, Magwitch is sustained. He is given a heroic gesture at the outset, when he throws away his chance of liberty to ensure that Compeyson will not escape too. To such a man, the boy who brings him food and drink and a file on that freezing Christmas morning will become an unforgettable memory. Even the reader's blood chills at the ghastly, dank cold of those winter marshes. With Pip's gift of food and brandy, we register the same spirit of gratitude as that poor hunted devil of a convict. It becomes the whole motive of Magwitch's being. When he returns at last he is still the same tough, resolute man of the marshes, but exultant and softened, because the objective of his life has become a reality.

As there is no hero and heroine motive in this novel, so also there is no conventional villain. Compeyson is just an essential mechanism, to get Miss Havisham into the novel and get Magwitch out of it. He has no part in the narrative, and appears only for a flash in the act of being drowned.

Perhaps the episode in the sluice-house might have been dispensed with. It has a flavour of the thriller about it. But Orlick could hardly have been left to wander out of the novel into nowhere. His hatred for Pip is one of its motives and Dickens chose that episode to make a dramatic finality of it.

Once again, the construction of this novel is perfect. It moves by inevitability, not literary stagecraft. Every event in it makes a continuity of the next. Its style is modulated to the whole tonal key of the novel, which is in grey half-tones and low horizons and flat, colourless skies.

But Dickens's mastery over style is evinced in the peculiar tonal atmosphere he gave each one of his novels. *Oliver Twist* is as dingy and stinking as a black slum at midnight. *Little Dorrit* exists in the murk of a London fog. In *Bleak House* the decaying odour of wintry woods merges in the hot, close smell of back streets. *Dombey and Son* conveys somehow a stylism in paint, — a richly coloured impasto with all forms in full relief. The *Old Curiosity Shop* has a satanic atmosphere pervading it; an emanation from that tremendous dwarf, Daniel Quilp. *Martin Chuzzlewit* is lived in the dead air of shut-up houses, dingy offices and greasy brick walls, with murder lurking in a dark entry. *Our Mutual Friend* carries the rank stench of riverside mud into the gusty streets of respectable family residences . . .

Nicholas Nickleby does not count for style; it is a mix-up of *Pickwick Papers* and *Martin Chuzzlewit*. *The Tale of Two Cities* I pass. *Barnaby Rudge* is a good romantic novel with a style to match, though the book is immortal for Miggs, Mrs. Varden, Sim Tappertit and Denis the Hangman. Fortunately, there is no conscience problem in its love episode, which is trivial.

Calling over the vast achievement of that mass of work, and the delight I have had over it, I am forced to confess to an attack of conscience for the analysis I have made here of its one false quantity. No man, having worked through a lifetime, may be sure that corruption does not lurk somewhere at the core of his effort, or that he has not made concessions to false values that his conscience ingeniously avoided detecting. Time alone can make a valid estimate of values in art.

In the madhouse of war and primitivism that has overtaken the earth to-day, all values in life and art have gone to hell. A return to sanity in life and stability in art is possible only by an effort to clarify the fanaticisms and imbecilities that have overtaken both. If this analysis of a universal conscience-problem in the artist helps to that end, it will have served its purpose, and I can relieve my own conscience by returning gratitude to Dickens even for the shell of his lovely Edith Dombey.

An Emetic in Oil-Paint

The only puzzle about the exhibition of Modernist French painting now on the walls of the N.S. Wales National Gallery is why the trustees have elected to hold it at this date, when its imbecilities have long since reached satiation-point with any cultured response to plastic art.

I saw the first Post-Impressionist exhibition in London away back in the year 1911. Examples of the same crude infantilities have been scattered broadcast ever since in prints and art-publications till the publishers of these inanities have used up their public, and booksellers are no longer stocking their products, as nobody will buy them. Instead, there are now coming from the art-presses reproductions of the world's greatest paintings, and that in itself is the evidence that the cult of Modernistic Primitivism is defunct. Besides, the buffoons who inaugurated it are now either dead or old men, and that, again, spells finality to it, by the inevitable swing-over of one generation from the plastic creed of the one that preceded it.

Modernist art has never been an aesthetic but a studio

Published in the *Bulletin*, Sydney, 18 May 1953

ARGUMENT RAGING IN PARIS

Picasso — The Great or Joker?

From PETER GLADWIN

LONDON, Today: A furious argument is raging in the Paris art world. Its theme: Is Picasso really one of the greatest or is some of his early work a gigantic practical joke?

THE MAN WHO STARTED THE DEBATE IS PABLO PICASSO HIMSELF.

The gnome-like near legendary Spaniard has become more famous and richer in his lifetime than any painter who ever lived.

To people who know nothing about art, but know what they like, the name Picasso conjures immediate visions of nudes with eyes, bosoms and other features rearranged in eccentric patterns.

Picasso has now shocked his idolators by telling an interviewer that he discovered as a young man that the path to success was "any kind of fantasy and intellectual charlatanism."

He says he tried to please the rich and the critics with bizarre, extravagant ideas, adding: "The less they understood it the more they admired it. By this sort of nonsense I rapidly became famous and I am now a very rich man."

These terrible statements, so devastating for so many critics and collectors, were published by Phillipe Barres in an Art Quarterly, The Living Museum.

Barres also credits Picasso with saying: "I am just a public entertainer who has understood his time.

This story from the Adelaide *Advertiser*, 18 November 1964, appears to vindicate Lindsay's view.

cultism, propaganded by newspaper art-critics and the astute art-dealers who capitalised the journalistic publicity to sell their wares to that section of the moneyed public (mainly rich Americans) who can be duped into paying money for anything popularised as a fashion-craze. Rich Americans with taste have bought nothing but works accredited by the highest standard of connoisseurship, so that America has now acquired some of the world's greatest masterpieces.

Modernistic art has always been rejected by the one source of authoritative opinion that can have validity, and that is from painters who have already achieved distinction on an established tradition of sound painting, and from the cultured art-buyers who have collected their works. It can't be repeated too often that there can be no other authoritative standard of values save this exchange between artist and buyer, for it is based on that unity between creation and perception without which art could not exist. Anyone who follows the resale of pictures from notable collections will see this process in action at any Australian auction-room today. The works by painters who have established the tradition of sound painting in this country continue to soar in value with every resale. To my knowledge no product of Modernistic art has ever found a buyer there.

For all the feverish tub-thumping by a few journalistic art-critics over the present exhibition of Modernist French art, that cult is as dead as mutton. I would not have crossed the road to look at it if I had not received a number of indignant letters from people whose taste I respect, and who are seriously concerned for the dignity of art in this country. For my part, a glance at the verbosities of the newspaper art-critics in praise of the exhibition was enough to assure me that its exhibits were worthless: and, anyway, I have long since lost any interest in the Modernist revolt, even from the one aspect that can be of interest, which is its pathological reversion to a state of infantilism. But I allowed myself to be coerced into paying a visit to the Gallery.

And I was really staggered to find again how incredibly bad the stuff was, even from its own acclaimed slogan of having discarded all standards of excellence in painting. I did my best to find some evidence that this insensate debauch of splodging paint on canvas had any genesis in mankind's prolonged struggle to develop the thumb which controls the use of a tool; but could only find two examples which showed some evidence of craftsmanship. One was a still-life with a certain harmonic quality by an accent of black on a basis of red and yellow, and the other a combination of blues, greens and reds toned down to give an effect of color-unity if viewed from a distance. It need not be added that any sense for form was lacking in both exhibits. Finally, with some reluctance, I performed that exercise defined in the studio idiom as putting my nose into the paint to examine the quality of its impasto. In the whole of that exhibition there was no evidence that its perpetrators knew that such a thing as an impasto existed. Which is to say, reverting from the plastic idiom to that which uses words as its medium the mental level which had produced these exhibits was hardly up to that of a child of eight, and a backward child at that . . .

I must pause here to comment on the one really exasperating aspect of the whole Modernist revolt from standard values in art, and that is not the drivelling nature of its works, but the affirmation of those works which has come from a number of writers who are themselves meticulous stylists in the métier of words. But, passing them for the moment, it may be well to dispose of the affirmation of Modernistic art by the newspaper critics.

The function of the newspaper art-critic is to attack all expressions of high quality in art. Defined roughly, this attack constitutes an endurance-test on the artist to ignore it, and his works to survive it. It springs, of course, from a fermenting state of frustration by a consciousness of inferiority forced on such mentalities in the presence of any high achievement in the arts.

I dare say it has always attended such achievements in the pre-newspaper past, but only since the beginning of last century, with its sudden and widespread production of newspapers and journals, have we been able to watch its procedure in action.

In poetry, Byron, Shelley, Keats, Wordsworth, and Browning have been selected for its most vicious attacks. In music, Beethoven and Wagner. In painting, Turner, Constable, Etty, Cotman, de Windt — and, in short, any painter who showed evidence of high quality in his works. I have gone to the trouble at times of digging up such evidences of journalistic spleen, and have discovered that the painters on whom those critics lavished adulation have never since their day been heard of. And therein is the doom of Modernistic art already constituted irrevocably.

The journalist attack continued through the 'seventies and 'eighties on the Impressionist movement, which was headed by Degas, Manet and Monet, and continued down to the 'nineties in the fury aroused by Sargent's portrait of Madame Gautreau, which drove Sargent out of Paris to settle in England. And that was a good thing for England, for Sargent may be accepted as the prime stimulus to that fine group of painters headed by Orpen, Lavery, Nicholson, Munnings and John. These are the real modern masters, and their works are extreme from Modernism. And they, also, were attacked by the art-critics, but by an ingenious reversion of their normal tactics . . .

It has generally been assumed that the present-day art-critics were aware of the ignominy that has since been bestowed on their past colleagues who had attacked the Impressionist movement, and that they were not going to be caught out in the same way over the Post-Impressionists. That is not the case. Journalistic art-critics are not constituted to act on an intellectual concept but on an emotional compulsion. They are recruited from the ranks of those literary frustrates who have failed to achieve any distinction as writers, so that they must seek to rehabilitate a deboshed self-esteem by resorting to the assassin's knife.

In Modernistic Art they found a superb opportunity of wielding it on serious values in art, not by the attack direct, but the attack oblique. With one glad howl of exultation the whole mob of them set out to acclaim Modernism as a new evangel in plastic art. And they are still tub-thumping the same stale old theme in an arbitrary jargon invented by the studio buffoons themselves.

For my part, I endorse the tactics of the journalistic art-critics. A lie has no existence, and their frenzied effort to affirm non-existent values in art merely exhausts itself in a vacuum. It may muddle a certain section of the public, but that is not the section of the public which has any effect on the cultural energy of a community. That is maintained by a very small nucleus of sophisticated intellects, and the exchange between creation and perception goes calmly on without taking any notice of journalistic splenetics or studio polemics.

But in dismissing any significance in the journalistic attack on serious values in art, I for one artist striving to do something with the gamut of those values, and concerned for the dignity of art itself, refuse to dismiss or condone the dirty work done to our profession by those writers I have already referred to, who are not journalists but prose-writers of distinction, and who have used the status acquired by their works to depreciate all that makes for distinction in ours. Of those I select Osbert Sitwell and Somerset Maugham, because both are meticulous exponents of literary style.

And what literary style is to a writer, the impasto of an oil-painting is to an artist. Precisely what a writer understands by a suavity of sequence between vowels and consonants, by a nice balance between the short and the long sentence to achieve lucidity or emphasise a passage, by using the paragraph to prolong or shorten a period according to its weight of subject-matter, and, most of all, by seeking to find the precise word which will convey the mental, emotional, or visual image the writer wishes to define.

All these things an artist seeks to express by the use of thick or thin paint to eliminate unessentials and to focus attention on a salient passage, by conveying the modulations between shadow and highlight in graduating brushwork from a smooth layer of paint to one where a loaded brush is used, by a gamut of values dictated by the play of light over surfaces and texture, and, most of all, by seeking the precise brush-stroke which will accent a form, finalise a tonal sequence, and convey to the eye the visual impact of a thing seen. Just as Conrad exhausted synonyms to find the exact word he needed, Sargent would make repeated brush-strokes in the air before committing to canvas the accent he needed on a form, a texture, or the crescendo of a light-passage. And this problem of the impasto has been the incessant preoccupation of all painters who have achieved mastership in paint from Da Vinci and Durer, who inaugurated the Renaissance, to Orpen and Sargent, who are the latest masters of perfect stylism in the use of oil paint. And that same preoccupation over a plastic use of words has been the major obsession of writers from Jeremy Taylor to Somerset Maugham.

I pause at Maugham, because, of all writers save Hazlitt, he has written the most lucid and understanding essays on style that I have read, and because he once studied painting, and does know good painting from bad. On that score Osbert Sitwell can be dismissed. For all his easy and graceful style as a writer, I've never read a word of his that indicates the slightest knowledge of style in paint. From the start he has acclaimed the whole lunatic output of Modernism without any discrimination between one studio clown or another, while he has jeered at Sargent by taking an air of tolerant derision to his painting, and has crudely stigmatised Orpen as a "supreme Irish carpenter and flashlight photographer", for which impertinence future annotators of *belles lettres* will administer a well-deserved kick-in-the-pants to Osbert, if his personal reminiscences endure on the bookshelves — which is doubtful.

But Maugham is seriously concerned for the dignity of letters, and has returned again and again to an analysis of style in his essays, using as examples all classic precedents of quality in writers, from the translators of the Bible down to Hazlitt. He is certainly reticent over ascribing stylistic virtues to writers of his own era, and in one of his novels makes a slighting reference to Conrad. It is because of his insistence that writers must study classic precedents in good style that his advocacy of Modernist painting becomes so offensive.

Take this from his latest series of essays, "The Vagrant Mood":

> The language of literature . . . if it is to avoid shapelessness and incoherence, must be founded on, and determined by, the standards of the period when English prose attained the highest degree of perfection of which it seems capable.

From which passage I turn to an essay on beauty in plastic art and find he has the immortal rind to write as follows:

> Even Greek sculpture, owing to the acquaintance we have now made with Chinese and Negro art, has for artists themselves lost the appeal. It is no longer a source of inspiration. Its beauty is dying . . . We grow tired of something we know too well and ask for something new.

So be damned to you, Mr. Maugham, for a treacherous renegade even to your own creed as a perfectionist in prose, which is to say, perfection also in poetry, music and painting. Allow me to translate into your own mētier of prose what a Picasso is saying to you in paint. Though there is not much profit to be gained by trying to separate rubbish from rubbish, I made a point of examining the Picasso in the present exhibition carefully, and observed that it was splodged in with oil-color thinned-out to the consistence of watercolor by turps, and apparently applied to canvas by a wad of cotton-wool. The imbecility of its subject I pass, but what it was saying to you, Mr. Maugham, was "Gug-gug-gug-bub-bub", which is the nearest I can get to an infant trying to exercise its vocal-chords in the cradle.

But enough of discussing these insensate fooleries. I observed that the average expression of the public inspecting them was one of dazed incomprehension, with a variation here and there to derision or a just indignation at a fraud imposed on the optic nerve, while the Gallery attendants looked extremely ashamed of themselves, as being forced officially to sanction a function degrading to their self-respect. For myself, I went forth to quell a slight sensation of nausea by having a look at the splendidly controlled brushwork of Ramsay's "Sisters", and to enjoy once again the staggering achievement of

Gruner's "Spring Frosts" and Streeton's "Fire's On". They were fortunately hanging side-by-side, so that I could turn from the tender welling-up of dawn light to the actinic brilliance of midday sunlight; Pan's hour. I never saw those two superb works look so lovely, for which, at least, I could thank the offence my eyes had been forced to endure in that Modernist inferno. Casting memory back over the galleries of Europe, England and America, conviction assured me that those two paintings are among the greatest landscapes this world possesses.

Before departing I had a look at the other Gruners, and if any writer is interested enough to study an example of what I have been trying to define of style in an oil impasto as used in Gruner's "Frosty Morning", let him observe how the weighted brushwork in the almost-colorless sky conveys the vibrant effect of pure light, while a certain quivering use of the brush into a rich impasto suggests the shimmer of frost across the surface of a field.

Once again we have the right to ask why the trustees have squandered money on this exhibition of rubbish which merely confuses the public at large, disgusts the minority of art-lovers with a cultivated taste in paintings, and pleases only a very small group of art students infected with Modernism, when they have the galleries of Europe and England at their disposal for a loan exhibition of genuine works of art. We had such exhibitions in Will Ashton's period as curator of the gallery, and vastly stimulating they were, selected by Ashton's impeccable taste and knowledge of the world's art.

I can think only of one excuse for inflicting this exhibition on the public, and that is to present it as an awful example of the state of moral decadence which reduced Europe to chaos. There is no separating art from life. When a people throw aside all reverence for standards of value which have slowly built up a civilised consciousness in mankind, it must revert to barbarism.

And in spite of itself Modernistic art has given us one irrefutable value in relation to the very values it has sought to destroy. If we accept, say, Rembrandt as the apex of all that is greatest in painting, then Picasso is the nadir of all that is rotten. With the exhibition now on the walls of the gallery, painting has reached its zero in worthlessness. It cannot get lower.

Bush Balladists

The anthology of *Australian Bush Ballads* compiled by Douglas Stewart and Nancy Keesing is a work that had to be done for the sake of Australian literary history as well as for the enjoyment of readers; and it could hardly have been done better. Out of a vast mass of material the best has been selected and produced in a handsome format which any Australian with a respect for his country's tradition must have on his bookshelves.

I handle this anthology with a pleasing sense of an aspiration achieved without any exertion on my part. For years I meditated compiling such a work, for it was obvious with the passing of the bush ballad that significant examples of it should be collected in book-form. The culture of every country begins with its folk-songs, and its later sophistication owes much to their inspiration. Burns turned back to the ancient Scottish minstrelsy for much of the form and spirit of his immortal lyrics, and Beethoven also drew many of his themes from folk-songs. But when I contemplated the labor involved

A book review published in the *Bulletin*, Sydney, 12 October 1955 in compiling a selection of the ballads resolution fainted into my boots. I have been in touch with the editors of this anthology while they were at work on it, and commended the discretion, or funk, which stalled me off from attempting such a laborious job. Every page of the big *Bulletin* files was turned for a possible item. Libraries were searched; a vast mass of defunct printed-matter sifted; hundreds of books of verse examined; in short, over 150 years of journalism and publishing brought under an exacting inspection. All that apart from the sifting and resifting of selected material for its precise relation to the ballad-form.

Now we have the ballads from the bushranging days down to World War I, neatly arranged in their relation to the various aspects of outback life, in a dozen or more sections ranging from "Bushranging" to "Tall Stories", from "The Irish" to "Horses and Horsemen". I read them through from first to last page, and was aware of a unity they made both in an outlook on life and on the aesthetic of the ballad itself. The better qualities of verse absorbed the lesser, but all were equally pregnant with vitality.

No doubt the great period of the ballad was in the 'nineties, with "Banjo" Paterson as its dominant expression. Not that the ballad in that era was greatly respected as a form of art. It passed as a casual product of journalism, and the poets striving for a more difficult and subtler verse-form hated it. That was inevitable, with a large public eagerly reading the balladists and the poems of those poets unread. I recall that I was ashamed to admit that I had a sneaking partiality for the ballads; but, then, my work did not come into competition with them. I illustrated a good many of them in the *Bulletin* and in book-form, and the fact that so many snatches of them remained in my mind over the years is the evidence that they had in them the stuff that endures. But now that major poetry is written in Australia, antagonism to the ballad no longer exists. Indeed, some very brilliant poetry has been written of late years in the ballad-form — but that has been the product of a technical command over poetic idiom. The ballad proper, as exemplified in this anthology, was a spontaneous outburst emanating from the people at large.

I do not think the balladists themselves had any sense of conflict between that poetry which seeks an image for reality, and the easy running verses which make a transcript of it. In my talks with Paterson I do not remember that poetry was ever mentioned, but I do remember him discussing the old bush songs that he was collecting at that time. And the only reference to verse that I remember Lawson making was that, in his opinion, "Mary Pity Women" was Kipling's greatest poem; which I think is a sufficient estimate of Henry's response to poetry. Though in the 'nineties every youth with an oppressed spinal-column was industriously writing imitations of Kipling's too-efficient machine-made verses, I'm glad to note that he had hardly any effect on the bush balladists. Gordon, it must be admitted, with his "Sick Stockrider" and his "How We Beat the Favorite", did set a key which vastly stimulated the writing of ballads, but the faculty and the urge to express it were there already; products of a tremendously enlivened sense for life as it was lived in the outback.

Life in the bush had already been established in a tradition by the men who had mastered its rough conditions. Theirs was no longer the haphazard struggle of the early colonists, who had no ebullient urge to chant ballads about it. But the subsequent generations, born into the bush, knew how to cope with it. Heroic figures emerged from them: drovers who brought the sheep overland in periods of drought; teamsters who got the wool-bales through, bogged to the axles in mud; mailmen who swam their horses across flooded rivers; prospectors who explored unknown country in quest of gold; ringers of the shearing-sheds and riders no outlaw could throw. Men were tested by a severe standard of excellence in all these vocations, and most of all by their courage and endurance under appalling hardships, where failure often meant a lonely death in the desert. The spirit engendered by such a life had to find a voice. Those tough denizens of the outback already had their oral tradition, carried from coast to coast of Australia by the drovers, shearers, teamsters and miners. So the balladists arrived to give their campfire yarns the enduring reality of the written word . . .

And an amazingly complete job they made of it. Every aspect of bush life is covered by this anthology. There is no pretence of psychological subtlety in the presentation of its inhabitants. Labelled Bill or Jim, the individual is submerged in the type. One set of characters does for all. Only the bushrangers are named as real identities; for the rest, a drover, a shearer, a teamster, a miner, a squatter, a cocky-farmer, a swagman, serve each balladist impartially.

It is almost exclusively a male earth. Women were few and far between in the vast, arid spaces of the outback. A drover's wife, a cocky-farmer's daughter or a shanty barmaid about make up the list of available femininity, and the barmaid is presented as a rapacious harpy rather than the gracious consoler of man's amorous ardors. Ladies of the squattocracy were of a social altitude not to be scaled by the tough denizens of the shearing-shed, though there is one dolorous ballad by a rouseabout craving one of those ladies to come down from Olympus and share his humble lot. A girlless earth is the inspiration of Lawson's enchanting "Shearer's Dream":

Oh, I dreamt I shore in a shearin'-shed,
  and it was a dream of joy,
For every one of the rouseabouts was a
  girl dressed up as a boy . . .
There was three of them girls to every
  chap, and as jealous as they could be —
There was three of them girls to every
  chap, and six of them picked on me;
We was draftin' them out for the homeward
  track and sharin' them round like steam.
When I woke with my head in the blazin'
  sun to find 'twas a shearer's dream.

I regard this as an inspired chant, for it is every man's dream. In short, casually written as most of the ballads are, they present the outback of their day with a vividness that no later reconstruction can hope to do. Most important of all, they compact in stark terms all that is admirable in the national ego. There is in them no taint of that sentimentality which sheds a tear for man's tragic lot. The major note of the ballads is a rejection of false sentiment. Death is a theme for sardonic humor. The bushman carting home the corpse of a mate who has pledged him to have it decently buried, when caught in the rain at night ejects the corpse from its coffin and takes cover in it himself. Two roistering drunks prop a dead mate at the bar of a pub and insist on buying drinks for him. In that little elegy for a mate who has perished in the desert (poetry in my opinion)

The coolibahs quiver,
The snakewood moans,
And the bower-birds play
With Lin Bower's bones,

sentiment is rejected with a shrug of humor:

They buried him there
With the Chinese cook

And for irreverence to Omnipotence and its pantomime heaven nothing could be better than the swearing bullocky "Holy Dan" and the rough-riding "My Mate Bill".

But in his admirable preface Douglas Stewart has said everything that need be said of the quality and significance of these ballads, and all I can contribute to it is some brief notes on some of the balladists I knew, ghosts of my own past. "Banjo" Paterson, who has the leading place in this anthology, I saw a good deal of at various times, but I could not claim intimacy with him. I never knew anyone who could. Emotional warmth of any sort was not a commodity he dealt in. A great horseman in his time, with his hawklike, handsome face, cut in hard, precise lines, and his slightly-hooded eyes, which looked past but not at one, he presents himself to me always as the living embodiment of the ballad itself; the national ego compacted in one man.

Ted Dyson, of the "Rhymes from the Mines", I knew intimately from my earliest days. He, also, was a typical product of the era defined by the ballads, with a pungent wit derisive of what Nietzsche called the vulgar display of generous emotion. He had worked as a miner in the big Ballarat mines of his youth, and still had the stocky, muscular figure acquired by hard physical labor when I knew him in his maturity. He made a considerable income from freelance journalism, turning out verse, short-stories, pars and articles with amazing facility. Too much facility. Of all his works, I think, only his best mining stories and his *Factory 'Ands* will live. Both should be republished.

Randolph Bedford, represented here by a goldmining ballad, "The Days of '84", was another who squandered a faculty for easy writing, but he had not in him the quality of mind to produce much of lasting value. As a mining engineer he covered all the early goldfields, and had a superb mass of first-hand material if he had been gifted with the art to use it effectively. Short and broad-built, with a bald head, a predatory hooked nose and a big blond moustache, he was a dynamo of inexhaustible energy. Arrogant, pugnacious, witty, with a Falstaffian sense of humor, he dominated any group he foregathered with. I never knew another man with such a command over swift incisive speech, and he was also the best raconteur I ever listened to, but when he wrote those yarns it was astonishing to note how pedestrian they were. No writer can be afflicted with a greater curse than rhetorical ease of speech. Bedford's novels are forgotten and his prolific output of verse has gone the same road. I could never away with his ballads myself; there was too much cloak-and-dagger fustian in them. He was much given to reciting them in bars, and I must admit that in that sympathetic setting the fire and energy with which he delivered one of his piratical ballads made it sound prodigiously well. It was the sound that bemused one's critical faculty. As a personality, Randolph was really a tremendous figure, and I would overload this review if I gave instances of the devastating things I have heard him say when flooring an opponent in a conflict of opinion.

Of the lesser balladists who appear in the anthology there was Alexander Montgomery, that gentlemanly man. Very erect, very precise of speech, with a clipped brown beard, his talk emanated a flavor of scholarly erudition, and he always seemed to stand apart from the Saturday-morning group of

Bulletin camp-followers who gathered at the front counter to collect small sums owing, or cadge something on account, before departing in a body to the pub two doors up George Street. He was on the *Bulletin* staff when I first joined it, but left later.

The name of "Steele Grey", of the ballads of "Post-hole Mick" and "The Girl at Native Dog", hooks out of the cheerful limbo of my student days in Melbourne a hazy, boozy, whiskered moonface wearing a high, flat-crowned boxer-hat, and the rest of it attired in respectable grey trousers and a black cutaway tail-coat; strange garniture for a bush-balladist, though he at least so far authenticated that profession by never going abroad without a bottle of rum — which he called his baby — in his coat-tail pocket . . . for which he was always welcome when chance doddered him into one of our student groups. Anybody in those days who had his verses published in the *Bulletin* was distinguished above the common human herd.

The name of Sorenson

> Though many ask; 'tis a nut to crack,
> Where old Bill Brown is now;
> He was heard of last on the Prospect
> Track
> Astride of a camel cow

fills another blank space in memory, but he was a genuine bush product: awkward, reticent, slow-spoken, with sleepy pale eyes and of such a general sandyness that his face merged into one tone with his hair, which was of such a fuzzy texture that it looked more like fur than hair. I recall that hair bringing down great confusion on me; for being with A. G. Stephens in his office, I chanced to remark that Sorenson reminded me of a native bear. Within a sort time of my making that casual comparison some imp of malice elected to lure Sorenson into the office, on which A.G. greeted him with "Lindsay's just been saying that you look like a native bear, and so you do." I never met Sorenson after that without seeing "native bear" in his eye.

Well, here they all are, balladists of mark and forgotten ghosts — Paterson and Lawson. Brady and Dennis,

"Dryblower" Murphy and John O'Brien, "Riverina" and Roderic Quinn, Dyson and W. T. Goodge, Ogilvie and Barcroft Boake, Adam Lindsay Gordon and "The Breaker" — compacted between the covers of a book destined to be the classic compilation of the bush ballads. Already they make a time-factor which has nothing to do with time as ticked off on clocks. Time is only measurable as a content of human consciousness, and now that poetry has reached its maturity in Australia, these bush ballads seem to have been written in a period as remote from us as the Border ballads were to the Elizabethans. Already they have acquired a patina of charm like Percy's "Reliques" of the Border ballads.

Greatest of Roman Novels

The mysterious portent of the greatest of Roman novels, the *Satyricon* of Petronius, is that, like the *Iliad* and the *Odyssey* in poetry, it was born, apparently out of nowhere, as a great novel. There is no traditional precedent behind the work of either writer.

Doubtless Homer had behind him the ballad-songs of the people, narrating the heroic deeds of kings and warriors, and doubtless Petronius had resources to those products of popular humour which deal with the common life of the people, in his time labelled Milesian Fables, and in our time smoking-room stories; a term derived from the 'fifties of last century, when the gentlemen gathered for a private symposium of bawdry and tobacco after the ladies had retired to bed.

No investigation, archaeological or aesthetic, has ever been able to trace the source of these anonymous products of popular fancy. They are handed down by oral tradition, and those which touch on present-moment affairs and personalities appear to be generated by spontaneous combustion, and to

Published in the *Bulletin*, Sydney, 5 June 1957

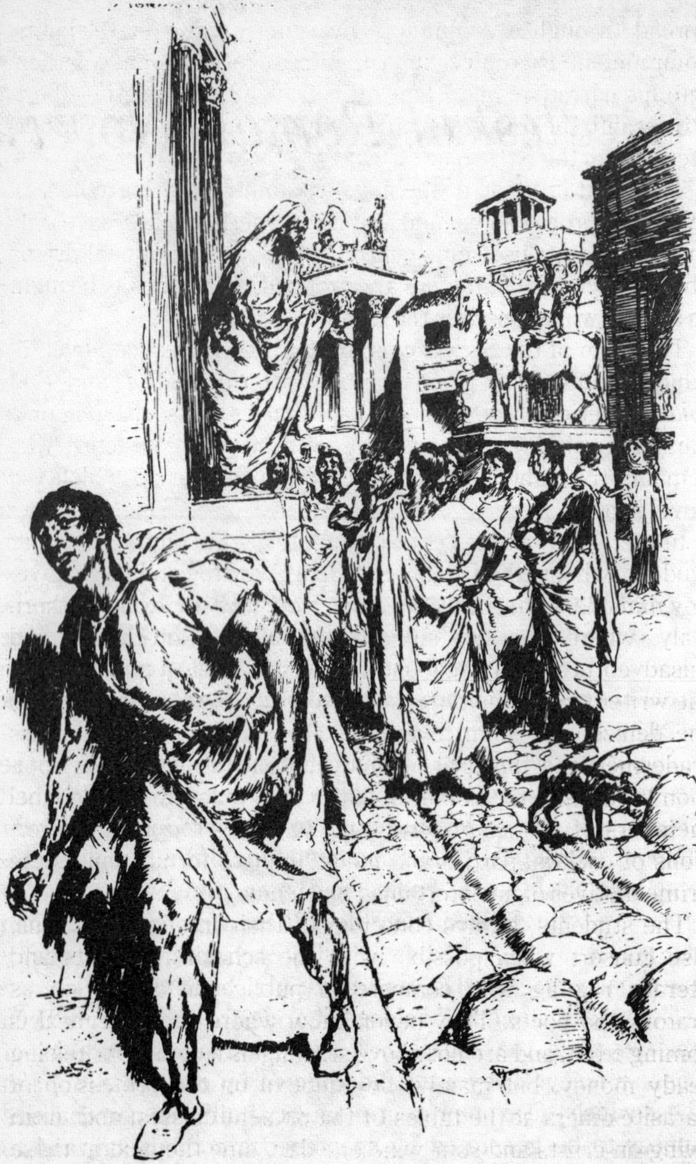

An extemporary declaration

spread through a community by some species of telepathic communion. Petronius himself introduces a couple of them into his narrative, and I fancy this trick of interpolating short-stories into the text of the novel, which lasted down to Dickens stems from the *Satyricon*.

That first creation of the novel contains every ingredient of the novel proper as we understand its mêtier today, save only that it does not use some centralised plot or emotional drama about which the characters are grouped, and which is brought to a crisis which finalises the novel.

The form of the *Satyricon* is that of the picaresque novel, of which the other two great examples are *Don Quixote* and *Tom Jones*. A series of more-or-less haphazard events is strung on a narrative relating to the actions of a central character, who remains throughout the constructive principle on which the novel is built.

In the *Satyricon* this central character is Encolpius, a beggar student, who, with his fellow-student Ascyltos and their slave-boy minion Giton, strolls the roads from city to city in southern Italy, where they are subjected to all the adventures and misadventures of a vagabond existence. Their journey allows the writer to give them free entry to all classes of society, from the denizens of slum taverns to the society of middle-class tradesmen and financial magnates, from the women of common brothels to the homes of ladies who today we would label members of the smart-set; those who seek the hectic diversions of cocktail-parties and indiscriminate fornication as the prime motives of an entertained existence.

The students, always conscious of their intellectual status, also consort when possible with the scholars, pedants and literary rag-tag who compete in public for distinction as orators and poets. They never know where the next meal is coming from, and are not above stealing as a device for raising ready money, but mainly they depend on the profession of parasite-diners at the tables of the opulent classes; and, from living on crusts and sour wine one day, dine the next at those monstrous Roman dinners which allow them to gorge themselves to a state of satiation on rich foods and rare vintages.

The narrative is in the first-person — singular. Encolpius being the narrator, and, in my opinion, this novel is one of the few successful experiments in that most difficult, and also most slovenly, method of telling a story. It automatically involves the "I" who tells the story with the "I" who writes it, and partisanship for the teller by the writer is thereby inevitable. Cool detachment from personal prejudice for or against the other characters is corrupted, and no good fiction is ever written unless that detachment is maintained.

Encolpius is quite immune from any posture of self-esteem. He tells everything about himself, no matter what ignominious exposure it may involve. He may lament the lambastings and indignities bestowed on him in such exposures as evidence of a malign destiny, but he never palliates any evidence which presents him as its buffoon.

In the breath of chanting high-minded sentiments in poetry he descends to antics very much in reverse of such sentiments. He can denounce Ascyltos in terms of outraged morality for tampering with Giton's virtue while indulging his own amorous ardors in private with that young catamite, who appears to be the property of Encolpius, though whether by purchase, abduction, or as a hired servant, is not quite clear. The two students are constantly brawling over the lad, denouncing each other in scurrilous terms as base fellows who put no decent restraint on their salacious urges, even to the extent of exchanging blows and lashings; and, in the breath of such strawfire furies, reverting to amicable relations, which are maintained till the next row breaks out between them. This, it would seem, is the febrile way those sports on the norm of human bisexuality, labelled homosexuals, conduct their emotional dramatics; on a top-note of frenzy one minute and all causes of offence forgotten the next.

Today their antics are subject to solemn investigation by the pundits of psychopathology, but in the Rome of the Caesars they were accepted as a commonplace in the spectacle of life, and Petronius gets an immense amount of fun out of them as comedy-figures. It is to be remarked that whatever lyrical sentiment Encolpius may indulge over Giton he never fails to load him with their luggage when taking to the road again.

Encolpius pays allegiance so far to the exclusively-masculine by having affairs with women, in one case bringing down on himself the most ignominious of all nightmares to male dignity, a collapse of potency at a crisis of the embrace amorous. Over Circe, the lady of that event, he indulges lyrical raptures. She is presented as a charming creature, with a wit to match her charms. The affair takes place in a flowering garden, that all the graces may adorn it. And also accentuate its awful debacle.

Outraged at such an insult to her feminine self-esteem, Circe has Encolpius beaten by her servants, spat at by her scullion-wenches and hurled into the street, whence he flees to hide himself in his apartment, and give himself over to all the furies of a degrading exposure, raving at the gods, or at his own treacherous body, in alternate outbursts of poetry and forensic declaration, and collapses into abysmal gloom. With all that, Encolpius remains a likeable fellow, and the sympathetic bridge is maintained between him and the reader, since it is through his eyes that we are given the spectacle of life as seen by Petronius.

Though every character in the *Satyricon*, however small a part he plays, is drawn with those swift word-imageries only to be matched by Dickens, its great central figure is that of Trimalchio, the slave-born emancipist, whose commercial cunning and rapacity have raised him to the millionaire class. He is painted so richly in the round that he ranks as one of the greatest character-creations in fiction, along with Falstaff, Mrs. Gamp, Don Quixote, Squire Western, Dugald Dalgetty, Panurge, old Grandet . . . There are others, but those are the ones which jump most readily into memory.

Trimalchio is a full-length portrait. Every facet of his personality is explored and exposed. We are not told about him; he is exhibited before our eyes by speech, gesture and action.

Like all parvenus of great wealth who dominate a horde of servants and sycophants, he has the illusion of being immune to derisive criticism and so exposes himself to it every time he opens his mouth. He is viewed at the summit of his concept of greatness, presiding over a dinner of monstrous proportions, ministered to by an army of slaves, and beslavered by the flattery of his parasites. His first appearance in the novel stamps him unforgettably on the reader's mind: a fat, bald-headed old man in a scarlet tunic playing ball with a group of long-haired boys, while a couple of eunuchs stand by, one with a bag of fresh balls as Trimalchio disdains to use one which has dropped to the ground, and the other with a silver chamberpot, in which Trimalchio relieves himself during the ball-game.

It is a notable touch that the eunuch in charge of the balls keeps a sharp eye on those which have been dropped. Obviously he will get into trouble later if those are not gathered up when Trimalchio departs. Petty economies are a constant constituent in rich men who have risen from penurious beginnings.

This little touch is typical of Petronius all through the novel. He never comments; leaving all such significances to detection by the reader.

When Trimalchio's wife shows a pair of gold bracelets to her friend Scintilla, Trimalchio calls for scales to weigh the bracelets and demonstrate their quality, though the place is littered with gold ornaments and utensils. When the guests commend the excellence of his cook, he tells of how he brought the fellow a set of carving-knives when last in Rome, and immediately calls for the carving-knives so that the guests may try their sharpness by shaving a cheek. He can't keep the balance anywhere between the exposures of puerilities like the above and his posture of the great man disdainful of the wealth he is constantly boasting about.

His steward comes in to read the account of the last month's commercial dealings in slaves and property, which refers to the purchase of Pompey's Gardens by Trimalchio. "When did I buy Pompey's Gardens?" demands Trimalchio. "Last year," says the steward. On that Trimalchio falls into a rage and commands that unless he is informed of such buyings within six months they are not to be recorded in his monthly accounts. In the breath of dismissing the purchase of Pompey's Gardens as

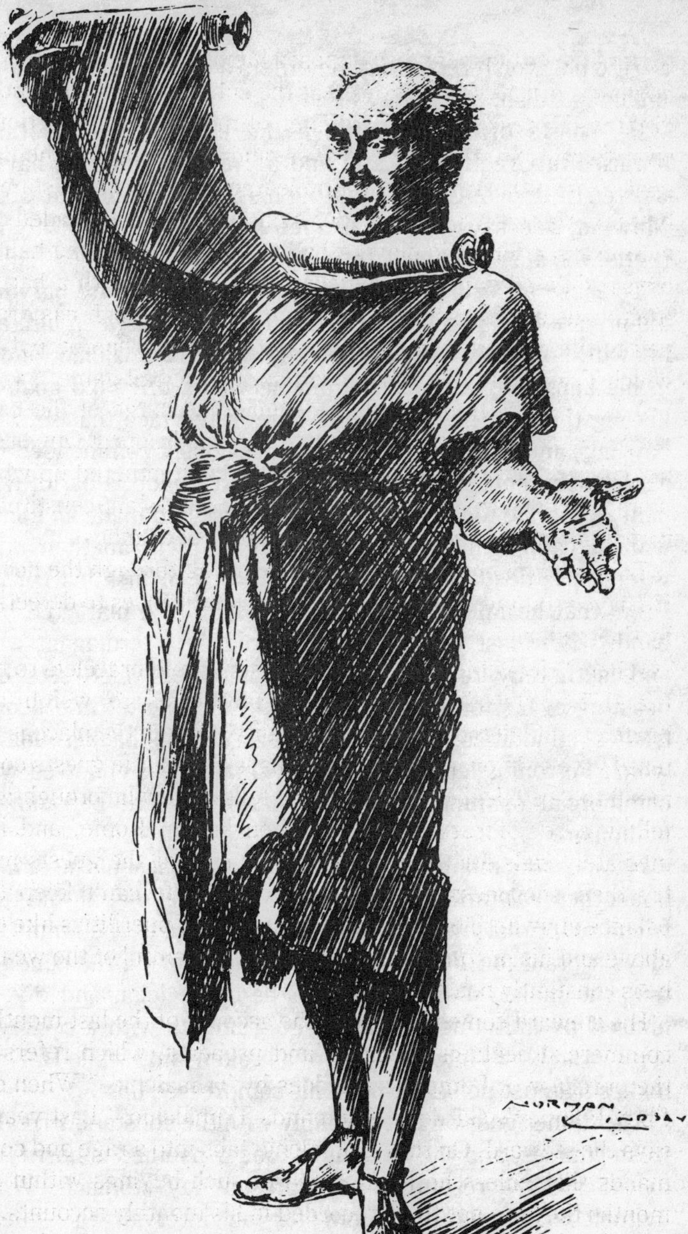

The Steward

a trifle not worth recording, he orders a slave to be beaten for breaking a dish.

He boasts of his learning in the classics and his three libraries in Greek and Latin and accredits Homer as having written the tale of Cyclops putting his thumb out of joint with a Mawkin, and says that at Cumae he saw a Sybil in a glass bottle who answered questions.

To these exposures of Trimalchio as the illiterate parvenu, his private life is presented to us in the row between him and his wife Fortunata over a slave-boy whom Trimalchio fondles in his cups. Denounced by Fortunata as a dirty old goat for kissing the boy, he deals her a slap in the face that sets her bawling, and then, though he has previously commended her as a worthy housewife, rants at her as a trollop, a harlot rampant, whom he took out of a bawdy-house and made an honest woman, capping his fulminations with the awful anathema that when he is dead she will not be allowed to kiss his corpse. From that he falls into the maudlin tears of a martyred husband, whose last years are embittered by a termagant wife: and is thereby revived to review his life, which sets him boasting of his foresight in cornering the market in essential trade-commodities; a compact itinerary of his background by which Petronius lets us see how a smart slave endowed with commercial cunning in his era may arrive at becoming a millionaire . . .

Habinas, the monumental-stonemason, a guest at the dinner, is another Falstaffian character. A jovial fellow, an old-time friend of Trimalchio, an established intimate of the family, he plays a prank on Fortunata, overturning her on the couch so that she makes an exhibition of her bare legs, and diverts himself by imitating the sound of trumpets with a cockeyed slave, who blows into the neck of a broken lamp while Habinas makes trumpet-noises through his compressed lips . . .

The dinner goes on interminably with the constant arrival of fresh courses, and the amount of food consumed is horrifying to the meagre resources of a present-day stomach. When Trimalchio leaves the room for an interval, the guests exchange table-talk freely among themselves, and their chatter, racy and colloquial, presents us with the daily life of the people in the very breath of living it, as no reconstruction by sociological historians can hope to do. I must resort to quotation as an example of its richness:—

> I don't bathe every day; cold water has teeth and eats away one's strength, but when I have a good dose of wine in my guts, I bid defiance to cold. Besides, I was at a funeral today. Crysanthus has passed out. Such a good fellow he was. We were together only last week; I think I can hear him talking now. But we're all no more than blown-up bladders on legs — mere bubbles. You'll say he wouldn't take advice, but not a crumb of bread or a drop of water passed his lips for five days. He died of the doctor, for what are doctors good for only to give us a bit of comfort? But in my opinion, his time was come. His wife didn't seem to care much, but women are a kind of kite; doing good to them is throwing money down a well.
>
> He only got what was due to him. As he lived so he died. He came of nothing and to his dying day he would have picked a farthing out of a dunghill with his teeth. I have eaten a dog's tongue and dare speak the truth; he had a foul mouth and was a brabbler — a mere make-bate, not a man. His brother was a fine fellow; a friend to his friend and kept an open table. He didn't order his affairs well for a start, but his first vintage set him up again. He was one of fortune's sons — lead turned to gold in his hand. He was seventy-odd when he died, but he bore his age well, was as hard as horn and as black as a crow.
>
> Talk of the living. What makes victuals so dear these days? So help me Hercules, I haven't had a mouthful of bread today. It's this drought we're having. A plague on those clerks of the market — they and the bakers juggle things together. You wink at me and I'll blink at you, and we hard workers get nothing while those jawbones make festival every day. I remember Sasinius; when I was a boy he lived down by the old arch. You'd have taken him for a peppercorn rather than a man. Wherever he went the ground smoked under him. When he was on the bench he tossed everyone like a ball — made no starched speeches — in the market-place his voice was like a trumpet — no hawking and spitting. And then, so ready to return a salute, and call everyone by his name, as if he'd been one of us. In his time, corn was as common as dirt; you could buy more bread for a farthing than two men could eat. Now everything gets worse day by day. If corn holds at the present rate I will have to sell my house.
>
> It's just the way things go; this way today and that way tomorrow, as the countryman said when he lost his speckled hog. If you were in another place, you'd say hogs walked about here ready-

> cooked. And now I think of it, we are to have a first-rate show these holidays; a fencing-match prize for the people, and not a lot of cheap bought slaves. Our patron Titus has a great soul, though he's the very devil when drunk; doesn't care a straw which side wins. They'll be given the best weapons and will fight it out to a finish; the theatre will be a butcher's shambles. His father left him a fortune, and let him play ducks and drakes with it, the estate can bear it. What sort of show is Mammea like to give us? The last one he gave us was of such a pitiful old mob of decrepit sword-players you could have blown them down with a breath. I've seen better at a funeral-pile, you'd have taken them for dunghill cocks fighting in the dark. One was a gouty, jolter-headed fool, another had a club-foot and a third had the stringhalt. The only one who put up a good show according to the rules of the game was a Thracian, the rest were just a block-headed rabble — mere runaways. And yet, says he, "I've given you a show".

In short, the price of food, politics, and the chances of sport — the three topics of perennial and eternal interest in mankind since wandering food-gatherers settled down into tribal communities, and evolved the same bedevilled system of bylaws, polemics, and social taboos under which we exist today. Stroll into any Sydney pub and you'll hear the buzz of talk at Trimalchio's dinner-tables.

And this is the only enduring substance of novels, the common life of the people played out in variations on a set theme, and in the lucid idiom of spoken words. Modernity in art is not, as the products of the studio-world intelligentsia assume, a revolt from established tradition, but the recapitulation of its eternal verities, for those are the verities of life itself, which never alter the pattern of human behaviour in any period or in any group of peoples . . .

The novel, in the state of its present text, ends abruptly. It has come down to us in a very fragmentary state, the only complete section of the narrative being the feast of Trimalchio.

The other fragments have been pieced together in a fairly effective sequence, but they leave gaps only to be filled-in by inference. There have been various seventeenth-century translations claiming to be a completed text of the novel, in so far as they make it a continuous narrative, which later Latinists denounce as forgeries. I am no Latinist, nor am I a purist or a

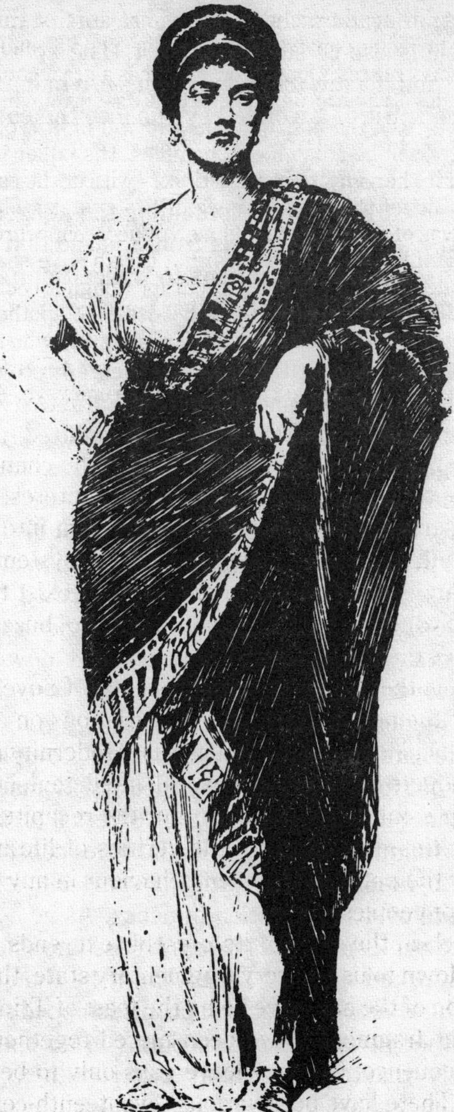

Tryphaena

perfectionist in academic stylisms. That sort of thing belongs to the preciousness of second-rate art. The spirit of a work comes first, and if a few trifling forgeries in a manuscript are in key with the spirit of a work, they enhance the entertainment value.

I first read the *Satyricon* in a Bohn edition, translated from the text of an earlier edition containing the alleged forgeries, and I found it excellent. It was from that edition I drew the subject-matter of the illustrations to the edition published by Ralph Straus and edited by Stephen Gaselee in London in the year 1910.

Gaselee was a strict Latinist, and an accredited authority on the text of the *Satyricon*; and, facing the Latin text, he selected a seventeenth-century translation and omitted from it the alleged forgeries, which was annoying, as it forced me to discard some of the illustrations which had reference to them.

I went to a considerable amount of trouble over those illustrations in respect to a factual reconstruction of the period, and never used any data that I had not verified from extant sources. Even in such a trifling item as a Roman razor I had to search several museums before I tracked down one, and thereby discovered that Roman barbers had forecast the principle of the modern safety-razor.

But there are some instances where complete factual evidence is not to be had, as in the case of a Roman merchant-ship. We can get a fair notion of its external structure from sculptured fragments, but for its inboard construction one must rely on rational probabilities. I came into conflict with Gaselee there over the question of decks. As he could find no reference to decks in the *Satyricon*, he assumed its ship to be an open undecked galley. I asked him if he thought that the Romans, a hard-headed, practical people, shipped silks, spices, corn and other perishable commodoties in an open boat. He said vaguely that they probably covered them with oiled fabrics of some sort.

Again, he refused to concede the Romans any sort of shelved furniture or wooden cupboards, as, of course, such febrile affairs have long since perished, and he could find no reference to them in Roman literature. I asked him what the Romans did with their rare vases and glassware and other objects-of-art, and he said they probably stood them on the floor. Of such stuff are the minds of scholarly precisionists made . . .

It was necessary to be as exact as possible in a pictorial reconstruction of Rome under the later Caesars, which was certainly not the grandiose Rome of the academic painters. The *Satyricon* itself derides a pretentious assumption that life as it is lived by the mass of a people *can* be a dignified procedure, and only moonstruck Utopianists are capable of indulging such a fantasy. On that score, the novel also repudiates the concept of reality in art as a present-moment experience in the action of life . . .

Petronius was an aristocrat. He detested the Rome of his era, with its corruption in all public affairs by boodling politicians and Governmental officials, its vulgar ostentation of the rich parvenu class which had ousted his own class of a cultured aristocracy, its decay of good manners and all the graces of social life, and, under all that, the crude rabble catered to by the bloody exhibitions of the arena. Yet, as a spectacle, it fascinated him. And as a great novelist he accepted its spectacle as its only enduring content to be re-created in art, leaving the sociological moralists to tub-thump a denunciation of all that they found obnoxious in it both as a spectacle and a corruption of civic integrity in the conduct of affairs.

Between these two outlooks on life as it is lived, the métier of a novelist is suspended. If he leans towards that of the social moralist he has infected his work with present-moment factuality, and that is an evanescent thing, changing with each generation. For that reason, the sociological novelist who appears most alive to his generation is most dead to the one that succeeds it. Only the novelists who remain completely detached from the moralistic outlook, and concentrate on the spectacle of life for its eternal pattern of human behavior and personality, will endure for what power they have to present it visually to the mental eye of the reader. Of such Petronius is one of the greatest masters.

The Great Sam Pepys

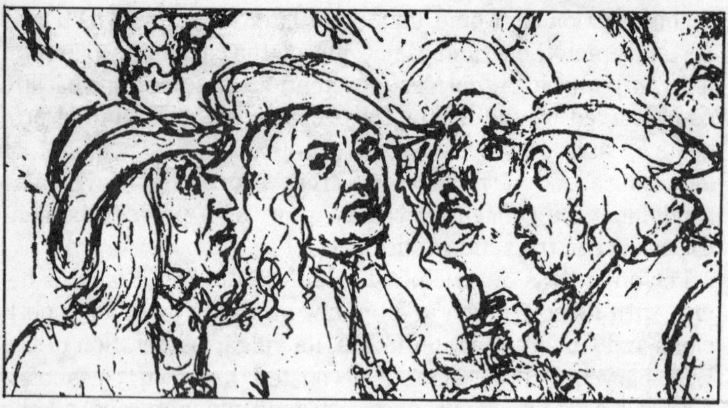

If I were required to answer that stock question about being wrecked on a desert island with only one book, my unhesitating choice would be the *Diary of Samuel Pepys*. Many greater works may be reread to satiation-point, but not Sam's diary. Its very form keeps curiosity constantly simmering, because it is impossible to retain a precise recollection of its many threads of action and the personalities involved in them.

The great character-creation of the diary is, of course, Pepys himself, but it seems to me that most commentators on it have overlooked a salient content in it. This is due to confusing Pepys's private presentation of himself to us with the presentation he made of himself to his contemporaries. In private Pepys dispenses with all false pretenses and postures over the petty, undignified and belittling actions which are the commonplace of every life that has been lived.

This ruthless frankness, this utter rejection of generous emotion on his own behalf over recounting such antics as slapping his wife's face, spying on her to see if she puts on pants

Published in the *Bulletin*, Sydney, 26 March 1958

for her dancing-lesson, squabbling over the kitchen-accounts or beating his page-boy till his arm ached are apt to raise a comedy-image of him in the reader's mind, thereby infecting him with a complacent sense of superiority to such ignoble behavior, and creating the illusion that the Pepys he sees in his mind's-eye was the Pepys under inspection by the people of his own period.

R. L. Stevenson's essay on Pepys is the best example of a reader's inability to separate the Pepys scribbling in his diary from the dignified Pepys in his character as Secretary to the Navy Office. To Stevenson, a self-idolator who exercised his literary faculty in presenting an idealised self-portrait to posterity, it was incomprehensible that Pepys could write about himself with such integrity unless he was such a simple fellow that he did not realise what he was doing. I have not read that silly and impertinent essay since I was a boy, but I recall a reference to Pepys as "a little cockboat" pulled about in the wake of popular events among "the stupid starers and the loud huzzas."

No concept could be further from the reality — the sound wisdom in which Pepys kept his stability in a difficult and dangerous world of public affairs. Amid the warring factions of that time no man might count on security in his office. The Navy Office itself was a hotbed of bickerings, backbitings and open enmity, and Pepys had to walk on eggs to keep out of open conflict with his colleagues. That he managed to do so while defending the rights and privileges of his office is evidence of his suavity of address.

Though he and Sir William Penn detested each other, their relations never came to outright warfare, and that must be accounted to the art with which Pepys handled that intemperate, hard-drinking, quarterdeck martinet. Very early in the diary Pepys gives us a sample of his temper when he and Penn were out riding on a country road, and chanced to meet two country fellows on one horse, "which I did, without much ado, give way to," writes Pepys,

> but Sir W. Penn would not, but struck them and they him, and so passed away, but they giving him some high words, he went back

> and struck them off their horse in a simple fury, and without much honor in my mind.

There is no question about the figure Pepys cut in the eyes of his contemporaries. He was Clerk of the Acts, Clerk of the Privy Seal, Treasurer for Tangier, a Brother of Trinity House and a member of the Royal Society. He mixed on equal terms with merchants on the Exchange; the goldsmiths, who were the bankers of that era; tradesmen who supplied commodities to the Navy; actors, artists and musicians; and, as spokesman for the Navy at the Privy Council, had personal contact with every notability at the court of Charles II.

Charles himself had a great respect for his abilities, and when, during the appalling year of the plague, Pepys ran the Navy Office practically single-handed, Charles said to him, "Mr. Pepys, I give you my thanks for your good service all this year, and I assure you I am very sensible of it." Lord Sandwich never moved in any affair of complexity without asking his advice, and Sir William Coventry, about the only man of genuine integrity in that era of almost universal corruption in affairs, never faltered in his respect and personal regard for Pepys.

The supreme instance of Pepys's ease of address in public is that of his great speech when he and his fellow-members of the Navy Office were called to the bar of the House of Commons, there to answer for their part in the disastrous war with Holland, which for the time being gave the Dutch mastery of the seas.

It was a time of panic for everybody who held any public office connected with the Navy. There was talk of impeaching Clarendon himself, also Lord Sandwich for breaching cargo in prizes taken by him, and Sir William Coventry for selling places. Many others went down under the wave of popular frenzy, and the Parliament's lust for fresh victims was insatiable. There were four months of it — nerves were frayed to breaking-point — till finally the commission inquiring into the mismanagement of the Navy Office demanded a full investigation at the bar of the House.

The command fell suddenly and there was little time to prepare a defence. Pepys shut himself up with his clerks, huddling together documentary evidence to make his case, till "quite weary and dull I could go no further, and resolved to leave the rest till tomorrow morning, and so in full discontent and wearyness went home, and without supper, vexed and sickish to bed." Unable to sleep, he woke his wife "to talk to me and comfort me . . . and made me resolve to quit my hands of this office and endure the trouble no longer."

In that desperate state of mind he went down to the House next day with his fellows, and was there called into judgment before a very full House, fomented with antagonism against himself and his office. A test of forensic ability, if ever there was one. The Speaker having read over the commission's findings against the mismanagement and corruption of the Navy Office,

> I began my defence most acceptably and smoothly [wrote Pepys] and continued at it without any hesitation or loss, but with full scope, and all my reason free about me as if it had been my own table, from that time (eleven-o'clock) till past three in the afternoon, and so ended, without any interruption by the Speaker, we withdrew.

An amazing performance, which cleared the Navy Office completely of all accusations brought against it. The personal qualifications which made it possible are apparent. Pepys had a fine voice — he sang with distinction. He had that fluent ease of speech which extemporises the phrase in a finished diction, and the emphasis which carries conviction. Without those assets he never could have carried an antagonistic audience with him for four hours, and won over its suffrages at the end of it.

On the theme of a successful career, that speech was one of its highlights, coming as it did on a long period of threat and suspense, and there is no pleasanter reading than the pleasure Pepys got out of the popular esteem it brought him. With breathless gusto he records all the compliments paid him. Sir William Coventry greeted him with, "Good morrow, Mr. Pepys, that must be Speaker of the Parliament House." When

Pepys met the King in the park, Charles said, "Mr. Pepys, I am very glad of your success yesterday." Lord Berkeley said he never did hear a speech delivered in that manner before. Prodgers of the Bedchamber "swore to me that he told the King I could teach the Solicitor-General." George Montague said "I was another Cicero, and all the world said the same of me." Mr. Godolphin said "he would go twenty miles to hear such a speech again." The Lieutenant of the Tower told Pepys that Mr. Vaughan "did protest to him that he had sat twenty-six years in Parliament and never heard such a speech."

There were many more such tributes, and Pepys "spent the morning walking in the Hall being complimented by everybody to admiration." Later, at the Privy Council, when the threat of a miscarriage in affairs was discussed as coming under the displeasure of Parliament, "Why," says the King, "it is then Mr. Pepys making another speech to them," which made "all the Lords and the Attorney and the Solicitor-General look at me."

A writer's capacity to communicate his own sense of pleasure to a reader is a difficult literary feat, and Pepys rarely failed to do so. Of all the arts, one's response to music is the most baffling to convey in words, yet Pepys finds the words which convince one of that ecstatic emotion which only harmonic perfection can arouse in us:

> But that which did please me beyond anything in the whole world was the wind-music when the angel comes down which is so sweet that it ravished me, and indeed, in a word, did wrap up my soul so that it made me really sick, just as I have formerly been when in love with my wife; that neither then, nor all the evening going home, or at home, I was able to think of anything, but remained all night transported, so as I could not believe that ever any music hath that real command over the soul of a man as this doth upon me.

During the ghastly year of the plague, when London was practically a deserted city, with nothing in the streets but the tumbrils carrying corpses for burial in the fields, a little group came to dinner at Greenwich, among them being Evelyn and

Sir John Minnes, both accredited wits at any social gathering. News had come of the capture of some rich Dutch prizes by Lord Sandwich, which, wrote Pepys,

> put us all into such an ecstacy of joy, that it inspired Sir J. Minnes and Mr. Evelyn with such a spirit of mirth, that in all my life I never met with so merry a two hours as our company this night was. Among other humors, Mr. Evelyn's repeating some verses made up of nothing but various acceptations of "may" and "can," and doing it so aptly upon occasion of something of that nature, and so fast, did make us almost die with laughing, and did so stop the mouth of Sir J. Minnes in the middle of all his mirth (and in a thing agreeing with his own manner of genius) that I never saw a man so outdone in all my life; and Sir J. Minnes' mirth in seeing himself so outdone, was the crown of our mirth. In this humor till ten at night, and we to bed, it being one of the times of my life wherein I was fullest of a true sense of joy.

That gay little party shines like a bright light against the black horrors of the plague surrounding it. For a few hours its tension is lifted, and the brief release from nervous stress inspires an emotion of pure delight.

The whole picture of the plague is drawn with terrific realism, and in that way alone adds dignity, courage and integrity to the full stature of Pepys himself. All through the diary he castigates himself for cowardice at any threat of physical danger, but the way he, alone of the Navy officials, stuck to his work during the time of warfare at sea and pestilence on land evinces an indomitable moral courage. And at last, on one count, it rewarded him well. At the beginning of the plague year he had £1300 to his credit. At the year's end that credit had amounted to the sum of £4500 . . .

An instructive sidelight on the universal system of bribery by which all business was conducted in that era.

It was an established precedent, and the only obligation imposed on it was that it should not be practised too blatantly. This was bad taste, and offensive to a general act of oblivion over its procedure, and no one was more discreet than Pepys in keeping decorum on that score. His system was this: he only took bribes when sound business justified the whole transaction.

All his colleagues on the Navy Board took bribes from anybody, no matter what shoddy they imposed on the king's purse and service. Pepys would have none of that. He never bought a commodity without first assuring himself personally of its quality. He learned to measure timber, evaluate bunting, canvas, tar, cordage or any other goods essential to the upkeep of the Navy, so that nearly all purchases recommended by him were endorsed by the Admirality Board sitting under the Duke of York, much to the exasperation of his own colleagues who saw their tenders turned down as being of inferior quality. But they had cause to bless Pepys for his astuteness at the expense of their pockets when the Parliament came to examine the alleged misuse of public money by the Navy Office during the Dutch war. Pepys had his books in perfect order, and was able to prove that the money advanced had been economically expended in the king's service . . .

The entertainment-value of the diary has been universally acclaimed but its literary qualities overlooked, which is a failure to observe that its entertainment is derived from its literary qualities.

Matthew Arnold once said, "People think I can teach them style. What stuff all that is. Have something to say and say it as clearly as you can. That is the only secret of style." And Pepys had that secret.

For stark realism, his picture of the great fire of London matches his account of the plague. There are pages of it, all sustained at the same pictorial clarity, meticulous observation and emotional tension:—

> So near the fire as we could not breathe for smoke, and all over the Thames, with one's face in the wind, you were almost burned with the shower of fire drops. This is very true, so that houses were burned by these drops and flakes of fire three or four, nay, five or six houses one from another. When we could endure no more upon the water we to a little ale-house on the Bankside, over against the Three Cranes, and there stayed till it was dark almost, and saw the fire grow; and as it grew darker, appeared more and more in corners and upon steeples, and between churches and houses, as far as we could see up the hill of the city, in a most horrid, malicious bloody flame, not like the fine flame of an ordinary fire . . . We

> stayed till, it being darkish, we saw the fire only as one entire arch of fire from this to the other side of the bridge, in a bow up the hill for an arch above a mile wide, it made me weep to see it.

That is most excellent writing, and only a genuine literary faculty could have produced it . . .

One extremely precious content of the diary which a commentator must not overlook is Pepys's adoration for the beauty of women, and his various amorous affairs with them.

However unreserved a man may be about his private love-life in talk it is the one subject he is most furtive about when writing a personal record of his life. No doubt most writers shy off it because it is the most difficult subject to handle with ease, assurance and a lack of self-consciousness, but its blank space in nearly all autobiographies deprives them of a first essential to self-revelation, for we can't know a man truly till we know something about his relations with women.

Pepys is hampered by no such reticence in the picture he gives of himself as an amorist:—

> I to the Swan and dined upon the rabbit, and after dinner to Mrs. Martin's, and there find Mrs. Burroughs, and by and by comes a pretty widow, one Mrs. Eastwood, and one Mrs. Fenton, a maid, and here a merry kissing and looking on their breasts, and all the innocent pleasure in the world. But Lord; to see the dissembling of this widow, how upon the singing of a certain jigg by Doll, Mrs Martin's sister, she seemed to be sick and fainted and God knows what, because the jigg which her husband (who died of this last sickness) loved. But by and by I made her as merry as possible, and towsed and tumbled her as I pleased . . . Mightily pleased with this afternoon's mirth . . .

For the most part, once Pepys has established a casual love-affair, it is passed-off in the diary with some such formula as "To see Mrs. So-and-so, and there did what I would with her," but with several of the women he had to do with, what he did is censored by a series of dots. When in London first I met old Wheatley, the editor of the diary, and asked him why he had made these exceptions between one woman and another. His answer was that these censored passages had to do with women whose descendants were still extant, and it was in deference to them that he had thought fit to delete from the text anything tendering to the disrepute of their ancestors. A fatuous explanation! The blank space of dots evidences that amorous antics are being censored, thereby leaving a libidinous impress on the reader's mind which a plain statement would dispense with.

I suspect Wheatley submitted to snobbery over those censored passages. He has no concern for the post-mortem reputation of Mrs. Bagwell, a carpenter's wife, or of Mrs. Martin, a purser's wife, while Doll Lane, a trollop, and anybody's property, has no reputation to be protected. The censorings have only to do with ladies of middle-class respectability, and Wheatley endorsed its interdictions against any violation of a code of decorum.

It was the novelist as much as the amorist in Pepys which so fascinated him with the world of femininity, for he has something revealing to say about every woman who came under his inspection, from the lovely Lady Castlemaine to a slatternly virago like the Duchess of Albemarle. His greatest life-size feminine portrait is, of course, Mrs. Pepys, though it lacks only one ingredient to complete it, and that is the precise nature of her offstage relations with men.

Those are left to what sapience the reader may have in estimating the value of circumstantial evidence, and there is a good deal of that to suggest that Mrs. Pepys also went off the marital rails when chance offered her a pleasing amorous interlude. Though Pepys was tormented by jealousy over any evidence of illicit behavior in such an interlude, he always shied away from trying to verify his suspicions, unable to face the disruption to his peace of mind which confirmation of them would inflict. He confesses as much in that notable affair between Mrs. Pepys and young Mr. Somersett, son to Lord Somersett.

Mrs. Pepys had known the youth in France, and chance brought them together again in a London theatre as a result of which Mrs. Pepys met Mr. Somersett next day at the 'Change where he presented her with some rings and a bracelet. Next day, being abroad with Pepys, Mrs. Pepys was accosted by a

French footman with feathers, who spoke privately with her though Pepys heard her promise to go some place next morning. And to some place she went next day, refusing to tell Pepys where she was going or, on returning, where she had been and though Pepys was in a ferment of jealousy, he refused to trounce her into confessing. He did not want to know.

That event set the pattern for all future indiscretions. Mrs. Pepys always maintained the same feckless, or reckless, refusal to concede any right of intrusion by Pepys on her private affairs, notably those which had to do with Pembleton, her dancing-master, and Brown, the painter who gave her drawing-lessons. The best Pepys could do to assert his marital authority was to refuse to have Brown dining at his table, much to Mrs. Pepys's indignation, and when Pembleton was alone in the house with her, and the exasperations of jealousy became unbearable, to hurry home from his office and shuffle papers in his closet, just to let them know he was on the premises.

When Pepys sent his wife down to Woolwich during the plague she had unlimited freedom to consort with Brown, as Pepys only chanced a visit there at intervals. On one of those he arrived during a furious quarrel between Mrs. Pepys and her maid Mary, who told Mrs. Pepys to her teeth that she would tell Pepys something about her which would stop her mouth, which Pepys suspected to be about Brown, and, as usual, refused to hear about, preferring to bolt out of the house in a mighty passion of jealousy.

Then again there was a letter which Pepys found in his wife's bed, which put her in a fluster of alarm to discover whether or not he had read it. Beyond noting that it acknowledged some great favor from Mrs. Pepys, he refused to read further and threw the letter away, making the excuse that it was too ill-writ to be worth the trouble of deciphering. Finally there was the gracious condescension of Lord Sandwich to Mrs. Pepys during her stay at Brampton, which was close to the Sandwich mansion of Hinchingbroke. During that tremendous uproar over the exposure of Pepys's affair with Deborah Willet, Mrs. Pepys threw at Pepys, as evidence of her chaste conduct as a wife, her rejection of amorous advances by Lord Sandwich himself . . .

That won't do at all. Credulity refuses to see Mrs. Pepys austerely repulsing the august ardors of Lord Sandwich. And the really insensate furies of jealousy she let loose on Pepys over the Willet episode are perfectly in key with her immature mentality, which would find them a justification for her own illicit antics . . .

Consider Mrs. Pepys, as revealed in the diary, and by Hales's portrait of her. She was a pretty little half-witted moron with plenty of sex-attraction but with the mentality of a girl of eight, and that is a combination no man competes with in terms of rationality, as witness her proposal to take Pepys by the nose with a pair of red-hot tongs when in a rage with him. Her intellectual status may be measured by her predilection for the "Grand Cyrus"; Pepys had to check her from boring the company by recounting slabs of its interminable drivel. Hales complained that her nose gave him as much trouble to paint as another person's face, and that completes for me, the knowledge that Mrs. Pepys was one of those women who never grow-up. It is a child's nose, without any definition of form between the aquiline and the retrousse. It is the human nose which determines personality, and no one can predict, looking at a child's nose, what that personality will develop into. If the nose refuses to grow up, the mind behind it remains that of a child . . .

Normally Mrs. Pepys was contented enough to run her house and squabble with her maids, and have an occasional outing at Vauxhall or Spring Gardens, to eat cakes and drink milk. But any special event of social pleasure made her discontented and avid for more, as Pepys frequently complained. One cannot see Mrs. Pepys's doll's-stare and her infantile nose permitting any ridiculous interdictions by a husband to intrude on an event of pleasure inspired by the flattering ardors of a lover . . .

Only one other work can be compared with the diary in the

whole range of English literature, and that is Boswell's journal. Out of hundreds of diaries, journals and autobiographies these two creations alone have succeeded perfectly in self-revelation and self-portraiture: a remarkable instance of the universal urge in mankind to escape facing the stark reality of its being. These are the only two men who ever told the truth about themselves.

The diary is not only a book read — it is a life lived, fully, richly, with impassioned gusto. There is hardly an emotional issue in it which does not awaken in us the consciousness of a personal experience. That is its universal appeal, quite apart from its enchanting entertainment.

The faculty of a fine novelist went into the making of this diary. In spite of its irresponsible form, it develops into a constructed work. Historians acclaim it for the intimate picture it gives of the affairs and personalities of its period, but its major value is that it is a literary work of rare distinction. It has all the essentials of a novel — character-creation, psychological divination, interest sustained by action, and drama brought to crisis against a vivid, pictorial background.

Most of all, it has a dominant theme based on a universal aspiration: that of success in the struggle for existence. Its narrative is held together by a single thread which runs through it from beginning to end — the acquisition of money, which also implies the advancement of Pepys from a beginning as a minor clerk to that of an outstanding figure in the Government of his country.

Regrets have been expressed that the diary was not continued into the reign of James II, but that is to confuse the métier of the historian with that of the novelist. As a novel the diary has completed its theme of a successful career. Pepys has acquired an opulent income and a distinguished place in public affairs. He has a fine house, stored with valuable portable property, a library of rare books, his walls are hung with examples from the best portrait-painters of the period. He dines off gold plates, his cellar is stored with wines of quality and the menu of his dinner-parties is enough to stagger the enfeebled stomachs of the present era. Finally, he has his own coach and horses; the caste-mark of social distinction in his day.

That other dominant motive in the novel, success in love, is also brought to a dramatic crescendo by the domestic cataclysm brought down on him over his affair with pretty little Deborah Willet, his wife's maid. This crisis arrives precisely in its right place in the novel, for something of the sort had to happen over the simmering jealousies between husband and wife, and its development is one of the diary's unique literary achievements. A husband detected in adultery by a jealous wife may be a shopworn theme, but it is rarely treated in fiction with such a sense of its emotional reality as it is in the diary, nor with such sustained drama. Never has the superiority of the wife in marital conflict been so ruthlessly vindicated as in the satanic vitality Mrs. Pepys draws from a distracted situation which drives Sam into a craven subjection to her for the sake of peace at any price.

Thereafter the diary draws to a close on a selected note of finality, a fear of failing eyesight which will not permit Pepys to carry it on any further. There was no need to carry it further, for it is a completed work of art, and the fear of blindness was groundless.

The Delicate Art of Bawdy

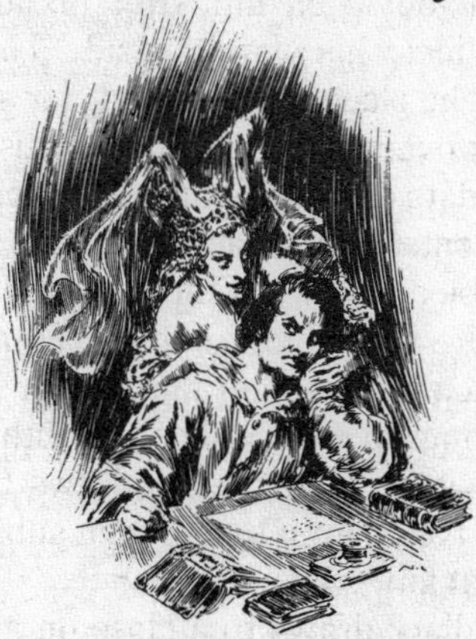

In the telling of bawdy stories, man shows one of the most urgent needs of his being. They are a relief from the decorum imposed on him by social and ecclesiastical codes of behaviour, and they gratify the itch of concupiscence in talk which is denied the release of action. They derive from the major theme of gossip between all peoples, which is the exposure of scandals, mainly sexual, detected in the private lives of others, related with gusto by the gossip-mongers, who are oblivious to a procedure which brings their own private lives under inspection and detection.

If art proposes to ignore this universal manifestation of human behaviour, it has rejected one of its most vital contents. It has also dodged facing one of the most difficult technical achievements, which is to use the idiom of ribaldry with ease, wit, and humour. The crude, colloquial terms used by the people in retailing the bawdy story are of no use to it. Only a fine artistry in prose and poetry can turn the Milesian Fable into good literature.

Published in "Norman Lindsay Number", *Southerly* No.1, Sydney, 1959

Antiquity succeeded in doing this with perfect good taste. All its writers, whether in prose or poetry, drew enchanting material from ribaldry in the key of humour and lyricism. Aristophanes is the greatest master of its idiom whose works have come down to us, though in all the lesser Greek writers, whose writings survive only in fragments, its gay note is rarely lacking. Among the Romans, save only for the cold and academic Virgil, there is not one poet or prose-writer who does not use its freed imagery where a theme calls for it. All of them, Catullus, Horace, Ovid, Martial, Juvenal, Apuleius, Petronius, would have regarded a ban put on such a salient aspect of the spectacle of life as a rank absurdity, which it is.

That ban arrived with the blight of Christianity, with its priestly hatred of the body and its obscene obsession with sin, which spread a dark miasma of joylessness over all experience which makes life worth living. Life became a penalty inflicted on man for being the thing he is, and which he was designed to be by the constitution of his being. Only the East, from which Christians derive their God, could have evolved the monstrous amalgam of sadism, masochism and nihilism which for so long corrupted all sane and clear thinking in the Western mind. Is there any need to question a mystery in the hatred of the Jew, the only Eastern race which has penetrated Western civilization and imposed on it its own religious cultisms and its racial cunning?

Sanity returned to life and art with the revival of Greek and Roman culture. And with it the gay note of bawdy was heard again in the poetry of Chaucer and Villon, the stories of Boccaccio, and that Homeric roar of laughter we call Rabelais, because the man and his book are inseparable. From Rabelais to Montaigne, who clarified self-knowledge in man so long befogged by religious fanaticism, we arrive at the superb achievement of Shakespeare, who once again presented man at full length in living portraiture, as Homer and the Greek dramatists had left him. And Shakespeare's bawdy is one of the most potent facets of his work. Its cheerful key survived into the Restoration, for all the frenzied efforts of the Puritan to stamp it out. It was given a brief rebirth by Congreve and

Fielding, and a glorious revival in the poetry of Burns and in Byron's *Don Juan*. Since then, it has been banned by English literature, with an extremely devitalizing effect on that same literature. We must turn to France and Balzac for the greatest and gayest work to the glorification of bawdy as a supreme achievement in the most difficult of all idioms in the written word.

The accent here is not on bawdy for itself alone, but as defining an understanding of man without which he has about as much significance as a eunuch. And a writer who presents men and women as creatures truncated below the waist is exposed as one who goes about without trousers, saying: "See, I have had my testicles removed."

Bawdy in art is extreme from pornography, and therein the gods have imposed on art its most infernal complexity. Pornography is the product of the vulgar herd, whether in the written or the spoken word. It is dull, boring and humourless to any mind sensitised to the intonation of wit and humour. The original Milesian Fables were tales. Petronius interpolated a couple in the *Satyricon.* They were well constructed and had wit. In that form they were handed down by oral tradition to the era of the printing press, when a few of them got into type under the title of Jest Books.

A bastard product of the Jest Book is that enfeebled pretence for after-dinner wit recently labelled the "smoking-room story" by male lewdsters, but now common property between both sexes. It is not a story at all, but what in journalistic argot is called a "gag", and depends for what entertainment value it may have on the raconteur's ability to spring an unexpected anticlimax on the listener. Harmless stuff in itself, it is harmful when the plebeian literary mind proposes to transfer its crude cant terms for the physical functions of the human body to the printed page. Their effect there is of a violent discordance, like a screech in the mental ear. In speech, intonation, gusto, the personality of the speaker may carry off such crudities without offence, but in the cold formality of type they are offensive to a degree.

Almost as bad technically and aesthetically are the

psychoanalytical and pathological terminologies dragged in to define the motives of human behaviour, for their barbarous phonetics convey no sense of reality to the mind. The American novel of these days has become so debased by these effects of Puritanism gone rancid that no reader who has the integrity of literature at heart can bear to read such scabrous stuff. Its evil is that the people's censorships can see no distinction between it and bawdy as an essential content of art when used by the masters of the written word, both in prose and poetry. Since those must use the spectacle of life provided by the people themselves, this conflict between the people's codes of behaviour and the revelation of that behaviour in the freed imagery of art is inevitable and will never cease.

The short story, as a distinctive art-form, may be said to date from the *Decameron*, through the tradition of interpolating it in the novel lasted down to the time of Dickens, who used it freely in *Pickwick*. From whatever source Boccaccio took the themes of his stories, they are shaped by a high literary faculty, and for that reason have the substance of immortality in them. They are an act of creation, not of compilation, as are the stories of the *Heptameron* which derive from them. Marguerite of Navarre was a gay lady, and we are in debt to her for the stories she collected and made into a book. Whether she rewrote them herself or had them contributed by others is not known. They have grace and wit and have none of the crudities of the Jest Book, but they remain rather a period piece than a permanent contribution to world literature.

If Balzac used the tradition of the *Decameron* and *Heptameron* for the spirit of the *Droll Stories*, the comparison need go no further. And if he took something of their style from Rabelais and their psychology from Montaigne, he had no need for either stimulus, for the stories are a derivative of the most fecund creative power in the whole range of prose fiction. They are Balzac at his best, for he has sent the severe ordinances of form and construction which hedge about the novel to the devil of gravity. For once he has slipped the chains of the galley slave: the daemonic lash is off his back and he is free to have a lark with work. This is the rarest of rewards given to one so driven as Balzac to get work done and done with. It was the obsession of his whole being, from which he derived the monstrous conception of covering every aspect of human life in his novels. A dozen Balzacs could not have completed his forecast of the *Human Comedy* yet to be written. Even on his deathbed, when told he had only a couple of weeks of life left, he cried, "There is yet time."

A mind so satanically driven, which burned itself out at the age of fifty-two, did at least take one gay holiday from work by shifting its accent from one of dramatic intensity to one of humour. Dramatic intensity in the *Droll Stories* is never allowed to impose emotional intensity on the reader. At a crisis of drama, its stress is always lifted by a version to humour. "The High Constable's Wife" is one of the best of the stories. Its drama is superb, but its nice detachment from stress is the key in which all the stories are written.

Savoisy is the lover of the countess, and comes secretly to visit her by the postern gate of the castle, when the High Constable is away elsewhere. Discovering the adultery, the Constable lays an ambuscade for Savoisy, giving orders that no one else is to be allowed into the castle and only the Countess herself permitted to leave it, though attended by her maid and a guard of soldiers, that she may have no chance of warning Savoisy of the doom prepared for him. In desperation for some device that may avert it, the Countess goes to High Mass in the Cathedral, where she knows the court gallants will be assembled in attendance on their ladies. Among these is a poor gentleman, named Boys-Burredon, who has long adored the Countess in silence, afraid to risk a rejection by making an overture to her. Inspired by her need to save Savoisy at any cost to others, the Countess now gives Boys-Burredon ardent glances, and by little signals gives him to understand that he is to follow her. Enthralled by her siren allure, he is drawn after her into the castle by its front portal, and into her private apartment. Here, touched by remorse for her treachery to him, the Countess confesses that she has brought him there only to die.

"Alas, sweet sir," said she, "I have acted vilely towards you. Listen. On your departure from this house you will meet your death. The love which I have for another bewildered me, and without being able to hold its place, you will take it before his murderers. This is the joy to which I have bidden you."

"Ah!" replied Boys-Burredon, interring in the depth of his heart a black despair. "I am grateful to you for having made use of me as something that belonged to you. Yes, I love you so much that every day I have dreamed of offering to you, in imitation of the ladies, a thing that can only be given once. Take, then, my life."

And the poor chevalier, in saying this, gave her one glance for all the time he would have been able to look at her through the long days. Hearing these brave and loving words, the Countess rose hurriedly.

"Ah! were it not for Savoisy, how I could love you," said she.

"Alas! my fate is then accomplished," replied Boys-Burredon. "My horoscope predicted that I would die for the love of a great lady. Ah, God!" he said, clutching his good sword, "I will sell my life dearly, but I shall die content in thinking that my death assures the happiness of her I love. I shall be better in her memory than in reality."

At the sight and the gesture of the courageous man, the Constable's wife was pierced to the heart. But also she was wounded to the quick because he wished to leave her without asking for the smallest favour.

"Come, that I may arm you," said she, making an attempt to kiss him.

"Ha! my lady love," said he, moistening with a tear the fire of his eyes, "would you render my death impossible by attaching too great a value to my life?"

"Come," cried she, overcome by this intense love. "I do not know what the end of this will be, but come — afterwards we will go and perish together at the postern."

The same flame leaped in their hearts, the same harmony had struck for both, they embraced each other with rapture in the delicious access of that mad fever which you know well, I hope. They fell into a profound forgetfulness of the dangers of Savoisy, of themselves, of the Constable, of death, of life, of everything.

Meanwhile Savoisy has arrived at the postern gate. The Constable is summoned, Savoisy enters the courtyard and the whole ambuscade rushes on him, and with the shouts of the men-at-arms and the clash of swords, the groans of the dying Savoisy mingle with the sighs of ecstasy from the lovers in the apartment above the courtyard, who are startled back to reality by the uproar below them.

> "Ah!" said the Countess, turning pale with terror. "Savoisy is dying for me."
>
> "But I will live for you," said Boys-Burredon, "and shall esteem it a joy to pay the same price for my happiness as he has done."
>
> "Hide yourself in the clothes chest," cried the Countess. "I hear the Constable coming."
>
> And indeed M. d'Armagnac entered with a head in his hand and, putting it all bloody on the mantel shelf, said "Behold, Madame, a picture which will enlighten you concerning the duties of a wife towards her husband."
>
> "You have killed an innocent man," said the Countess, without changing colour. "Savoisy was not my lover."
>
> And with that speech she looked proudly at the Constable, with a face marked by such dissimulation and feminine audacity that the husband looked as foolish as a girl who has allowed a note to escape her below, before a numerous company . . .
>
> And the Countess turned lightly on her heel like a weathercock turned by the wind, pretending to go and look after her household affairs. You can imagine that D'Armagnac was greatly embarrassed by the head of poor Savoisy, and for his part Boys-Burredon had no desire to cough while listening to the Count, who was growling to himself all sorts of words. At length he struck two heavy blows on the table and said, "I'll go and attack the inhabitants of Poissy." Then he departed, and when night was come Boys-Burredon escaped from the castle in some disguise or other . . .

As a tailpiece, we are told casually that the Queen, charmed by the devotion Boys-Burredon had shown for the Countess, lured him away from her to become her lover, till the King, discovering that Boys-Burredon was cuckolding him, had him sewn up in a sack and thrown into the Seine. Thus a nice balance is kept between drama, exalted sentiment and humour. Sardonic as may be many of the episodes, the key in which they are related is never sardonic. It gives everything to passion and nothing to sentimentality. For that reason there is vital reality in these stories which has nothing to do with a realistic idiom, for the imageries of fantasy run riot through them. Because all passions are reduced to their stark essentials, men and women were never so alive elsewhere in fiction as they are here.

It is the women who dominate action in these stories, and who dedicate men to the service of their desires. Husbands of the nobility, ferocious and intemperate as mad bulls, are cuckolded with audacity by their ladies; citizens, cunning in the chicanery of their professions, are invariably outwitted by their wives. So in his novels, it is in the creation of his women that Balzac's greatest achievement is manifest. They are alive with desire and desirability, infused into them by Balzac's adoration for women. The images of feminine allure that he pours out in their portraiture are inexhaustible; they are complete women, from the tops of their heads to the tips of their toes; the key of their presentation is that of a lover's caress.

> "A lady most dazzling white, most delicately wanton, with long tresses and velvet hands, filling out her dress at the least movement, for she was gracefully plump, with a laughing mouth, and eyes moist in advance, a woman to beautify hell."
>
> "What lovely thick hair hung over her ivory back, showing white places, fair and shining, between so many tresses."
>
> "The Maid of Thilouse, whose arms were red and firm and her breasts hard as bastions, which kept the cold from her heart — her waist round as a young oak, fresh, clean and pretty, like a first frost, green and tender as an April bud."
>
> "Joseph inspected the pretty white of the girl's breasts, which a modest grace covered with an old rag, and looked at them as a schoolboy looks at a rosy apple on a hot day."
>
> "Believing herself alone with her maid, she made those little jokes that women will when undressing. 'Am I not worth 20,000 crowns tonight? Are these overpaid by a castle in Brie?'
>
> "And saying this she gently raised her two white supports, firm as rocks, which had well sustained many assaults, seeing they had been furiously attacked, and had never softened."
>
> "And the page noticed his lady's foot, which was delicately slippered in a little laced shoe of a blue colour, a true foot of delight — a virginal foot that merited a kiss, as a robber does the gallows; a roguish foot, a foot wanton enough to damn an archangel; an ominous foot, a devilishly enticing foot, which gave one a desire to make two new ones just like it."

There never was such a harem of vital femininities caged between the covers of a book. Peasant girls, street girls, citizens' wives, young virgins, great courtesans and great ladies of the court: to each is given an imagery drawn from the status of whatever rank of the social order she was born to. One thinks of the great army of serious-minded novelists who have sweated midnight oil to find variants for the shop-worn clichés about hair, skin, eyes, noses and mouths, to create the illusion of lovely women in cold type, searching the dictionary for synonyms of desirability which only the warm embrace of a woman's body can evoke . . .

Fantasy must insist that desire is inexhaustible, and so it is, as an image. That image must be drawn from the flesh, even though the flesh is so swiftly exhausted of desire. But if the writer, the artist, allows the flesh to make a fool of him there, so much the worse for his art. Creation in art must have a full experience of life, but if it allows that experience to dominate creation it is creation which becomes exhausted. Physical chastity is as essential to the image of desire as experience in desire is essential to the creation of its image. A balance must be maintained between the factuality of all experience in life and the imagery by which it is re-created in art. As evidence of where that balance is maintained, and where disrupted, contrast the lives and works of Balzac and Hugo.

Balzac had few love affairs, and those only with mature women of highly cultivated minds. From them he derived his subtle knowledge of feminine psychology. In the action of work, he lived a celibate existence, shutting himself up like a monk in his cell and sometimes working eighteen hours at a stretch, keeping himself mentally alert with cups of black coffee. Between novels, he plunged into the world of affairs, squandering money earned by his novels in those wildcat schemes for making money which kept him constantly on the verge of bankruptcy, pursued by duns. From those affairs he drew his vast knowledge of finance, commercial rapacity, sociological conflict and political corruption, as well as the army of characters which people the stage of his *Human Comedy*. Biographers have failed to see in his seeming feckless behaviour over money the hard and ruthless logic which threw it away recklessly that the bare need for it should drive him back again to work.

Hugo, to put money first, was a mean fellow who hoarded it,

audited his wife's kitchen accounts, and allowed Juliet Drouet, his mistress, to live in penury after she had thrown up her profession as an actress at his command. He made immense sums by his novels and plays and left a large fortune.

Physically, he was endowed with the potentialities of a satyr and a stud ram combined. The number of women he possessed is countless, and he did not care where they arrived from; shop girls, street girls, minor actresses, dancers, with a sprinkling of women from the higher social classes. And he never created one desirable woman in the whole mass of his work. He vitiated the image of desire for them by incessant copulation, giving over his gloomy and overstressed novels to a Jesus cultism for suffering humanity while gloating sadistically over imageries of physical torment — the effect of an iron constitution which never suffered a physical ill in the whole course of his long life, save a twinge of toothache in old age, which staggered him as something incomprehensible. To such a man, the gay earth of Balzac's *Droll Stories* was equally incomprehensible, since the spirit of delight can come only from a black abyss of the spirit endured in secrecy.

Most critics of Balzac's work pass the *Droll Stories* as of little consequence compared to his novels; a work tossed off as a diversion rather than a serious contribution to literature. To me, it is one of the greatest of his works. Will the illusion never be dissipated that humour is an inferior quality to gravity in art? For the very few prose works of high quality dedicated to the spirit of humour there are scores and scores of works created in a serious idiom, or, to use the cant term of critical virtuosity, "works to be taken seriously". Is the *Satyricon* not to be taken seriously? Or *Don Quixote* or *Tom Jones?* As a supreme act of creation, is Falstaff to be taken less seriously than Hamlet, or Mrs. Gamp than Lady Dedlock? It seems to me that these sapient critics of works to be taken seriously are confusing the humorous with the comic.

The comic consists of satirical comment on the passing scene and is as ephemeral as the social habits, customs and conventions from which it is drawn. Almost every decade brings in some variation in an outlook on human behaviour and states of mind dictated by whatever may be the prevailing fashions and opinions of the moment. Since the era of illustrated journalism, we are able to observe that what one generation found extremely funny in these external facets of behaviour the next generation found nothing whatever to laugh at. All literature derived from the comic is destined to an abysm of dullness.

Humour is that supreme clarity of vision that sees mankind precisely as it is and not as false sentiment and human dissimulation assume it to be. It is aware of the incongruity of human behaviour as distinct from its pretensions; it sees in the idiosyncratic individual the prototype of it in the mass. It is the rarest of all gifts, for its spiritual content is a delight in the whole spectacle of life, whether that inspires laughter, horror or pity. It may not always use the idiom of humour, but its approach to the spectacle of life is always in that sane detachment from emotional histrionics which is the most subtle expression of humour. The "serious" novel, however competently done, which lacks this detached approach to a drama of the emotions will not endure.

The *Droll Stories* compact both aspects of the approach humorous; outright comedy and dramatic intensity. That balance is maintained throughout the whole book, and for that reason it is an inexhaustible treasure-trove of entertainment.

It is preferable to leave this tribute to Balzac at the *Droll Stories*. No single essay could encompass the achievement of his great novels alone, even by discarding the greater mass of his work thrown off recklessly and indiscriminately till he found the form and outlook he was looking for. It may be a praiseworthy industry to labour through all those early experimental works, or even those blatantly turned out under the heading of potboilers, but I have never attempted to do so. I stop at *The Bachelor's Establishment, Eugenie Grandet, Cousin Pons, Old Goriot,* and some of the lesser tales, such as *The Ass's Skin*, for a frequent re-reading. And this, I don't doubt, is what all genuine Balzacians do, leaving his other literary lumber to the academics.

Attention to the *Droll Stories* is stressed in this essay because they are the last great contribution to bawdy in literature — bawdy in the Elizabethan key of gusto. If any earnest academic intrudes the names of James Joyce here, he is promptly consigned to the people's limbo of the pornographic. There is no place for Joyce in the gay Olympus of bawdy, which is generated by delight in the spectacle of life expressed in terms of wit, lyricism and humour, Joyce is the product of a puritanic Catholic hell. One has only to read his *Portrait of the Artist as a Young Man* to see starkly exposed the sin-haunted terror of its flames excited by the pulpit rantings of a hedge priest.

Another essential to bawdy is that it must exalt the feminine image; it must love women. A strange ordinance, no doubt, in this era of the eternal war between the sexes, when in modern literature one would say that its most dominant attitude to women is one of dislike, even hate. Yet, if fantasy cannot retain its image of desire for women as that is reflected in art, the very source of vitality in life is vitiated.

I hesitate to include the stories of de Maupassant under the heading of bawdy. There is no facet of human behaviour, sexual or otherwise, that he does not handle with inimitable artistry. He has humour, and women fascinate him, but his approach to love for them is rather clinical than lyrical. On the other hand, though Chevalier is not of the full stature of Balzac or de Maupassant, his *Clochemerle* must be accounted a superb contribution to the high spirit of bawdy. It will endure, that work, when those of Proust and Gide have floundered back into the Freudian morass from which they emerged.

I refrain here from evidence that the spirit of bawdy is alive in the best poetry produced in this country. It is a depressing business affirming the high quality of that poetry to a generation which does not read it. Or reads so little of it that the poets themselves must take journeyman jobs to earn a living. A later generation, we trust, will have the wit to discover what the dull dogs of today are missing in the gift of major poetry to this country. And possibly that generation may be given a prose avatar in the delicate art of bawdy.

The Mask of Robert Browning

No man setting out on the adventure of art can be sure what his objective is till he has attained it. If he sets out on the wrong foot, he will very soon be aware of it. If he is not sure of what he wants, he will have no doubt of what he does not want. If he has a resolute and individual outlook on life, he will find the conventionalised art movement he has arrived in of no use to him. That, in Browning's youth, was the tail-end of an impetus given to poetry by Byron, Shelley, Wordsworth, Coleridge and Keats, and its idiom had become stale by repetition. Those poets had been evaluated and their place in the tradition of English poetry established. To break away from their stylisms and their used up subject-matter was the problem that faced Robert Browning . . .

Like all first essays in the use of a medium, Browning's were derived from the shop-worn idiom of the preceding generation. *Pauline* stems from the two poets he admired most, Byron and Shelley, and is poor stuff, as Browning was well aware. Anything Browning wrote at that period of immaturity must

From *Southerly* No.4, Sydney, 1959

have been poor stuff. Only a sophisticated experience of life could give him both the material and the key to its expression he needed.

Wisely, he set out to acquire that by travel and by mixing at large with all types of people. His itinerary covered Russia, Germany, Italy, the Low Countries and a sea-voyage, and he returned from it to try another bout with poetry. This was his *Paracelsus.* So far as it sought to deal in psychological portraiture, it was on the right track, but its smooth versification lacked the vigorous, spoken word idiom he needed to vitalise its problem of character-creation. Though it was hailed as a work of "unequivocal power" by that critical pundit Foster, and it introduced Browning to the intellectuals of the day as a poet to be taken seriously, it left him restless and dissatisfied. His poetry was still hobbled by conventional shackles, and by an act of desperation he sought to free himself from them. In short, he wrote *Sordello.*

Instead of escaping from his shackles, it now seemed that Browning had encumbered himself with them to the paralysis of any movement at all. The critics who denounced that work as a deliberate piece of obscurantism were only wrong in the motive which drove Browning to perpetrate it. Even his circle of admirers refused to swallow it. No mental gullet could have gulped down that craggy, indigestible mass of involuted parentheses. Browning himself got muddled in trying to elucidate some of its most entangled passages. His prose explanations of them are rather more obscure than the text itself. But, for Browning, it had achieved its objective. There was no going back to what in later life he described as "scented poetry". As an exercise in character-creation, it had the germs of that vital idiom he used later in his magnificent dramatic monologues. There is no need to take it seriously in estimating the great qualities of Browning's poetry. An essential preliminary exercise in a difficult métier, and nothing more. But by throwing that literary brickbat at the public's head he brought down on himself a denunciation for obscurantism which lasted for fifty years . . .

I think that the long endurance-test Browning had to face in waiting for any sentient response to his poetry is the only way we can account for his abundant good health, the easy conditions of his life, and its apparent freedom from all emotional stress and conflict. The gods are not given to awarding their poets in such gracious terms. The lash is their usual implement for stimulating an imagery in poetry inspired by a conflict between the damnable and the desirable in life. In the action of life, Browning seemed to have escaped most of the normally damnable as a personal experience. Moreover, he lived through a period which was singularly free from war, cataclysm, and the eternal threat and suspense which have been the common content of life since the 1914 world war.

Did that compensate him for the way his poetry was constantly attacked, or (what was more depressing) ignored? And, finally, for which he got no return in money till he was beyond any particular need for it? Only a very strong spirit can go on doing its work under such a vicious or stagnant response to it, and with a stoical refusal to voice the anger and disgust which it must have inspired. That superb equanimity was one of the concessions allowed Browning by the parsimonious gods. Or else it was the defence by which Browning defeated their malice. If there are readers of Browning still duped by the equitable mask he presented to the world, let them go to "Childe Roland to the Dark Tower Came" to discover what was going on behind it.

Browning's mask! No man who took so large a place in the life of his era, and who was — or appeared to be — so frank and open in his exchanges with others, had such an impenetrable mask. A subtle mask, which hid all privacies behind a pretence of having no privacies to hide. Most subtle in Browning's chosen pose of the average man of affairs who had no use for the esoteric refinements of thought and preferred to pitch exchanges to the level of dinner-table small-talk — a device which lured that fat clown Chesterton into labelling Browning "the man in the street". To be sure, by that device Browning also lured the furtive human ego out from cover, assured that there was no danger of detection from this hearty, friendly gentleman, who had the art of inspiring those confidential relations from which Browning derived so much material for his poetry.

In the end, a confusion between the mask and the man behind it did develop in Browning an almost morbid dislike for any intrusion on either the privacy of his thoughts or his life. His refusal to discuss his poetry, the seeming tolerance which endorsed any drivel written about it, and (most of all) his rejection of any pose as a poet, which made the sour Lockhart say that he liked Browning because there was nothing of your damned literary man about him, were only other facets of that passion for privacy which made Browning burn every letter or scrap of paper which might have contained some hint of his private life. Even the letters he wrote to women he was intimate with were written under proviso that they be burnt when read.

Does a man make such a fuss about hiding his private life unless he has one to hide? And, in that prurient and prudish age, what privacies could he have had other than affairs with women? Quite apart from Browning's dislike for baring his heart to a public he had a contempt for, we must go to another of his major obsessions to account for this determined effort to smother up any revelation that might have disparaged it. This was his desire to leave behind him the legend of a perfect love-marriage.

A great deal of sickening sentiment has been written about that marriage. It was entirely the wrong sort of marriage for a poet so engrossed with femininity as Browning. I can't think what the compulsions of his destiny were about to let it happen. It put such a blight on Browning that for over five years he never wrote a line of poetry. He had been going strong up to his marriage. With it, inspiration dried up in him. The isolated life which Elizabeth B. B's invalidism forced on him cut him off from the bustling activity of social affairs from which he drew so much material for his poetry. He was not allowed out at night and his days were devoted to male-nursing Elizabeth. He was cut off from his men friends with whom he could enliven his mind by the exchange of ideas. They might have disturbed Elizabeth. Moreover, she had the arrogance to dictate to Browning on the themes he selected for his poetry. He put aside that of *The Ring and the Book* because she objected to its motif of murder. He had to wait till she was dead to write it, as well as *Mr Sludge, "The Medium"*, which would have offended her fatuous belief in faked spiritoidal phenomena. He never would have written *Fifine at the Fair* while she was alive. A prunes-and-prism prude, she must have had a corrupting effect on a free sex imagery in Browning's poetry.

In short, she kept Browning slavishly to heel by the device of self-imposed invalidism which had kept her own family in sycophantic attendance on her and exalted her as a chosen Sultana in the domestic harem of that incestuous old Sultanic parent, Edward Moulton Barrett of Wimpole Street. Having no physical attractions to compete with other women in the battle of sex, and being endowed with a precocious facility for scribbling verse, she early discovered that, in her invalidism, which created an illusion of mystery about herself, in the publicity of her poetry and the exclusive privacy of her life, she had a perfect system for gratifying her feminine vanity by imposing all responsibility for its needs and aspirations on others. Her resistance to Browning's activity in detaching her from that fusty, dusty, close-smelling seclusion was not dictated, as she protested, by the fear of imposing an obstruction on his life but by the fear that he might disrupt the satisfactory nature of her own.

On that score, her practised art of invalidism might have reassured her. Browning was the perfect instrument to be practised on. It is a psychological commonplace that very robust men are attracted to invalid women. The masculine imperative has no defence against the insidious compulsion imposed by feeble, sickly and very often infantile femininity. The robustness of the husband constitutes his abject subjection to the invalidism of the wife. It commands that he pet and protect her and submit to all her whims and caprices, as if she were some rare and exotic creature, instead of the purely selfish and self-engrossed egotist that she is.

Browning's case as the subjective husband to the invalid wife is complicated by its disruptive effect on his poetry. How far he was the dupe of the adulation he lavished on Elizabeth's verses it is hard to say. It was the sort of poetry he particularly disliked; the conventionalised product of his era which his own poetry was in revolt against. Moreover, he had to endure the ordeal of hearing it eulogised by the critical imbecility of the time as being equal to the poetry of Shakespeare, while his own poetry was subjected to scurrilous abuse. One effect of this situation is apparent enough. He became so sickened with the profession of poet that he ceased to practise it, and turned to music and sculpture for some release for the ferment of irritation going on within him. Not that he was likely to show anything of that, or possibly admit it to himself. So complex are those inner conflicts between what Yeats calls the True Mask and the False Mask in those who are endowed with the creative faculty that the creator himself is the most confused about which mask he is wearing in the action of work. All we can do, as spectators looking on from without, is to try to divine from the subject's actions which particular mask inspired them. And from those it becomes pretty clear that there was a great deal of False Mask in Browning's efforts to maintain the legend of a perfect love-match in his marriage with Elizabeth.

By the time she had managed to bear a son, after a couple of abortive pregnancies, it is clear enough that Browning's posture as the subjective husband was wearing a bit thin. After five years of it, he had managed to escape from the cloistered seclusion it had imposed on him into the brisk bustle of a social life, with its colour, vivacity and conflict of personalities so essential as a spectacle from which the material of art can be drawn. And by it he got back to poetry again. It was now Elizabeth who stayed at home, nursing her infant and her invalidism, while Browning was abroad, chasing diversion in the rather hectic social gatherings of expatriate society in the Rome and Florence of his era, from which he rarely got back before three o'clock in the morning. Not that he did not always maintain towards Elizabeth the graces of a devoted husband.

And those were genuine enough. He was extremely fond of her. But fondness of that sort does not imply any strict observance of the marriage pact. Certainly not with a man as physically vigorous as Browning, and one so fascinated with the world of femininity, and who was himself so fascinating to women. Did not Elizabeth herself say peevishly that it was indecent the way women chased Browning?

The biographers of Browning are an exceedingly futile lot. I have more than a dozen works dealing with his life and poetry on my shelves, and not one of them worth reading. They have nothing to reveal about the off-stage part of Browning's life — or, if they had, they are such congenital liars that they would not reveal it if it touched, even dimly, on the code of respectability maintained by suburban gentility. Browning, in his poetry, covers the whole gamut of human passion, and to assume that he acquired this profound knowledge of life by living the life of a respectable grocer is to degrade the whole adventure of life and art. A man who knew so intimately the relations of men and women, in all the complexities of sex-conflict, drew that knowledge from personal experience, and that experience is largely gained in the most impressionable years of life, from puberty into the twenties, when youth is at its most vital and its curiosity over the adventure of sex unappeasable.

What little we know of those early years of Browning's life makes evident that he went through the normal procedure of a youth avid for all the experience he could extract from it. The picture we have of him is that of a handsome, black-haired vivacious fellow, self-assured and at ease in any society, and a bit of a dandy. He danced, rode, fenced, and boxed well. His special intimates, the Silverthorne cousins, are described as wild youths. Other intimates, Alfred Domett and Joseph Arnould, were intellectuals who aspired to literature. They both wrote poetry. With others, they formed a club called The Colloquials, which met weekly and dined at a hotel. They frequented the theatres and dance halls, and strolling home to

Camberwell at night they often visited the gipsy encampments, where no doubt Browning first got an armful of some Fifine. He also attended lectures at Guy's Hospital, which made him free of the medical student mentality, always a rowdy and ribald product. By the time he had completed the grand tour of the Continent, Browning must have acquired a fair assortment of casual love affairs — for, however slight those may be, they are the substance of which the image of femininity is created in art.

It is only the legend of that damned idyllic love-marriage that obscures our understanding of Browning's virile masculinity, which needed something more vital to satisfy it than Elizabeth's unfeebled, undeveloped body. Sex could have played very little part in that unequal union. With the arrival of her infant, any exchanges of that sort must have ceased between them. I imagine Elizabeth herself to put an end to them. Any sort of emotional or physical stress was beyond her endurance.

And, in any case, Elizabeth was about the last type of woman to inspire sexual desire in Browning. He was one of those lucky men endowed with a taste for strongly flavoured femininity. In reference to some Abyssinian girls he saw at an Exposition, he wrote to Isa Blagden: "You know my rotten cheese taste in women." Brown Dolores, squatting outside the convent tank and steeping in it her tresses, "blue-black, lustrous, thick like horsehairs", was much more to his taste physically than poor little Elizabeth with her hand like a bird's claw. No doubt he did get from Elizabeth the sort of feminine outlook on masculinity, which he expressed in "Any Wife to Any Husband" and in "James Lee's Wife", and in those poems, it is well to note, it is the husband who goes off the marital rails and has affairs with other women. Since Browning expressly tells us, if we want to know anything about him personally, to search his poetry for it, we may take "Any Wife to Any Husband" as definitely autobiographical.

Poems sprang from a mood — a detached memory-image, or

from some event which suggests the subject of a poem. A poet such as Browning, whose material was Man and Woman, was in himself all men and all women. Investigation of his poetry can't pin down self-revelation in him to any particular poem, since the whole mass of his poetry is self-revelatory. Autobiographically, he may be the tenderly reminiscent husband of "By the Fireside", the remorseful husband of "Any Wife to Any Husband", the husband who claims his right to possess all women, from Helen of Troy to a gutter drag in *Fifine at the Fair*, or the husband of "Dis Aliter Visum" who is jeered at by the mature woman who had shyly offered herself to him as a young girl and been rejected; a theme of regret for a lost opportunity over which we all maunder in our latter years.

The sentimentalists who have searched Browning's poetry for any autobiographical revelation have picked on only such instances as may be applied to the legend of an idyllic marriage with Elizabeth, befuddled by the illusion that there was only one love affair in Browning's life, and that, in all other relations with women, he deported himself like a respectable suburbanite. No doubt Browning was largely responsible for this fatuous assumption, which his generation's universal furtiveness over anything relating to sex allowed him to try to impose on posterity. His eternal preoccupation over that imposition made him command that any intimate letters he wrote to women should be burned. It was a condition he imposed at the outset of any exchange of letters, which the ladies in question mendaciously endorsed but had the wit to ignore. Browning burned their letters to him, while they preserved his to them. Thus we had to thank Isa Blagden for the only intimate and off-guard letters that Browning wrote. Naturally, they do not establish what his sex relations with her may have been; no letters from a man to a woman ever do. If there is such a relation, it is understood between them; if there is none, there is no call to affirm it.

Isa was a lively little lady who wrote very mediocre novels, which gave Browning considerable trouble to dispose of with the publishers. They also inflicted on him reticence over their manifest shortcomings. His intimacy with Isa dated from early days in Italy, and the letters were exchanged between them when Browning returned to England. They arranged to write one a month, on the sworn condition imposed by Browning that she destroy his letters. He destroyed hers, which is a great pity, for they would have thrown a much needed light on Browning's social relations with others, as revealed by gossip. His letters in return include that pleasing ingredient, as well as some light sauce of ribaldry, instanced by the smoking-room story he tells, as whispered to him by a lady at a dinner party. A husband returns home after an absence to find that his wife has been having an affair with their pastor. On the husband demanding how many times adultery had been committed, the wife coyly confesses that, before indulging, they always read a chapter of the Bible and turned down the leaf. On the Bible being consulted, it is found to be dog-eared from Genesis to Revelations. Apart from such lighter exchanges, Browning airs some caustic comments on contemporary poetry, notably that of Rossetti; a thing he never allowed himself to do elsewhere. They are the only frank letters Browning wrote, and for that reason the best written letters. In all other letters that touch on self-revelation, he is so much on guard against letting out anything relating to his private life that some passages are rather more obscure than contestable passages in his poetry. This is very much the case in his letters to Julia Wedgewood, when he did have a very valid reason for smothering up his private relations with her.

Mrs Browning was three years dead. Browning had settled in London and was a prominent figure in society when he met Julia Wedgewood. Within a few weeks of meeting him she made a direct overture towards intimate relations with him. "A woman who has taken the initiative in a friendship with a man, as I have done with you, has either lost all right feeling or has come to a very definite decision on the issue of all such friendships . . . I prefer the scorn which falls on those who say too much to the price which may have to be paid by those who say too little."

That is definite enough, and it catches Browning, who

replies to it with a warm emotion, mitigated by precaution against saying too much himself at such an early stage of the affair. In his letters, as often in his poetry, Browning generally piles up half a page of parenthesis before getting to the point of what he is saying. He commits one indiscretion only. Julia has recently lost a brother; Browning has recently lost a wife. Referring to a friendship between himself and Julia, he says "I dare believe that you and I shall recover what we have lost." What else could Julia assume from that but that she might become the second Mrs Browning? There is no understanding Julia's later behaviour unless this objective is accepted as the driving urge behind her intimacy with Browning.

That intimacy is at once pitched up to a state of lyrical ardour. There is almost a daily exchange of letters between them, with frequent afternoon tea visits by Browning to the Wedgewood home. To ensure the decorum of those visits, Julia shows Browning's first discreet letter, addressed to "My dear friend", to her mother. The later "Dearest Friend" letters are not shown to Mama. Within a month of their first meeting, there can be no question that their intimacy has arrived at that "definite decision" hinted at in Julia's first overture to it. Writing to Browning from the country house where she had spent many of her early years, she is astonished to find that all the regrets and frustrations of those years have ceased to be. "Are they really gone? Will they not return? Surely I think they must — but meantime what a strange wonder, what a foretaste of immortality to feel oneself without them . . . I look round at the shrubs and the distant hills as if I should find some change in *them*, that I had ceased to feel 'Oh Earth, release me'."

A woman does not write in that dithyrambic style to a man over a mere intellectual intimacy begotten over the afternoon tea cups. Browning replies that her absence has made a hole in his life. His letters, while assuring her of his enduring affection, are careful to insist that it must remain a clandestine affair between them. He writes: "You know the difficulties will begin soon enough: my visits will seem importunate — be remarked on, the usual course of things must be looked to.

And then, you yourself, let me speak plainly — keep you in mind, for justice sake, what my claims are — arising from your own free gift."

Julia retorts that it is all very well for him — he is not surrounded by a horde of prying, suspicious relatives. Besides, his grey hairs would reprieve him from insinuations of loose conduct which her youth would not exempt her from. She adds to that: "You see, I will not let you escape from the contrast of my exultant youth. Ah, I wish I was young. But at least, I am a great deal younger than you . . ."

The graces of coquetry were not in Julia. To keep her shares up, she constantly twits Browning about his age. Annoyed at the assumption that he has any intention of competing amorously with her exultant youth (Julia was thirty to his fifty-two) he writes "Palm-wine is not proof-spirit, of which I am not without experience of certain thimblefulls. Ah, the *Vivandières* will press *le petit verre* on us old grey *moustaches*, for 'love', if we flaunt a *chevron* or two, and have arms presented to us by the sentinels."

In precise terms: "A man of my distinction has no difficulty in picking up casual love affairs, as I know by experience." There is no need to go on adducing more evidence that this was a full-length love affair, though greatly cramped by the stringent ordinances of social decorum under which it had to take over. The letters soon drop any reference to the emotional side of their intimacy, which remains at the terms insisted on by Browning, and Julia is forced to realise that he has no intention of offering her marriage. An occasional hint of the terms under which the affair was maintained escapes from Julia, as in the instance where she puts off a visit from him because "the house is full of young cousins running in and out, and it is well to be cautious".

The situation may have suited Browning well enough, but it was putting a considerable strain on Julia, and a study of her photograph suggests that the element of stress in the affair was not altogether due to keeping up appearances. She has no good looks. Her forehead is bumpy and her brows jut beyond the bridge of her short, cocked-up nose, while her mouth is large and coarsely shaped and the lips slightly relaxed. Julia may have been a highly intellectualised product of her generation but her face is that of a peasant hoyden. Good looks are not essential to sex-appeal, and one would say that Julia was a good deal troubled by that dynamic. Aesthetically, Browning adored beauty in women; but physically he liked a coarse, strong element of sex in them, as he frankly confessed to Isa Blagden.

There was another disruptive facet in their intimate relations; Julia was deaf. For small-talk over the afternoon tea tray, Browning's resonant tones may have competed with that disability in Julia, but they were hardly suitable for the keyed-down conspiracies of a clandestine love affair, even if Julia's old mother was out of the house and the drawing-room door shut against intrusion by servants. With all that, she had to endure the incessant naggings of her wretched relatives over the nature of her intimacy with Browning. That was inevitable, as Browning himself had forecast. In the end, Julia's nerves cracked, and she wrote suddenly to Browning that his visits to her must cease and there must be no future relations between them . . .

Browning is not greatly perturbed at his dismissal. "I thought from the beginning it was too good to last," he says, but suggests that the sudden termination of their intimacy after a year of more or less constantly seeing each other will be rather apt to set tongues wagging. "That will not cure the evil, whatever it is. Two people who suddenly unclasp arms and start off in opposite directions looks terribly intimate. But you know the circumstances . . ."

The circumstances are not disclosed and Browning does not press for them. He was at work on *The Ring and the Book*, which was much more engrossing than a pleasing enough love affair. It took him three years to finish, and the first book was in the hands of the printer when he finds himself involved again with the Wedgewood family by a note from old Mrs Wedgewood inviting him to dine. In return, Browning writes Julia a formal note, addressed to Miss Wedgewood, saying he can't accept the invitation as it would put him in a silly position after her dismissal, and requesting her to make what excuse she pleases to her mother over his inability to accept her invitation. He adds that he has finished the long poem he had begun during their intimacy and, since he had promised her then that she would be its first reader, he will shortly send her a copy.

Julia snatches at this opportunity to begin another correspondence with him, and its only interest to us, psychologically, is its revelation of the simmering condition of belittled self-esteem which Julia has been enduring over her affair with Browning. She had offered herself to him and Browning had accepted her, but on his own terms. She was a conceited woman, given some standing as an intellectual by articles and reviews in the literary journals of the time. She was a woman of wealth and social position among the higher middle-class families. Once she had arrived at a final intimacy with Browning, she doubtless assumed that he would regularise it by marriage. All that happened was that she had got herself into a complicated situation which invited scandalous inferences and her family's antagonism to the ambiguous nature of her relations with Browning. Under her boring pretences to being a cultured intellectual, she was a vulgar woman, as her face attests, and *The Ring and the Book* gave her a fine opportunity of venting the spite she felt for Browning by attacking it. It is altogether a vile work, grovelling in the mud of all that is most evil in the human soul, with only one redeeming figure in it, the martyred Pompilia, whom she likens to "a snowdrop growing out of a dunghill". She writes pages to express her abhorrence of the work and the exposure it makes of Browning's morbid preference for the horrible and brutal in life rather than for all that is pure and beautiful.

Browning accepts all this abuse of himself and his work with a tolerance that must have exasperated her. It is quite true, he admits, that he finds evil a much more engrossing study than what may be good in the human ego, and thanks her for noting that the printer had misprinted a passage, which he had overlooked. With the next letter she is at him again over the poem, and yet again after he has answered that tirade, till

Browning has had enough of it and rejects further controversy over the poem by asking her point blank why she had suddenly cut off relations with him without explaining why.

That demand flusters Julia. She can't accuse Browning of compromising her by those relations, because she has expressly invited them. She can't say that only marriage would have regulated them under her code of middle-class social decorum. The only excuse she can pump up is that "some refracted words of yours made it possible for me to do what I did".

Browning retorts indignantly that he does not know what she means by "refracted words". If her name had chanced to come up in conversation with others, all he had ever done was to express his esteem for her. He dismisses her accusation by remarking that gossip of some sort was inevitable over their affair, and adds a postscript to say that he is off to the Continent and letters will not be posted after him; a sufficient hint that he does not want any more letters from her. She tails up the affair with one which is not answered . . .

Since her letters have been preserved along with his, it can only be assumed that Browning posted them back to her; another definite finality to any more exchanges between them. She survived until 1913, and the letters were not published until 1937, so that earlier biographers were debarred from this documentary evidence of Browning's method of conducting a casual love affair; of which, he assures Julia, he has had considerable experience. The letters are of value for two reasons. One is that they contain Browning's analysis of the Franceschini murder-trial as subject matter for *The Ring and the Book*, and the other is that they demolish sentimental drivel about his remaining austerely faithful to the pact of an idyllic marriage with Elizabeth.

His later mix-up with Lady Ashburton can't be classed as a love affair, though no doubt he was strongly attracted by her. She was a lovely woman, judging by Landseer's portrait of her and by many contemporary tributes to her beauty, her richly modulated voice and her superb figure. She was an aristocrat, a rich widow and a dominant figure in society. Browning did go so far as to propose marriage to her, and the indiscretion which exploded any possibility of it was his explanation to another woman that his main reason for taking a rich wife was that it would be of service to the advancement of his son Pen, then at Oxford. In a letter to the same lady, he confesses to having been frank enough on the same score to Lady Ashburton. What she may have taken from Browning in private very naturally infuriated her when made the subject of public gossip, and she wrote a couple of vitriolic letters to Browning which abolished all further relations with him.

The whole episode is so puzzling in its evidence that Browning did apparently hint to Lady Ashburton that her fortune was a major inducement to marriage with her, and this is so far out of key with his knowledge of feminine psychology, that one wonders how he could have had the indiscretion to do it. My own opinion, for what it is worth, is that, when it came to the point of marriage with such a formidable lady, Browning's courage, as well as his discretion, funked the issue, and therefore he gave her a valid excuse for rejecting him.

Added to that was the reflection that marriage at that date with a lady of fortune would rather tarnish the lyrical legend of his love-marriage with Elizabeth. Also, he was a man of sixty and Lady Ashburton was at the best of her early maturity. And, if Browning's own portrait of her is a valid one, she was a dangerous lady for a man of sixty to take a risk with. It indicates that Browning's resentment against her was balanced by the strong sexual attraction she still had for him:

What bade you come, brisk-marching bold she-shape,
  A terror with those black-balled worlds of eyes,
That black hair bristling solid-built from nape
  To crown it coils about . . .

My queenly impudence, I cover close,
  I wrap me round with love of your black hair,
Black eyes, black every wicked inch of those
  Limbs war-tower tallness . . .

There again we have the image of the sort of women who physically attracted Browning; the sort of women in a lower social stratum it was so easy to pick up for a casual embrace in the Italy of his day, with its complete amorality to any interdictions against casual copulation. The Italy of Browning's day was no different to that of Byron's, and Byron's journal gives us some delightful sketches of the girls he had affairs with. No particular stress need be placed on that aspect of the little comedy of love, which may go no further than a kiss or a hug in passing, but it is an essential content of the life of any poet, painter or musician who made man and woman the major theme of his art.

And it is especially essential in Browning's case to know something about his extra-marital love affairs, because the legend that he led a celibate existence prior to, during, and after the cessation of his married life has done a great deal of harm to his reputation as a poet. Great poetry is not given to poets who regulate their sex lives to the ordinances of English middle-class conduct and morals. If Tennyson is brought forward as an instance of one who did live such a sexually drab existence, the answer is that he was not a great poet. A great artificer in the technique of poetry, if you will, but of men and women, and the whole drama of human passion, he knew nothing.

Browning's "respectability", to use the term in its debased sense, has helped to engender the assumption that his poetry was infected with Victorian prudery in any relation to sex, whereas his is the only poetry of that era free from such a taint. There is one instance only where he made a concession to its universal moral cowardice when faced with the conscience-problem of integrity to reality, and that was in his presentation of Pompilia in *The Ring and the Book*. The concession there is to the word *"Purity"*, which needs both italics and the capital letter to emphasise the devastating effect it had on all Victorian art, wherever that touched on any psychological revelation of the feminine ego.

It was used as a bludgeon to trounce any hint that women, and especially girls, were not sexually anaemic creatures devitalised of all sensory responses to the prime function of their being. Browning's Pompilia is a product of the popular fiction of the day, which ordained that its heroine must be "pure" and that she must suffer unjustly. The real Pompilia of the Franceschini murder case had plenty of suffering inflicted on her, but she was not the pallid dummy of Browning's poetry, which rejects the documentary evidence that she was a vital warm-blooded girl, determined to escape with a lover from the husband she detested. Caponsacchi and Pompilia were unquestionably lovers. They exchanged love letters; the driver of the carriage in which they eloped saw them clasped together, face pressed to face. At the inn where they stopped, they spent the night in the same bedroom. When Franceschini arrived hot in pursuit of them, Pompilia snatched up a sword and rushed at him, "calling him a traitor and a tyrant, and threatened his life" and so drove him from the inn.

How much better *The Ring and the Book* would have been if Browning had made Pompilia a real girl, instead of the mushy product of popular melodrama! Where there is not a strong passion for life, there can't be much significance in a death.

There is another aspect of Browning's concept of life, defined in his poetry, which has drawn to it an extremely obnoxious type of reader: those who have sought to extract from it an invidious content which they choose to label his "message", implying thereby that its major objective is the scavenger's job of saving their miserable souls.

At the core of all Browning's thought lies the conviction that the image of desire is a greater reality than the actuality from which it is drawn, since the image is an indestructible content of the mind while the actuality is a shadowgraph passing into non-existence in the event of its happening. All expectations of happiness exceed their realisation; all aspirations of achievement fall short of their attainment. The image of desire is insatiable but its rewards are swiftly satiated. The spirit eternally dances ahead of the flesh, which toils in pursuit of it, doomed to frustration.

All those pessimistic outcries denouncing the flesh for its inability to satisfy desire are based on the acceptance of its image as a basely inspired fantasy, treacherously luring the flesh on to a quest destined to be defeated. They come mainly from the East, whence all evils of the spirit which have infected the West are generated. Browning's concept of the image of desire as the only enduring reality utterly repudiates them. What has been fatuously labelled his optimism is, in effect, an outlook commonly accepted as pessimistic, since it accepts the frustrations of the flesh as a first essential to the aspirations of the spirit. Without its eternal quest for happiness, life would offer no adventure worth having. That quest alone is its objective, for out of it are born a full experience of life and a completed content of the ego. The image of desire is perfected because of its unattainment in the flesh, and since its image is indestructible, concreted in the very substance of the mind, it is therefore attainable elsewhere.

At "elsewhere", Browning's concept of the mind's eternal continuity in time and space stops short. He will have nothing to do with all puerile concepts of that continuity devised by religious and occult fantasy-mongering. He uses its anthropomorphic vocable of God because there is no other save God which may infer a controlled cosmic principle underlying the creation of life. In spite of its obnoxious association with priestcraft and mankind's lunatic asylum of religious hatreds, it is simpler to use God as a cosmic symbol than to bedevil thought with cosmic metaphysics or scientific polemics of the indestructability of force and matter. If first-hand evidence is necessary that Browning did not use it in any relation to man's anthropomorphic deities, it is his answer to a point-blank demand by a journalist named Buchanan as to whether he was a Christian Browning shouted an infuriated "No!" at him.

The various gods scattered about Browning's poetry make a joke of the assumption that he gave any credence to the multifarious gods of religious dogma. The innocuous god of Pippa (responsible for the stigma of "optimism"), the malignant god of Caliban, the impersonally detached god of Karshish, the pagan god of the Bishop, ordering his tomb, the polemically astute god of Bishop Blougram, are facets of the personalities they have to do with. The theological mentality fascinated Browning. He was able to extract vast entertainment out of its exercises in logistic acrobatics based on premises of pure imbecility. To his psychological profundity he adjoined the gift of a satanic faculty for forensic analysis.

Half the inspiration that drew him to study the Franceschini murder was the material it gave him to present the case from all angles, speaking in the voice of each character involved in it, from the Pope himself down to the man in the street. That work culminated his greatest achievements in poetry, the dramatic monologues. It was a form he created and in which he reached Shakespearian stature. He failed as a dramatist; he failed in dramatic narrative, as in *Red Cotton Night-cap Country,* but wherever a character of his takes the stage in the first-person singular he created a masterpiece. Long before Yeats pronounced his dictum that the idiom of poetry should use words in the order in which they are spoken, Browning had exploited it in his dramatic monologues.

The facility with which he adjusted the spoken idiom to the character speaking is one of the greatest feats in character-creation. In the compact space of the fifty-six lines of "My Last Duchess", he draws a full-length portrait of a Reinaissance duke. Changing his idiom to the long, rambling, distracted monologue of *Mr Sludge, "The Medium",* he plays on every variation of intonation of that exposed imposter; cringing, obsequious, whining, persuasive, belligerent, down to that sudden, terrified outcry:

> Had I seen, perhaps, what hand was holding mine,
> Leading me whither, I had died of fright . . .

in which Browning, by the way, gives credence to occult forces duping the impostor who makes a pretence of controlling them to dupe others.

In any great creative achievement, its inspired content is rather less than half its mass, which is otherwise made up of exercises in its special métier. The exercises are essential as the generative source of inspiration, but in themselves they may have little virtue. It is no tribute to a creator to make a conscience-problem of accepting with equal reverence the uninspired content of his work.

This is especially the case with Browning, who lived so long and did so much work. The test of its values is in those which excite an impassioned interest and in those which fail to sustain it. For me, its richest rewards are the *Lyrics,* the *Men and Women,* the dramatic monologues, which include *The Ring and the Book,* and *Fifine at the Fair.* Most of the rest I pass, and I daresay that the accusation of obscurity in his poetry has a good deal to do with that portion which we find unreadable. We may say that all poetry which transforms factuality to its imagery is obscure unless we bring a sustained interest to it. Where Browning's poetry reveals the profundity of his thought, it is never obscure. In those two little verses "Love in a Life", he has packed his whole concept of the image of desire as the supreme reality, and not its quest in actuality:

Room after room,
I hunt the house through
We inhabit together.
Heart, fear nothing, for, heart, thou shalt find her,
Next time, herself! not the trouble behind her
Left in the curtain, the couch's perfume!
As she brushed it, the cornice-wreath blossomed anew:
Yon looking-glass gleamed at the wave of her feather.

Yet the day wears,
And door succeeds door;
I try the fresh fortune —
Range the wide house from the wing to the centre.
Still the same chance! she goes out as I enter.
Spend my whole day in the quest, — who cares?
But 'tis twilight, you see — with such suites to explore,
Such closets to search, such alcoves to importune!

The theme is carried over to "Life in a Love", with its delighted cry of

Escape me?
Never —
Beloved!

and its tolerant acceptance of present frustration with "So the chase takes up one's life, that's all."

Very often, in many of Browning's poems, the artistry which evokes an emotion in the reader has been labelled obscurity. That is to confuse the lucidity of prose with the emotional idiom of poetry, whose highest function is to startle the mind out of its inertia by the mystery and profundity of life and the intensity of human drama and passion.

Three poets only have covered the whole gamut of human passion — Homer, Shakespeare and Browning — and each in turn has enlarged on its psychological profundities inspired by his forerunner. Each has sought an answer to that enigma which was the driving impetus of Greek civilisation. All its art, its thought, its restless questings into the unknown, demanded an answer to one question: "What is Man, and why is he the creature of those eternal dualities of love and hate, exultation and despair, desire and disgust, terror and delight, baseness and nobility, craven fear and heroic courage?"

It took seven hundred years for Homer's concept of man to become an integral content of mass-consciousness, and to engender its effect in the great Greek dramatists. That mass-consciousness, slowly penetrating the European peoples in contact with it, was given its next great answer to the enigma of Man in the dramas of Shakespeare. It has taken three hundred years for Shakespeare's concept of man to penetrate the mass-consciousness of today. On the basis of such time-factors, we may assume that it will take another hundred years or more for Browning's thought and his concept of man to penetrate the inertia of the mass-mind.

No one knew better than Browning the slow progression of consciousness eternally opposed by that inertia. It explains his whole mask — his indifference to all the imbecilities written about his poetry.

In every great creator's lifetime there are the few, the very few, who respond at once to his profundity. Perception is the other half of creation. Without it, creation would function in a vacuum. If there is any response to it from the mass-mentality, it is one of suspicion, resentment, or outright antagonism.

It pleases me to account myself Browning's fool who anticipates. After all, I was born in his era, being ten years old when he died, and I was wearing an edition of his lyrics in my pocket in my early teens, as part of my daily garniture. A fool one must be, to treasure the illusion of another Renaissance in the arts; but, without that illusion, effort would perish. Affirming that illusion, I affirm that Browning will be the great "Next Poet" he disdained any claim to being in his own lifetime.

The Art of the Profile

I would like, if I could, to put an accent on profiles quite apart from their literary qualities. It has to do with those two questions posited by the Greeks, on which we may claim that the whole Greek civilisation was built. *What is man, and why is he the creature he appears to be?*

To the first question, there can be no answer; it is one in part with the enigma of life itself. But from the Olympian heights of a Homer or a Shakespeare down to the murk of the Freudian dialectic, all creative thought has sought to find an answer to the second. It may take many forms and wander into obscure byways, that eternal query, but its restless quest is never sated. By what man does it seeks to find some solution to the compulsions of his being, but what man does may have very little relation to what he is.

In this era of newspaper publicity, when all notable or notorious individuals having to do with world affairs are constantly headlined in the world's press, the public is under

.An extract from Norman Lindsay's preface to *Australians: Nine Profiles* by John Hetherington, F.W. Cheshire, Melbourne, 1960 an illusion that it knows a great deal about them. Any man in the street will tell you off hand what this or that national figure is doing, intends to do, and what sort of a fellow he is. In reality, he knows nothing whatever about him. He does not know whether de Gaulle is an inspired leader of the French people or only an egocentric clown; whether Kruschev is a machiavellian imperialist or only a peasant-minded demagogue; whether Macmillan is a statesman with a sound grasp on world affairs or only a glib party politician. And so with all the others who are stage properties in newsprint, which seeks to envision a world as unstable as running water or shifting sand. When time sifts all the rubble of factuality it collects for the few grains of reality which are left, we find that events do not make history, but people. And all we can know of the past is what has been written about those people by the few who had them under immediate observation, and had the capacity to reveal or expose just what sort of people they were. Historians are not to be trusted when recasting from events the characters who figured in their action. Where political and personal prejudice are involved, historians are the rankest liars.

In recreating the past, there are only three sources we can rely on for the truth. Those observers referred to above who wrote down their impressions of notable or notorious personages at first hand, or who gathered data about them from others who had personal knowledge of them. The second source is from private journals, in which were scribbled intimate revelations of the people whom the journalist had to do with. The third source is from letters which survive from one period to another, and which are vivid with the present-moment life of a period, and with the most revealing of all ingredients — gossip.

Surprising how little survives of these three sources of information, yet without them we would know nothing of the past save its bare bones in chronicle and legend. What would we know of the Greek and Roman dominant figures if it was not for Plutarch's *Lives*, or the incidental sketches of them in the works of Suetonius and Tacitus? Or of what life was like in medieval times if it was not for the Paston letters? That we know more about all the prominent personages of the Stuart kings than any other period in history is due to two sources, Aubrey's *Lives* and the *Diary* of Sam Pepys. Walpole has peopled the early eighteenth century in his flippant and stylistic letters, while Boswell has left us immortal character creations of the notabilities who figured in its latter half. The great age of the letter arrived with Queen Victoria and the penny postage, and today biographers and social historians are delving into its accumulated hoard of private letters. For that reason it will be the best known period in history.

We may well pause to ask what intimate data about its notable personages the twentieth century is going to pass on to posterity. Of late years, much has been collected and stored away in libraries. I'm sure that my generation has added a rich quantum to it; at least in its earlier years, when the post office was still the focal point of communication between countries and peoples isolated from direct contact with each other.

But at a given point in time that source of personal exchanges between peoples dried up dramatically. One small gadget abolished it, the telephone. Why go to the trouble of writing a letter when one has only to ring a bell, and establish immediate contact with another in speech?

A dolorous subject of meditation, to think of all the intimate exchanges between people by the written word — all the gossip, scandalous or otherwise — all the splenetic antagonisms — all the conspiracies over affairs which once bulked the postman's bag, evaporated into thin air; dead in the very sound of gabble which vibrated it across a telephone wire . . .

And what gabble! For myself, I loathe the wretched gadget, and never use it, save over a matter of immediate business, which can't be avoided. Otherwise, the exercise of trying to talk in sentient terms to a disembodied voice is a ridiculous procedure to which I would not subject my vocal chords. But perforce I have frequently had pressed on my ears one-sided exchanges over the phone, and such a misuse of the English language would hardly be tolerated in an infant class. Never a formed sentence, never a selected choice of words, truncated exclamations, auditory misconceptions, constant repetition — a perfectly exasperating procedure which only a telephone addict would endure.

Today, nobody keeps a journal or a diary. If the resources of the letter are denied posterity, where is it to look for a clarified understanding of the life lived by its parents and grandparents, and some intimate knowledge of its notable personages? There is only one reliable source left, it seems to me, and that is the art of the profile.

For it must be understood that the profile has nothing to do with the newspaper article, or with the documentation of the biographer, or with personal reminiscence which leaves some account of its notable contemporaries. The profile is a strictly defined literary form, and its principles were laid down by Harold Ross, who inaugurated and edited The *New Yorker*.

First of all, the profilist must know his subject personally, and must garner from him something of his background, his interests and aspirations, his intellectual status, his achievement in whatever may be his special mĕtier, whether in the arts, the professions, or in the direct action of life. He must also gather data about his subject from those who know him intimately, whether they like and admire him, or are antagonistic to him. To all this he must add the spoil of his own observation of the subject's peculiar psychology; his place in the category of human identities.

The profilist will, of course, gather much more material than he needs, and the test of his artistry will be his ability to select only those salients of personality in the life, speech, habits, gestures and external appearance which will allow him to present a full length portrait of his subject to the reader. It is needless to say that the profilist's intellectual integrity and psychological astuteness will also be involved in this difficult exercise which recreates in typematter the character of a living human being, very much in the same way as a novelist creates a character in fiction.

The pressing need for the art of the profilist in this country has been much driven upon me these latter years because of my status as one of the few survivors of my generation who met and knew personally most of its notable writers and artists, and many others who had something to do in building up the genesis of a national culture. I find an eager curiosity in the youth of the present generation to know what sort of men they were, what they were like to talk with, what were their particular quirks of temperament and character. I have been much urged to write about them, and convey my impressions of them as living identities.

Well, I have at times written some brief sketches of them, but only I can say how inadequate these are. Memory is a wretched faculty for reliable data on people and events. One may have had long and intimate talks with a man, but all that remains of them are a few arid phrases, arbitrarily retained in memory without any selective sense of significance in the man who uttered them. All reminiscence which presumes to recall talk in any volume and in sequence of dialogue is fraudulent; a mere exercise in literary reconstruction. Talk must be jotted down almost in the breath of its utterance, or it will fade from memory within a few days. And talk has so much to do with revealing or exposing the constitution of the human ego.

All we can expect from reminiscence is a blurred impression of the personalities it deals with. For a valid presentation of them, we must go to the writer who has studied them at first hand, working from the living model, as a portrait painter does.

The Question of Ned Kelly's Perfume

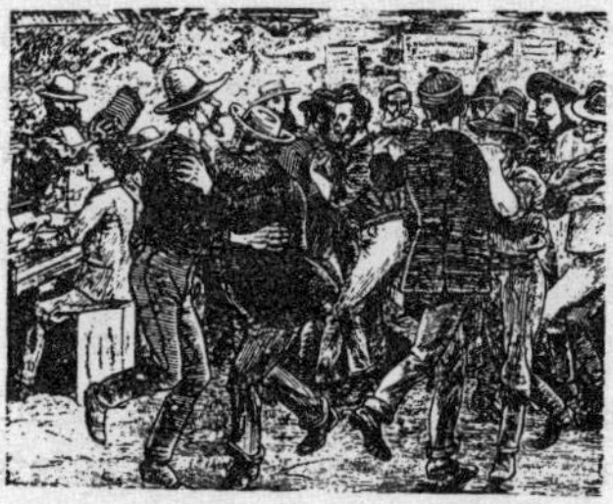

Lindsay appended this woodcut from a journal of the 1870s to substantiate his argument

As I live outside the postal delivery area, which also includes delivery of the daily newspaper, I rarely see one, unless it arrives as tradesmen's wrapping paper. It was, therefore, only by the courtesy of my butcher that I read of Mr. Sydney Baker's stigmatisation of Ned Kelly as a homosexual which so justly outraged the citizens of Jerilderie, a township which reveres Ned as its national hero.

I have not read Mr. Baker's work on the new Australian Language, which contains his assumptions of Ned Kelly's homosexuality, but if, as I understand, it is based on the use of perfume by Ned; and that the Gang was given to selecting each other as dance partners, then Mr. Baker is accusing a very large section of the male population of the Kelly era as homosexuals.

I was born in that era, being, I think, about the age of eight when Ned was hanged, but I am not to be relied on in respect of dates. And I don't think any trial at law, before or since that of Ned Kelly, has taken possession of the Australian people

Norman Lindsay's last contribution to the *Bulletin*, Sydney, 18 March 1967 with such a passionate intensity. It touched on a content of the national ego which is as potent today as in Ned Kelly's time, and that is the amalgam of reckless man and dangerous man, which becomes heroic man when a people is threatened by war or conflict with other nations. This is in part the theme of Douglas Stewart's superb verse drama "Ned Kelly".

And no section of the population of this country was more obsessed by the exploits of the Kelly Gang than the small boys of my generation. With us the eternal game of cops and robbers became that of Police and Bushrangers. We played it to the exclusion of all other diversions, though with considerable grudging from the junior members of my nonage, of which I was one, for we were forced to sustain the role of police, while our elders took over that of the Kelly Gang, who, with the unerring marksmanship of cork-popping pistols, shot down the ignoble police to a man.

We had the whole saga of the Kelly Gang from my father's groom, Dennis Denny, who claimed to possess Dan Kelly's saddle, though how he came to inherit this historic relic was not revealed. I see him now, seated on the chaff bin, surrounded by an admiring group of small boys, while he recounts to us how the police would have had Kate Kelly for what that era solemnised as a fate worse than death, and of how Dan Kelly, nobly defending his sister's honor, shot a policeman in the arm. Or was it that the policeman shot himself in the arm in order to prove a case of criminal assault against Dan, forcing him to take to the bush and join his big brother Ned, who had already fled there to escape a pumped-up charge of horse-stealing by the malignant police?

I have reverted here to the biographical, as it is essential to refuting the charge against Ned Kelly of homosexuality because he used perfume. Nearly all men of that era, irrespective of class, used perfume. My father, an Irishman, a horse and buggy doctor, and as a dominant a male as ever wore whiskers, always finished off his morning toilet by dabbing his handkerchief freely with perfume. When my parents gave a dinner party it was the men guests who loaded the atmosphere with perfume and hair oil. It was, in fact, almost a male prerogative, for women, or those who classified themselves as ladies, used very little perfume. At most, a lady dressing for any social event dabbed a little eau-de-cologne behind her ears. A woman who overdid the use of a scent bottle was considered "fast".

Men had other rituals which if practised today would make them suspects of a sexual kink. They wore a considerable amount of jewellery, heavy signet rings, jewelled tie-pins, watch-chains from which dangled lockets, medals, charms, and other trinkets. Also they wore flowers in the button-hole, nosegays they called them, and some perfectionists, to keep the flowers fresh, had their stems inserted into a small bottle of water fastened by clips under the lapel.

Here I have dealt only with the gentry. Let me turn, then, to the toilet of one of our many grooms, for, like most tolerably decent small boys of that era, the stable was for me a chosen domicile within the home and the company of grooms preferable to that of other members of the home circle. The groom I have in mind was a notable member of the local football team, and, in his own estimation, an amorist of distinction among the professional tarts from Ballarat who frequently weekended at a sort of bordello run by old Jimmy Ah Wah at our Chinese camp. Herewith is his Saturday night's toilet, for that was the week's gala night, when shops and pubs remained open late. It began with a stiffly starched white shirt, a polo collar, and a narrow, red tie fastened to his shirtfront with a brass clip. He then inserted his stockinged feet into a pair of bell-bottomed pants which were too skintight at the knees to permit the passage of boots. His boots were very elaborate, with high heels, decorative toecaps, and brass lace-up tags. His coat was of the flash pattern known as a ducktail, because it had two buttons designed to cock its tail upwards, while its very small lapels made another class distinction from the long-tailed coats of the gentry with their wide spread of lapels. But the culmination of his toilet was the way he brushed his well-oiled hair. This was parted at the side and brushed down in a curve over his forehead. With that he placed a forefinger about midway on the curve and brushed the ends of the hair upwards in a curve over his finger. When this was adjusted to his satisfaction he carefully inserted into the curve the tail feathers of a drake to preserve its upward curl. His high-crowned boxer hat was adjusted about an inch above it so that the brim should protect this final perfection of his toilet. It need hardly be added that the perfume bottle was up-ended on his handkerchief that he might go forth imposing on all noses an aroma of the barber's shop.

I am not implying a lack of erudition in Mr. Baker that he failed to discover that perfume was a property common to all men of the period he deals with, because I had forgotten it myself till he called it back to memory. When digging up material about any past period the hardest data to unearth is that of the trivialities which writers in the period rarely record, because they are conventions accepted as understood by their readers. The reason for a lavish use of perfume all through the Victorian era is not far to seek. Anyone who reads *Bleak House* or Henry Mayhew's documentation of London life during the 'fifties will realise how much the squalor of the slums impinged on all main thoroughfares. Even in those the open drains were clogged with refuse, so that the whole atmosphere must have been equally clogged with stenches, carrying with them the germs of typhoid and cholera. In such a miasma men, hurrying about their affairs, had no other resource but to clap a handkerchief loaded with perfume to their noses.

In answer to Mr. Baker's other inference of homosexuality in men dancing together, I have appended to this article a woodcut of the 1870s of men dancing together at a pub. How else could they work off the exhilaration of liquor, lacking women to dance with?

The use of perfume by men petered out with my father's generation. The custom had been inherited from England and the generic cause for it forgotten, since there were no city stenches in Australia to demand a prophylactic against them.

A Letter

TO MARY LINDSAY, 1959

Over the years, I have seen the Sydney I arrived in, a real sailor's town, with the tradition of its past still extant in its waterfront, its streets, and its people, gradually lose all individual distinction and sink into the dull cosmopolitan convention of any city anywhere else which existed on the retrogressive procedure labelled progress.

At the same time, what the hell does Sydney mean to me these days? I never go there — I think it is eight years since I set foot in it, and that visit gave me a bellyful of disgust for it. It had destroyed the last remaining section of its nostalgic charm for me — Circular Quay. When I painted at that studio in Bridge Street after taking up oils, it was my habit, of a Sunday afternoon to stroll around the Quay and lower George Street — an area more or less deserted by people on a Sunday. In the late afternoon I liked to watch the ferry-boats arrive with their mobs of surfers from the ocean beaches, and indulge biological meditations on the human species by observing the grand procession of noses as it passed; male noses, female noses . . .

Besides, the Quay to me was holy ground: Conrad had walked it, ships in which he served had berthed at it. He had drunk at the hotel to the right of it which was still there till quite recently. The Quay that he describes in *The Mirror of the Sea* was the one I arrived in. I have eaten at the Chinese restaurants in Lower George Street that he writes of, and bought tobacco at the little shop round the corner from the Quay in George Street which was kept by the Frenchman who had lost both his hands, and who tried to roll cigarettes with his stumps. A marvellous scoundrel he made of that Frenchman as a character in his story "Because of the Dollars", though he only took the externals of them from the real Frenchman.

The Quay of today is too obscene to be described. Only a few remaining ferry-boats berth there. An overhead railway mounted on crude brick pillars roars across it. A vilely designed Opera House is being built at one end of it.

Yet here is something that gives my detestation of it pause. Jane*, I find, likes it. She likes its noise, its flood of speeding cars, its sense of existence pitched up to an excitement of the nerves. In short, it belongs to her earth, and mine has ceased to exist. And I know perfectly well that if I were offered the possibility of returning to it even for a day I would refuse to do so. It would become again a present-moment factuality, and I would be as indifferent to and unaware of, its nostalgic charms as I was when it was just a commonplace figment of the days of my youth.

This is one aspect of conflict between the generations which we, at the tail-end of our generation, are apt to forget, when we are bored to hell with a stale procedure long left behind us, while the young of this generation are charging into it as something new and interesting, to be explored and exploited with avidity.

*Jane Glad, Norman Lindsay's daughter

The Literary Works of Norman Lindsay

NOVELS

A Curate in Bohemia, N.S.W. Bookstall Co., Sydney, 1913.
T. Werner Laurie, London, 1937. Illustrated.

Redheap, Faber & Faber, London, 1930.
Published as *Every Mother's Son*, Cosmopolitan Book Corporation, New York, 1930. Banned on publication in Australia. Ban lifted 1958. First Australian edition, Ure Smith, Sydney, 1959.

Mr. Gresham and Olympus, Farer & Rinehart, New York, 1932.
Published as *Miracles by Arrangement*, Faber & Faber, London, 1932. Title and ending were changed with consent of author on suggestion of Brian Penton. Later author regretted change and stated American edition is the correct one. No Australian edition.

The Cautious Amorist, Farer & Rinehart, New York, 1932.
T. Werner Laurie, London, 1934. Banner & Korch, Copenhagen, 1962. Illustrated. Banned in Australia on publication. No Australian edition.

Saturdee, Endeavour Press, Sydney, 1933. T. Werner Laurie, London, 1936. Illustrated.

Pan in the Parlour, Farer & Rinehart, New York, 1933. T. Werner Laurie, London, 1934. Illustrated. Hudibras Forlag, Copenhagen, 1946. Paperback without illustrations.

Age of Consent, Farer & Rinehart, New York, 1938. T. Werner Laurie, London, 1938. Illustrated. Banned in Australia on publication. Ban lifted 1958. First Australian edition, Ure Smith, Sydney, 1962.

The Cousin from Fiji, Angus & Robertson, Sydney, 1945. Random House, New York, 1945.

Halfway to Anywhere, Angus & Robertson, Sydney, 1947. Illustrated.

Dust or Polish, Angus & Robertson, Sydney, 1950.

Rooms and Houses (Autobiographical novel), Ure Smith, Sydney, 1968.

SHORT STORIES

Micomicana, Melbourne University Press, Melbourne, 1979.

CHILDREN'S BOOKS

The Magic Pudding, Angus & Robertson, Sydney, 1918. Hamish Hamilton, London, 1931. Farer & Rinehart, New York, 1935. Penguin Books, in Puffin Story Book Series, Harmondsworth, UK, 1957. Kodansha, Tokyo, 1979. E.G. Anaya, Madrid, 1988. P.C. Barcanova, Barcelona, 1988. Illustrated. *The Magic Pudding* is always in print in Australia, although the prospectus for the first edition states "only one edition will be published and it is sure to sell out at once."

The Flyaway Highway, Angus & Robertson, Sydney, 1936. Lansdowne Press, Melbourne, 1973. Illustrated.

CRITICISM AND PHILOSOPHY

Creative Effort: An Essay in Affirmation, a limited edition book of 120 copies published by *Art in Australia,* Sydney, 1920, with original etching as frontispiece. Revised edition Cecil Palmer, London, 1924.

Hyperborea: Two Fantastic Travel Essays, Fanfrolico Press, London, 1928. Illustrated. First appeared in *Vision* magazine, Vision Press, Sydney, 1923.

Madam Life's Lovers, Fanfrolico Press, London, 1929. Frontispiece by Norman Lindsay.

Scribblings of an Idle Mind, Lansdowne Press, Melbourne, 1966.

REMINISCENCES

Bohemians of the Bulletin, Angus & Robertson, Sydney, 1965. Illustrated.

My Mask (Autobiography), Angus & Robertson, Sydney, 1970. Published posthumously.

LETTERS

Letters of Norman Lindsay, Angus & Robertson, Sydney, 1979.